D1295601

WHO SPEAKS FOR THE SOUTH?

Books by the Same Author

Pee Dee Panorama (with Carl Julien)

Southern Heritage

The Road Home

Who Speaks for the South?

WHO SPEAKS FOR THE SOUTH?

by James McBride Dabbs

FUNK & WAGNALLS COMPANY, INC.
NEW YORK

Library of Congress Catalogue Card Number 64-20965
Printed in the United States of America

Jacket photo by Dominic Capezza

To
The South: My Land and People

PREFACE

"Except as the inhabitant of a certain geographical area, the Southerner doesn't exist." I've been told this but I disagree. Like Lee, faced by Grant before Richmond in '64, he may be hard to corner. But, also like Lee, he is there. Or was. One thing that makes him hard to corner is the fact that he came into being over a long period, and has always been in process of change, a change that is taking place rapidly at present. Daily he becomes more American. At what time, if ever, he will be simply an American, no one knows. This suggests that the ideal type, the character toward which the Southerner tends, must be sought for at some time in the past, and perhaps a basic question is, when?

Granted that the figure of the goateed Southern colonel is a myth, myths do not grow, like Spanish moss, on trees; they are rooted in earth. Southern in his formality, his courtesy, and his military air, the colonel is too simple; and, in spite of Henry Adams's comment on his Harvard classmate Rooney Lee, son of General Lee, that the young man was simple beyond all comprehension, simplicity is about the last thing to expect of the Southerner. History has warped him strangely. But though this makes his characterization difficult, it does not make it impossible. Non-Southerners visiting in the South sense the character, Southerners visiting beyond the South recall it. It is as distinctive as the balmy air blowing inland across the sea-islands of South Carolina.

Not that everyone born and bred in the South is Southern; nor is everyone born and bred outside the South non-Southern. But there's a predominant Southern type, the product of history, still existing though daily being modified toward the American norm.

Friends tell me, "There may be a half-dozen types you can call Southern, but not just one." With this I disagree. You define the half-dozen only by possessing a sense, however vague, of the one. It's true, we can sense things we cannot define, and it may be that no one can define satisfactorily the Southern type; but, if so, it is not because it does not exist, it is because of the limitations of the writer.

Because of the rapid changes occurring in the South today, more rapid than at any time during its history except for the years of war and reconstruction, it would seem that the ideal Southern type would be found somewhere in the past. By "ideal" I mean not what should be but what tended to be. But I am not sure about this; the Southerner may still be in process of formation even while he is also being Americanized. If, however, we take 1820, the year of the Missouri Compromise, as a landmark, we may say that before that the Southern section of the Union prospered; after that it lost ground until it collapsed under military defeat and occupation and nearly a century of decreasingly stringent colonialization. Excepting its Negro slaves, the people of the South of 1820 had not known defeat; whatever else may be said of the South today, it is, as C. Vann Woodward, one of our leading contemporary historians, has pointed out, that part of America that has suffered defeat and frustration. Yet, long before

1820, the South was recognized as a region, and the Southerner as a type distinct from the Yankee and the Puritan; and, long before 1820, the seeds of the South's disaster had been planted, though they were hardly recognized, certainly not by Southerners. Jefferson was an exception. Referring to slavery, he said, in 1784, "I tremble for my country when I think that God is just, and his justice will not sleep forever." When, in 1820, the Missouri Compromise was enacted—the first indication that the country might be divided into free and slave states—the aged Jefferson heard the news like "a fire-bell in the night." For the most part, however, no portent of defeat had yet touched the Southern mind. Such portents were to cloud increasingly the succeeding forty-five years, and defeat itself the century after.

But, along with the defeat of the white South, went the rise, however faltering or broken, of the Negro South. After the false dawn of Reconstruction, there was a long period of darkness. Now we are in the midst of the real dawn; the Negro, long defeated and frustrated, is coming rapidly into his American heritage. But the Southern Negro is also the South, and the South is also the Negro. The Southerner has been created largely by the relationship between the two races, by both their separate and their common victories and defeats. He is still in process of creation; and although he is losing perhaps a certain sharpness of distinction from the accepted American type, perhaps he is also, because of the rising importance of the Negro in the American scene, and the major importance of the Negro in the South, coming at last to himself.

If this is so, the Southerner is still being born, and Southern culture is still alive. To understand this Southerner, however, we shall have to go back to the beginning, and trace to the present the major steps in his development.

Perhaps the critical step was the introduction of Negro

slavery in 1619, only twelve years after the settling of Jamestown. Except for the episode of Reconstruction, it is only during the last decade that the Negro has been a clear and public force in the shaping of Southern life. He was, however, from early years a secret force, pressing continually upon the mind and the character of the white South, and being molded himself by that character, until out of this pressure and counterpressure, combined with outside pressure, the South was born and with it the Southerner. That we may follow more easily this complex development, I shall begin with a tentative summary of what seems to me the Southern character as it has been, is, and is becoming. But this caution should be borne in mind: though the influence of the Negro in the formation of this character has been of steadily increasing importance, it has generally been unrecognized or, at least, unadmitted.

A personal note should be entered. Though there is, in my opinion, a characteristic Southern attitude, my analysis of it is probably influenced by the fact that I was born and have lived in a seaboard state, a part of the original South, and not in one of the later Southern states, such as Alabama or Mississippi, which were part of the Old Southwest of ante-bellum days. The seaboard South experienced the liberal eighteenth century, and, though it fell from grace as it took its place in the Cotton Kingdom about 1800, it has never entirely forgotten its early history. The Old Southwest, never having had this history, succumbed more completely to the violence inherent in the slave system. The last ten years have shown that though violence is far too common across the South, it is greater in some parts than in others. The tone of this book may be influenced by the fact that I come from the quieter part.

The book falls into three natural parts. In Part I, "The Formation of Southern Character," I shall sketch the development of the Southerner up to the Civil War; in Part II, "Its Bitter Testing," the modifications caused by military defeat, Reconstruction, and colonialization; and in Part III, "Its Present Possibility," the Southerner as he is today—and what he may become.

—*J. McB. D.*

ACKNOWLEDGMENTS

I wish to express my appreciation

To the Field Foundation for the grant-in-aid that made it possible for me to spend most of my time for two and a half years on this book, and to the Southern Regional Council for sponsoring the project;

To the Library of the University of North Carolina for the use of its facilities, including an office, during the 1961–62 session;

To my wife for her complete cooperation both in my presence and in my absence.

CONTENTS

PART II
Its Bitter Testing

PART III
Its Present Possibility

PART I

The Formation of Southern Character

CHAPTER 1

PRELIMINARY VIEW: THE ESSENTIAL SOUTHERNER

It must be understood that in all I am saying there is nothing absolute. The Southerner is also a Westerner and an American. All of his characteristics appear in other Americans but less emphasized and less complexly interrelated. It's a question of a little more and a little less. But when closely interwoven, these produce a distinctive character, easily sensed but hard to define.

Of all Americans, the Southerner is the most at home in the world. Or at least in the South, which, because of his very at-homeness, he is apt to confuse with the world. At its best, this attitude leads him to improve but not to deny or destroy the world; at its worst, it makes him, like an uncouth guest, indifferent, careless, soft to the allurements of the world or harsh in taking advantage of it. But these are faults of love, or at least of liking, not of fear or distrust. Generally, the Southerner moves through the world more easily than other Americans and regards it with greater satisfaction. To say it more clearly—he loves the world more. Loving it more, he spends more time in observing it, less time in changing it. When he does change it, as of course he does, he is working to make it not more valuable but more satisfying.

The sense of at-homeness extends ideally beyond the bounds of the physical world. The sense of security, an essential element in at-homeness, rests upon the feeling of belonging, in the first instance to the family, but, more largely, to the human community and to nature—which includes the mysterious depths of the universe. No one is completely at home, no one completely secure—we live by faith—but the deepest security belongs to him whose home is the most deeply rooted.

This concern with the world as something valuable in itself was the basic force in the creation of a Southern culture. If, as the theologian Paul Tillich argues, culture is the form or shape that religion takes, and the essential religion of a people is the spirit of its culture, then the essential religion of the South was strongly focused upon this world. This was its strength and its weakness. The tensions that created the Southern culture were, at least primarily, within the world, and consisted of the setting of time against time and place against place. This was not true in New England nor generally in the rest of the nation. There this world was set against another, and the extremity of the opposition created a tension that approached conflict. Consequently, men tried to escape the too-great tension by becoming advocates of either this world or another, that is, Yankees or Puritans, the latter becoming in the course of time extreme idealists. In such an atmosphere, one could use the world either for material or for so-called spiritual advancement; but one could hardly love it. In the South, the opposition was less basic, and the tension therefore less urgent; a man could live with it. He did not have to choose this world or another; it was not a matter of *either-or*. It is significant that no two contrasting types developed in the South to correspond to the Yankee-Puritan dichotomy of the North.

The chief tension in the South has not been between time

and eternity but between past time and future time. Southerners have sought a future both like and unlike their past. Time, therefore, has been neither the unworldly timelessness of the idealist nor the clock-controlled time of the materialist; it has been the organic time of the complete man, the man who shapes his dreams from the actual world around him. This is another way of saying that the Southerner has been at home in the world.

This at-homeness appears in several ways. First and most importantly, a quality of relaxation. The Southerner's life is less strenuous. This relaxation is not only of the body but also of the spirit. Physically, it may be an effect of the climate; more fundamentally, it is the expression of the spirit. The Southerner's spirit is less taut. Whatever he does, he does with a certain ease or even abandon, responding not to a theory but to the suggestions and exigencies of the moment. He has a strong inclination to accept things as they are, even if he isn't entirely pleased with them; he is not by nature a rebel. If he is reputed to be one, it is because of certain chances of history.

Being relaxed and at home, he is consequently slow to change. He is essentially a conservative, inclined to think of the world and society as it is, not as what he or others can force it to become. Like any man living close to nature, he assumes that change is inevitable, but a good part of this will be the slow, rhythmic change of day and night and of the seasons, part the decay or growth due to the passage of time.

Living more relaxed and slowly, he lives in a richer present. Since he has not subjected his world to violent change, it contains numerous mementoes of the past and promises of the future. His life is strong and steadfast in memories and hopes. Having accepted the flow of time as natural and inevitable, he has become in a sense the master of time. His time is within himself, not on the face of the clock.

Lingering in time, he necessarily lingers in a place. Indeed, the abstract and, from the human point of view, empty spaces of the world become under his hand distinct places. Between these places and the untouched space around them there is no absolute division. His rich sense of place spreads out and colors, however faintly, the bare spaces of the world, sometimes even the endless space of the universe. Yet that which is close is more richly endowed with meaning, and continually gives back to him an echo—or is it more?—of his own concern. He was ready at the beginning of our national history to make the nation the *locus* of his love, but failing disastrously in this, he extended, at least to the borders of the South—if he was white—a devotion unusual among the several regions of the nation.

Lingering thus in time and space, enriching the present and some particular place with memories and hopes, he developed a social order wherein place was important. In this order there were higher places and lower; the order showed marks of an aristocracy. These places, however, did not crystallize as they had in Europe; there was too much freedom of mind and movement, geographical and social, to permit this. But there was an aristocratic ideal, and, especially in the eighteenth century, an aristocracy; and faint evidences of that ideal still linger, though the aristocracy is long gone. Belief in social place and belief in geographical place express the same inner spirit of stability and community. The belief of the whites in the changeless place of the Negro was, in the dynamic American air, a distortion of this basic belief.

Such a people would tend to cherish the concrete and the local, and to have little dealing with, indeed to be suspicious of, the abstract and the universal. They would observe carefully and lovingly the people and the things about them. But if the Southerner had observed these local objects—people and things—with an intelligence equal to his fondness, he might have realized their universal implications and been saved from the weakness of his provincialism. He did not do this; he found his world satisfactory and felt no urgency to subject it to sharp scrutiny. He avoided the abstract because of his interest in things as they were, in the complete world about him. Not deeply concerned to change that world, he did not need to reduce it to an abstraction.

Out of his continued and accustomed relations to people and things, his life became a tissue of sentiments. He was sustained by these sentiments, but because he felt little need to analyze them, he was finally enslaved by them. Here lay the cause of his weakness: he accepted the world too easily, too uncritically. Consequently he was bound to it, and, in time, enslaved by it. He had the strength of those who live close to the earth, but he heeded too unquestioningly its whispered suggestions. He often fell into error and sin, from an uninformed heart rather than a wicked heart, from perhaps slothfulness of flesh and spirit, rather than from spiritual pride or deliberate intent.

Even his critics do not deny him a certain wholeness in his tendency to accept life and himself, the evil with the good, a wholeness that was accompanied by a certain innocence. This may be the secret of a kind of goodness in the South, the goodness of a socially oriented personal life, which exists, paradoxically, within a flagrantly unjust social order and beyond individual pride and passion.

Yet he, too, has had from the beginning, though less clearly than other Americans, the individualistic, competitive spirit that was to mark the modern man, a spirit that was sharpened in the eighteenth century by the settling in the South of some two hundred thousand Scotch-Irish immigrants. The Civil War was indeed a civil war; the Southerner was fighting not only against the North but also against himself and was therefore fated to lose. He had never been really wholehearted. The most delicate part of our task is to define the inner flaw, relate it to the world beyond the South, and raise at the close the question as to whether it is at last being remedied.

CHAPTER 2

EARLY SETTLER

The Southerner, like the rest of us, is the product of history—which, as he became a Southerner, he both suffered and directed as a Southerner would. When did he become a Southerner? Not recognizably so for a long time, but he had the makings in him when he landed in Jamestown in 1607. He had certain basic tendencies, which, under the influence of sun and land and other lures and pressures, would make him the distinctive person he was to become.

The simplest way to get at that seventeenth-century "Southerner" is to set him beside the figure of his contemporary, the New England Puritan. They were both English but with a difference. The advantage of using the early New Englander is that of all American types he has been most clearly and completely drawn; New Englanders themselves began to draw the picture at the very beginning, and have continued through the centuries, with help, not always friendly, from the outside. They were that kind of people; they thought about what they wanted, they wrote it down, and then they thought about it some more. Consequently, we know them fairly well. Because their wants were relatively simple, to purify or abstract God out of the world, they serve as a good standard by which to measure the vaguer and less frequently analyzed Southern settler.

Let us admit the injustice of using any group as a measuring rod. The varied humanity of the group is forgotten, a few notable and widespread traits remembered. But this injustice was indeed invited by the early New Englanders when they simplified and intellectualized life as they did. The complexity of real life, with its tensions and its contradictions, tends to recede, and the simple explanation to be remembered. But many men over the years have tried to do justice to the Puritan mind, and certainly the hardiness of the Puritan character can bear the chance of some misunderstanding on our part as we use that mind and character, not to illumine it further, but to bring into a clearer light another distinctive American type, the Southerner.

Probably John A. Doyle, author of the classic *The English in America,* makes too sharp a contrast between the Virginia and the Massachusetts settlements when he says: "Virginia was the offspring of economical distress, as New England was of ecclesiastical conflicts."[1] Nevertheless, the contrast was there. The Puritans may have been seeking a larger world, but they believed themselves to be seeking a *better* world. They were ill at ease in the religious world of England. As their religious oppression grew, through the reign of James I and into the reign of Charles I, they increasingly lost their hope of purifying the church at home, and increasingly looked to America as a land in which they might worship God as they chose.

The England they were dissatisfied with, from which they were uprooting themselves, was an England still strongly marked by the Middle Ages: an England with an official church still close to the Roman Catholic, a church burdened—so the Puritans felt—with excessive and idolatrous forms. They were for stripping these away, even though this meant the stripping away of age-old communal practices. Though they did not realize it, in thus turning against the community, in thus making religion increasingly a matter of the individual's inner encounter with God, they were inaugurating the modern world. They were beginning those uprootings and those separations that, continued long enough and, in their case, across the wide American frontier, would result in alienating modern man.

It is true, the individual was not deprived of the support of a church; in fact, for more than half a century a theocracy was maintained in Massachusetts: the church not only supported men in their struggle with Satan, it forced them onto God's side. Nevertheless, the individual's encounter with God was still the heart of life, and for a long time the man who wished to become a church member and a townsman had to affirm that he had experienced this encounter and had received God's grace.

The Puritans said of themselves that they had crossed the Atlantic on an "errand into the wilderness"; they had been sent by the Reformed forces of Europe to establish in the New World the Kingdom of God, and thus "to vindicate the most rigorous ideal of the Reformation, so that ultimately all Europe would imitate New England."[2]

The single most important aspect of the group was this intense spiritual concern and this high aim. Regardless of the effort and the cost, they intended to cut themselves off from the world, to purify themselves of worldly lusts, and to find God in the wilderness. They meant the physical wilderness of America. Unhappily their search led them, through the centuries, into the wilderness of the individual heart, which, isolated from its world, became a natural core for those wildernesses of steel and stone we call modern cities.

Speaking of the extreme height of the Puritan's aim, and thinking especially of Jonathan Edwards' famous disciple Samuel Hopkins, Harriet Beecher Stowe says: "There is a ladder to heaven, whose base God has placed in human affections, tender instincts, symbolic feelings, sacraments of love, through which the soul rises higher and higher, refining as she goes, till she outgrows the human, and changes, as she rises, into the image of the divine. . . . This highest step, this saintly elevation, which few but selectest spirits ever on earth attain . . . has been seized upon by our sage [*i.e.*, Hopkins] as the all of religion. He knocked out every round of the ladder but the highest, and then, pointing to its hopeless splendor, said to the world. 'Go up thither and be saved!' "[3]

Though the Puritans came to America with impossibly high ideals, I am not suggesting that they scorned the land or the people they left. The courage of the adventure was undoubtedly mixed with regret. Indeed, there is hardly a greater passage of mingled heroism and nostalgia in American literature than the following words from William Bradford. He was of course writing of the coming of the Pilgrims to Plymouth, but the later Massachusetts Bay settlers were their spiritual cousins. Says Bradford of that first Massachusetts autumn: "For summer being done, all things stand upon them with a wetherbeaten face; and the whole countrie, full of woods and thickets, represented a wild and savage heiw [*sic*]. If they looked behind them, ther was the mighty ocean which they had passed, and was now a main barr and goulfe to seperate them from all the civill parts of the world. . . . May not the children of these fathers rightly say: Our fathers were Englishmen which came over this great ocean, and were ready to perish in this willdernes; but they cried unto the Lord, and he heard their voice, and looked on their adversatie."[4]

They brought with them not only emotional but also intellectual intensity. The leaders of Massachusetts Bay were highly educated men, who sought God also with their minds. To be sure, a man could be saved only through faith, but how was he to know whether he had faith or not? Only by continuous self-examination. Such self-knowledge could not bring the redemptive flash—this was God's free gift—but it could at least prepare a man for its reception and for its recognition when it came.

But the ideal of early New England education included more than this. It included the whole new world of science that was opening up during the seventeenth century. Here, too, men might behold the glorious works of God. From the very beginning, the Puritans did not accept the world as it appeared to be. On the one hand, they were afraid of it, tried to flee from it, and purify their hearts of it; on the other, they were scientifically interested in it—albeit with the highly religious spirit of seventeenth-century science. When, within a century, their urgent God-seeking should weaken as a result of its very intensity and of their material success in the New World, they would still retain this early analytical interest in themselves and in the world; and they would have developed, out of their material success, and, more fundamentally, out of their awareness of the world and a man's duty therein, a new type, the New England Yankee. With the development of this type—though they did not know it then—they would become the directors of the American future.

Unaware of what they were doing, they built for this from the beginning: they built villages and towns. The importance of the New England town is suggested by the terminology itself—the whole area of countryside surrounding the town is the "town." From the beginning the town was dominant, and was destined to remain so until it became the industrial city of today.

In this matter, like the Virginians, the Puritans brought from England the memory of the agricultural town, a memory ineffectual, however, in Virginia. Also, they had geographical reasons for building towns which the Virginians, as we shall see, did not have. The New England land was not conducive to broad plantations; the bitter climate suggested close-set dwellings for social life. But one of the main reasons for the town was the Puritan desire for religious and moral control; this could be much better maintained in a town than in a sparsely settled countryside. Later in the eighteenth century, the leaders of the seaboard settlements sometimes opposed the growth of inland settlements because they feared the frontiersmen might become wild and immoral. According to Perry Miller and Thomas H. Johnson in *The Puritans*, "A preacher before the General Court in 1705 bewailed the effects of the frontier in terms that have been echoed by 'Easterners' for two hundred years and more; men were no longer living together, he said, in compact communities, under the tutelage of educated clergymen and the discipline of an ordered society, but were taking themselves into remote corners 'for worldly conveniences.' "[5] And, in 1758, Reverend Thomas Barnard "states the theocratic case against the backwoodsman quite clearly. Religion, he said, will flourish most where the arts of peace are cultivated, especially industry, among those born for labor."[6]

Having built the town, and being forced by the settler's need to provide himself with tools, the Puritan passed eventually, of course with the aid of Jefferson's Embargo, from a shipbuilding and trading order into a manufacturing order. The town created manufacturing, and manufacturing created the city.

Thus the Puritan settlers of New England became the advance guard of the modern world, projected onto the American shores by the radical, Protestant, dawning modern mind of Europe. They claimed they were reaching back across sixteen hundred years to pick up and restore the clear, simple image of essential Christianity, purified of all the earthly accretions of medievalism; they were cutting back to the roots, pruning away time's luxuriant growth. They ended by rooting religion in the thin air of the universe. This was bad, for religion must be rooted in earth, no matter how high the heaven wherein its branches wave.

They claimed—and they must have believed it—that by stripping away the material world, men could be brought closer to God. And they proceeded to discard the impedimenta that might hinder their rapid march into the New World, in which they would establish God's Kingdom. But as they stripped away the cumbersome garments of the Old World, they increased their speed and extended their activity in the world itself; and it's anybody's guess whether at a given moment a Puritan was stripping to meet God or to make money. God knows whether the Puritans met Him or not; we know they made money.

Of course, the money was made by the Yankees, not by the Puritans. But given an unexploited America, rich in natural resources, it was inevitable that the Yankees should appear. A basic Calvinistic tenet was that, though the world is wicked, it should be used by Christians—those called to be "saints"—for the glory of God. We are here *not* to enjoy the world but, in a kind of detached purity, to use it for God's glory. But when saints begin to use a wicked world which they do not allow themselves to enjoy, when they self-indulgently allow themselves to take pleasure in their power of using the world, they become something less than saints. Though their catechism tells them their chief end is to glorify God and enjoy Him forever, they now begin to glory in the world, and even worship it. Ceasing to be complete men, physical-spiritual beings in a physical-spiritual world, they become manipulators. They become Yankees. The myth of the New England Yankee existed even before the Revolution was fought.

Not all Puritans became Yankees. Some became idealists. Not the garden variety that most of us at one time or another have been, but the shimmering idealist, such as Emerson, or the practicing idealist, such as William Lloyd Garrison or even John Brown. Such men feel that their ideals are godlike; from our point of view they may be so high above earth as to seem hardly human, sometimes brutally inhuman, or humanly ineffective, like Matthew Arnold's Shelley, "a beautiful but ineffectual angel, beating in the void his luminous wings in vain."

All told, it took about two hundred years for the Puritans of the Massachusetts Bay settlement to become the supreme manipulators of the nineteenth century, remaking the world for the glory of God and for individual profit. But they brought with them the seed of this individualism, and they found in the rich new world a perfect field for exploitation. They did not call it exploitation; they called it "use for the glory of God." The world was not to them a home to be cherished, it was a property to be developed. They had come out of England because they had ceased to feel at home there. Though they did not know it, they were leaving the Middle Ages behind them; they were leaving a world they had suffered and enjoyed, and loved dearly, for a world they would control. They thought of themselves as colonists here, citizens of another country—not England, however—travelers traversing a weary land, or, as the Plymouth settlers called themselves, Pilgrims.

In a sense, all men are pilgrims, since it's the human fate "To look before and after,/And long for what is not." Walter De la Mare was right when he urged: "Look thy last on all things lovely every hour." Whether we flee from the world or not, the world flees from us. Nevertheless, it should be loved and regretted in its going. There is a difference between traveling through a land you love and hurrying fearfully through a land unloved.

This is an extremely brief, and therefore probably unfair, interpretation of the early Puritan culture of New England, the culture that became dominant in the United States, against which the South struggled and by which it was overthrown. Let us now measure by this Puritan standard the early southern settler, who was to become the Southerner.

There were, of course, Puritan settlers in Virginia as there were non-Puritans in Massachusetts. The laws enacted by the London Company for the government of the Virginia colony are about as strict as those of Massachusetts Bay; but Virginia was controlled by a trading company in London, while the Massachusetts Bay colony, guarding its charter here, controlled itself. Furthermore, religion was the main concern of the Massachusetts settlement. The Massachusetts Bay settlers, though narrower, were more single-hearted, more devoted to the religious ideal, more determined to set up in the new world a *new* England. Some Puritanism existed in the South from the beginning, and its spirit was deepened and diffused during the eighteenth and nineteenth centuries through the meeting of the Scotch-Irish and the frontier, but it was not dominant from the beginning, as it was in New England. The earliest Southern settlement occurred in a land appropriately called Virginia, out of personal regard for that incarnation of the English spirit, the Virgin Queen, Elizabeth. It would be over two hundred years before this name would flower in the personal and feminine culture of the South, but the seeds existed at the beginning.

Finally, regardless of the degree of Puritanism present in early Virginia, it was far more difficult to maintain puritan discipline on the scattered tobacco farms of that region than in the towns of Massachusetts.

This is not a retelling of the old myth of the Cavaliers and the Roundheads. The fact that such a myth arose, however, suggests a basis of fact or at least desire. A few Cavaliers did come to Virginia after Charles I was defeated by the Puritan Cromwell, but they were too few to change radically the temper of the colony. That temper had been set with the organization of the London Company in 1606. It may have been influenced by Raleigh's Lost Colony of twenty years before, for the London Company resulted partly from the prior failure of single adventurers, of whom Raleigh was the most famous. The settlement was also the outgrowth of the desperate economic situation in England due mainly to the land enclosures of the sixteenth century, through which a great number of small farms had been wiped out to make sheep pastures. Patriotism was also involved, for England was engaged in an imperial race with France and Spain. And as always, as in every venture in the early morning of the modern world, there was religion. The London Company said that its action concerned "God, and the advancement of religion, the present ease, future honor and safety of the kingdom, the strength of our Navy, the visible hope of a great and rich trade, and many secret blessings not yet discovered."[7] How real was the concern with religion, it is hard to say. At one place John Smith says that the Jamestown settlement was undertaken for the glory of God. At another he speaks of the foolishness of the Company's propaganda about religion; it was common knowledge, he added, that desire for economic gain was the chief motive for the undertaking.

Whatever part the religious motive played in the settlement of Virginia, it played a smaller part than in the settlement of Massachusetts. The paradox of this is that the God-seeking Puritan made far better economic use of his opportunities than the Southern settler did, perhaps because of the severe challenge of the New England geography and climate and the stern worldly code of the Puritans, which made of earthly business a heavenly vocation.

I have already suggested that the Puritan settlement of Massachusetts Bay, in its essential spirit, had retreated considerably from the more complex and full-bodied community of

Elizabeth's day. It is worth noting that the Massachusetts Bay settlement was made in 1630, twenty-three years after Jamestown, years which saw the rise to power in the Anglican church of the fanatical authoritarian Archbishop Laud. The Jamestown settler, though he came out of a hungry England, came out of a religiously more stable England.

Of course, the Virginia settler wasn't completely at home in England; had he been, he would hardly have left. But on the most fundamental level, the religious, he was at home. Because he had no desire to remake English religious customs or any other English customs, he gladly took his past with him. Mainly, he wanted a better economic chance in the world. He came out from England, seeking not a *new* England but a wider England: land for the landless, space, food, ease—after the first expectable hardship—and adventure. The dreams of Elizabethan England still influenced his life. Even that of the Kingdom of God—he would extend it among the savages. The individual would have a better chance because of the freer air and wider land. Since religion was a strict matter everywhere in those days, he transferred this strictness to America, even as the Puritan did. But he was generally satisfied with the forms of the Established Church, and, in even sharper contrast to the Puritan settler, he was indisposed to raise publicly questions of faith and belief. This was a matter between the individual and God. Unlike the Puritan, he did not see himself as a member of a community of saints, proved so by inner, personal experience. He was an Englishman and an Anglican; as a result of centuries within an established church, first the Church of Rome, then the Church of England, he felt himself a part of such a church.

The Virginian was not irreligious; he was only more conservative in his religion. Being therefore more under the influence of the vanished Middle Ages, he was more accepting of the totality of life than was the Puritan; he was not so deeply concerned to purify the spirit from all eartly influences and set the individual naked before God. As it turned out, he was less abstract, less modern; he moved more hesitantly into the modern world. This foothold in the past has always been the basic strength of the Southerner; it has also been his chief misfortune because it set him in opposition to the future-oriented Puritan-Yankee of New England.

In brief, the Southerner entered the New World, lured on mainly by the thirst for adventure and economic advancement. The Puritan added to this the immense force of a theology admirably suited to such an imperial thrust. In the rich New World that stretched equally before them both, the Puritan-Yankee was the better motivated and therefore gained the dominant power.

Here, at the very beginning, in the disparate temper of the two colonies, Virginia and Massachusetts, can be seen the traits that, modified by the vicissitudes of history, were to create two American types, the Northerner and the Southerner. The Northerner, eager to strip himself of the past, hurled himself into the future. The Southerner advanced also, but deliberately, hesitantly, carrying more of the past with him, continually held in tension between past and future. If, during the last century especially, he has been too closely bound to the past, this is but a distortion of the attitude he brought to America three hundred years ago.

It is true, of course, that both the Puritan and the Virginian removed themselves from their English homes and from the concrete evidences of their past: pulled up some roots, divorced themselves from old communities, drove toward the future, and began to be individualistic, rootless, modern men. There was no extreme difference between them, as there is no extreme difference between Northerners and Southerners today. We are all Americans; we are not Europeans. The northern American has no problem; he is simply *the* American, he sets the standard. But the Southerner has become, through time, a variant of the American type, and therefore has a problem: Just where and how much does he vary? And what can he do about it?

It is especially this quality of growth out of the past that produced the culture of the South. For culture is a growth, not wild, but still a growth. And though pruning is necessary and rerooting is possible, uprooting is dangerous. Such a tearing up of roots as Puritanism exhibited may be in the long run destructive—the long run, not the short. New England certainly produced a distinctive culture; but as New England spread westward, driven increasingly by its desire for the future, continuously putting down new roots, preoccupied with change and progress, it moved increasingly from a stable culture into the restless crosscurrents of the modern world, of urban and industrial America. The South moved too slowly, indeed became entangled in the past, and, in possibly inevitable conflict with the future-dominated North, it was as an entity destroyed. Yet from its beginning it was trying to expand its English home in the New World, to root the old culture in a new land.

Carrying with him this sense of England as home and the English social system as the model, the early Virginian, surrounded by boundless lands, naturally developed a landed aristocracy modeled after the English gentry. The laws of primogeniture and entail, which remained in force until abolished through the influence of the democratic Jefferson, are evidence of this. The purpose of the Virginian was to build and maintain great families, which the mode of settlement and the nature of the land and climate made possible, indeed probable. Again, we must not make too sharp a distinction between the Virginia and the Massachusetts settler: the sense of class may have been as sharp in the northern colony as in the southern. In the North, however, education and religious position conferred social distinction; furthermore, the soil and climate did not suggest the formation of a landed aristocracy. Finally, we must remember that Puritanism was an individualistic religion, focused upon the inner, private life while pushing the outer, institutional life into the background. Under the influence of the more relaxed Episcopalianism of the South, man was less the isolated individual struggling upward in a world of isolated individuals and more the social being accepting his place in a fixed social order.

Did the Southerner accept this place too easily? More importantly, did he accept the world too easily, with its mixture of justice and injustice? Did he accept men, including himself, too easily, with their mixture of good and evil? The Puritan temper of early New England inclined men either to flee from a fearful world or to whip it into submission. Did the Virginian, and his descendants, go to the other extreme, and accept the world too unguardedly? Was he too relaxed, perhaps too easily made at home?

This is what the region must have suggested to the Virginian. The suggestion, however, fell upon ready hearts and accepting minds. Having come away from England not fundamentally dissatisfied with life there, not religiously dissatisfied, he was disposed to be satisfied with life here. As it is natural for a man to relax at home but not on military duty, so the Virginia settler could relax as the Massachusetts Bay settler could not. For the latter had come on an errand to the wilderness, sent as a soldier of Christ in the ceaseless warfare of spirit with flesh.

Early life in Virginia, although the climate was more genial, was no less arduous than it was in Massachusetts. Virginians starved and died of disease and were killed by Indians. Perhaps they starved more frequently because they lacked the stern religious discipline of Massachusetts, just as they lacked a dominant religious theory that shaped the inner life to the military spirit. The Virginia settlers became fighters because their earthly ambitions brought them into conflict with the Indians; they were not at the same time soldiers of the Lord. In fact, at the beginning, they were generally indisposed to fight against the Indians, though this restraint was pretty well destroyed by the great massacre of 1622. Not entirely, however. The Virginia government continued to establish and tried to enforce peaceful relations with the Indians. In general, every American colonist had to keep trained for the fight against starvation, disease, and Indians; but the Virginia colonist, unlike the Puritan, was not also engaged in a fight against the world itself. Therefore, the quality of deeper inner relaxation, of at-homeness, could take hold within the Virginian.

Of course, relaxation can become laxness, and laxness can become looseness, even in the moral sense. There was always the danger in the South that men would become soft, and New Englanders were quick and persistent in pointing this out. From the strict Calvinistic point of view, says Max Weber, "the real moral objection is to relaxation in the security of possession, the enjoyment of wealth with the consequence of idleness and the temptations of the flesh, above all of distraction from the pursuit of a righteous life. . . . Not leisure and enjoyment, but only activity serves to increase the glory of God."[8]

The Puritan mind stressed intellectual tautness. The early mind of the South did not. There was, on the contrary, a relaxation even in the realm of thought. To the Puritan, stern self-inquiry was necessary if one were to find God and obtain grace; the non-Puritan of Virginia and the later Southern colonies did not believe this necessary. The more public, formal faith of the Southerner enabled him to view the world and himself as what they seemed to be. He was inclined, as we would say now, to accept his public image as his real image. He was not necessarily less religious; he merely thought of religion as a more public, a more inclusive, a more social matter. In this view, much more depends upon custom and ritual, much less upon study and solitary introspection. This relative lack of intellect has marked the religious life of the South even to the present.

As it has marked all its life. The attitude of acceptance is usually a nonintellectual attitude. Like the conservative of any time, the Virginia settler was carrying most of his past into new surroundings. The surroundings themselves—the new present—would suggest any necessary changes. He had no notion of creating a way of life that had never existed before; consequently, he gave little thought to his way of life. Around most of the past certain sentiments had grown up. Cherishing these sentiments, he could move with considerable assurance into the world he now faced. He carried what he needed in his heart. Only if he had wished to create a radically new world would he have needed more intellectual stamina.

The Puritan settler of New England, determined as he was to create a radically new world, needed—and probably knew he needed—that supreme modern instrument, the analytical mind. But the Virginia settler had far more need of such a mind, or of a poetic, imaginative mind, than he realized—or perhaps than his descendants realize now. For, far more than he knew, he too, was moving into a new world, the modern world of dynamic change, which was to be in sharp contrast to the relatively static past world of the Middle Ages. The Jamestown settler did not know what this dynamic world would do to him, how much it would change him and the very bases of his life. The Puritan was destined to draw from this rich world, and from himself, mainly the dynamic elements. The Southerner was destined to fail to understand the composite medieval-modern world which, largely unconsciously, he was making in the South. Too inclined to be complacent, he would lose himself in a new land with its new and insidious temptations. Unlike the Puritan, he did not hate the world; indeed, he didn't even mistrust it. There was open for him only one safe course—but no course is safe—and he can hardly be blamed for not taking it. Only the greatest saints and poets have taken that difficult road. This was not merely to accept the world but to affirm it. As Nietzsche said: "It is not enough to accept fate; you must love it." Nor is it enough to accept the world, you must love it, too. As the Southerner did, but not with an active intelligence. If the early Southerner had sensed the difficulties inherent in accepting the world, he would have recognized that a man taking such a stand would need an intelligence even greater than that the Puritan aimed at. To take the ascetic stance and either turn your back on the world or pound your way through it is relatively easy. Easy because simple. When the deed is done, it is done. But for a man, himself a part of the world, continuously to face the world, to move through it and not be overcome by it—this is almost impossible. The Southerner tried to do this, but failed to develop at the same time that form of intelligence—call it philosophic or imaginative or poetic—that might have protected the South in the dangerous venture. The Southerner let himself be made too easily at home. Like a child he entered the dark wood of the modern world and was tragically—or perhaps pathetically—lost therein.

CHAPTER 3

INVITING LAND

But it was a lovely land that engulfed the Southerner. And it is appropriate that he came to Virginia, and the Puritan to Massachusetts. To those disposed to be at home, the New World offered a home; to those disposed to fight the battle of the Lord, it offered a superb battlefield. Each group found in the new land its proper climate. The Puritan said the world was dangerous and one must fight against it. The climate of New England was—and the land broken and rocky. Though the Virginian often voiced the Puritan view of this earth, he felt deep down that the world was friendly; and this was the world he found. Unfriendly, of course, in the swamps of the lower South, with malarial fevers and the excessive heat, but generally broad-bosomed and balmy; and, as the years proved, productive of staple crops in great demand in Europe. The limited fields of New England encouraged only subsistence farming; the Newfoundland Banks, however, were rich in cod, which England relished; and therefore shipbuilding developed, and at last worldwide trade, and the men who had uprooted themselves from England now found their second home upon the moving waters. And when the imposition of Jefferson's Embargo Act in 1807 and the closing of the slave trade in 1808 handicapped shipping, they found in their native rivers and later in steam the power that through manufacturing would dominate American life.

In the South, on the contrary, the broad and fertile land encouraged men to stay at home. The preeminence of farming is suggested even by the towns the South did not build. The Virginians did not need them; indeed, they did not want them, though as transplanted Englishmen, they would have found the agricultural village congenial.

The London Company wanted such towns to be built, so that the colonists could be protected and controlled. But the land took over. Within a decade tobacco was the money crop; shortly thereafter it became money itself. Tobacco demanded land, ever new land, because of its impoverishing effect. Therefore, despite all the entreaties and commands of the officials, individual settlers moved steadily up the rivers. Governor Yeardly, in his address before the first house of burgesses, in 1619, warned the planters not to establish themselves so far from one another.[1] But the lure of tobacco-bearing land was too great, and the rivers encouraged the dispersion. The coastal plain of Virginia is crossed by many large and small streams. These were the highways, and few tobacco farmers lived far from them. The tobacco crop and the rivers of Virginia soon made countrymen out of men who had been village dwellers.

So the Southerner became a countryman, a farmer, an individualist. The life he lived, which was the life the land suggested, was the taproot of the individualism that has always marked the Southerner. This individualism accompanies the lack of institutionalism in the South. The institutional life as it later developed was a highly individual, or personal, institutionalism of which the family is the prime example. The individual—and his family—were important because formal institutions were scarce.

But this individualism of the Southerner was, at least in its beginnings, the result of circumstances more than of native temperament. As generally representative of an England that still showed the marked influence of the medieval community, the early Southern settler brought this sense of community with him and, as much as one could expect, maintained it in the isolated clearings of the New World. Indeed, the very isolation increased the desire for society. In time, the Southerner was to become in most things one of the most individual of Americans, but he has also retained longer than most the sense of belonging to a community, however loosely organized. It is probable that his extreme individualism is partly the result of his sense of security in a community. However much he isolated himself physically, he wasn't primarily interested in isolating himself spiritually; he had a strong sense of society even in solitude.

The land and climate of New England did not suggest to the Puritan settlers such dispersed lives; on the contrary, they suggested compact towns. Such settlements were also better suited to economic, educational, and even religious advancement. Indeed, they were instead essentially barracks of the soldiers of the Lord, and, in later generations when the service of the Lord became too arduous, domiciles for Yankee traders. But whether they housed the Puritan or the Yankee, or both, the dealer in souls or in merchandise, the town sheltered the modern individual on the make, the man who settles close to others because thus he can use them better. Such a man creates an unhappy solitude even in the midst of society.

I overstate the case against the Puritan-Yankee. The South has had plenty of "Puritans" and "Yankees," though being less abstract-minded, the Southerner was never able to become purely one or the other. My main point is that the Southern settler became an individualist primarily because the land suggested this to him, not out of concern for his eternal welfare.

But the Southern land and climate also suggested the plantation; and the plantation, though under strong individual control, was also a society of its own, in some ways comparable to the medieval village. It will be said immediately that if the New England town was organized to enhance individual advancement, much more so was the plantation. The charge cannot be denied, yet it needs to be examined. For it is my first illustration of what we often see in the South: institutions that appear to be purely exploitative, but that, upon examination, reveal nonexploitative characteristics resulting partly from the intention, partly from the structure of the institution.

The plantation arose in the South both because of land and climate and because of the intentions of the London Company and the other English businessmen associated with the Southern settlements. The London Company set out with the intention of founding a great plantation and controlling directly the land, but the policy was so unsuccessful that within eleven years the Company had surrendered its monopoly and was granting fifty acres to every man who transported himself and another to Virginia. Administered fairly, such a system might not have built up a great landed aristocracy. As it was, however, within a hundred years the system had resulted, to cite an extreme instance, in the three-hundred-thousand-acre estate of Robert Carter, who was known as "King" Carter because of his power and haughtiness and because the extent of his lands matched many a European principality. "There is no doubt," says Thomas J. Wertenbaker, "that the land policy of the Southern colonies was second only to the slave system in building up the aristocratic type of society. It was the vast landholdings of 'King' Carter, rather than the culture of tobacco or his mercantile ventures, which made his descendants a power in Virginia for over a century."[2] Farther south, in Carolina, in 1669, Lord Ashley, one of the noble proprietors, had the philosopher John Locke, then his secretary and confidential adviser, draw up the Fundamental Constitutions of the province. Though Locke failed to persuade Carolinians to accept the varied titles of nobility he named—cacique, landgrave, etc.—he did set the stamp of approval upon extensive landholdings and thus fostered the growth of aristocracy in the South.

As for slavery, it need only be said at this point that, as indentured labor became more scarce slavery became a necessity if the plantation was to prosper. With its coming, it became a powerful factor in the growth of the plantation, but, originally, it was the plantation that created slavery.

In its inception, and indeed in its development, the plantation was by no means merely a profitable device for modern individualistic man on the make. It was a copy, adapted for the New World, of the landed estates of England; and it was created by, and was instrumental in creating, landed aristocracy, who thought of themselves as English gentry. Men, that is, with the stamp of the past upon them, with the aristocrat's sense of community and of obligation to community. This was a powerful factor in transferring to the American South, to this new land where men were generally small farmers on lonely homesteads, a strong sense of human community.

Yet it must be remembered that, though one part of the early Southerner's mind looked back toward the past, the Middle Ages, and aristocracy, the other part looked forward toward the future in a new world, and to whatever gifts that world might hold. To those who, through wealth or influence, obtained vast acreages, it bestowed a continuation, and even an extension, of the social position of the English landed gentleman. And to all men, since the frontier was inconceivably vast (especially after the Revolution), the New World held out the possibility of land of their own, of democratic freedom, and—with luck and hard work—of vast holdings and aristocratic prestige. In such an open world, despite the inequities, aristocrats were being continually made, and—through carelessness or bad luck—unmade. To be an aristocrat was to possess power and influence; but seldom was this power so great that it could be wielded without regard to the wills of the numerous smaller landowners in the vicinity. Southern aristocrats customarily had to pay attention to Southern democrats, and even with the growth of democracy during the nineteenth century, the democrats also paid attention to the aristocrats, not only because of aristocratic power but also because they admired this power and the men who held it and often hoped in time to gain such power and influence for themselves.

The significant thing is that the ideal of the English country gentleman took root in the South as the ideal of the plantation master. The past was not denied and rejected but re-expressed. With the passage of time, this American expression of the English past became the prevailing ideal of the American South. Not that every yeoman farmer wished to become a plantation owner with numerous slaves; he may have been content to remain a yeoman farmer, with no slaves or a few. But if he did have ambitions of greater influence and power, he probably envisaged the plantation as the best way to attain them. If he had cut out his farm on the frontier, he remembered the plantations along the coast or along the lower reaches of the rivers as being something of the expression of what he was working for. Like the earliest Virginia settler, who was seeking *not* something radically different from Old England but only more of the goods that England offered, he was asking of the future only that it provide him more generously with what the past had already given him a taste for. His ideals were rooted in the past. He was re-building in a new environment.

The plantation is usually defined by historians as a farming establishment having twenty or more slaves. By this standard, the plantation was always relatively infrequent in the South. The great majority of agriculturists belonged to the so-called yeoman farmer class. Such men possessed no slaves or, at most, one or two. But the temper of a society is not set by what its people do; it is set by what the people would like to do, by their ideals. The plantation became the Southern ideal. Farmers striving to advance strove to acquire plantations. Professional men seeking prestige bought plantations and often managed them from their homes in town. In fact, the plantation became such an ideal that the late ante-bellum South spawned the myth that all Southern farming took place on plantations. Blanche Henry Clark points out in her book *The Tennessee Yeomen, 1840–1860,*[3] that the myth had become so strong by this time that even travelers saw only plantations and reported that this was just about the only type of farming. In this view the South was composed of aristocrats, poor whites, and Negro slaves.

But, though this idea of the prevalence of the plantation was a myth, it was created and took hold because it expressed a deep social wish. Granted that this wish existed most strongly in the aristocrat himself; granted also that as the leader and chief molder of society he had the power so to express and extend this wish as to make of it finally a myth. He did not do this against the will of the rest of society. For the sense of hierarchy, of the fitness of an aristocracy, existed in the early American settler; he brought it with him from Europe; and the growth of a landed aristocracy in the South seemed to most men both natural and advisable. Of course, as we entered into our post-colonial, national period and the transmontane world opened westward, the increasingly extensive frontier, with its necessary emphasis upon the individual, weakened this sense of the rightness of an aristocracy, and by the time of the Civil War, had pretty well undermined it. But for a while the aristocratic attitude was very strong, and even today, a hundred years after the Civil War, faint hints of it remain.

I remember a South Carolina woman, a leader in church affairs, who at a national meeting of United Church Women rose to speak against a proposed action: "Why, we couldn't possibly do this. Our governor has already taken an opposite stand." He was the anointed leader; her duty—and her pleasure—was to follow.

CHAPTER 4

DOMINANT PATTERN

There's an interesting comment, elicited by slavery in the South, in Harriet Martineau's *Society in America:* "A magic ring seems drawn round those who live amidst slavery; and it gives a circular character to all they think and do upon the subject. There are but few who think within it who distinctly see anything beyond it."[1]

Miss Martineau, an early Victorian abolitionist, meant this as a criticism: a kind of black magic imprisons every white Southerner; he rarely breaks through its walls. This may have been true during the period of slavery; a similar limitation has appeared during the recent civil-rights battles.

Doubtless, what Miss Martineau meant was that on the subject of slavery the Southerner repeated the same limited phrases like a broken record. He did this in part because he lacked the courage to break through the phrases and face the situation with a new word or in a new light from outside his magic prison.

But this circling quality of mind, this failure of a direct projection of thought, is probably a characteristic of the Southerner, accentuated though it may have been by the presence of Negro slavery. For the Southerner's mind, like his life, is inclined to move in circles about a particular situation or place located in present time. From his beginning in the South, he has had a strong sense of his life as being centered between the past and the future within a place whose expansible limits reach far into space. He does not move logically from one object to similar objects to abstractions of these objects until the original object has disappeared and only a formula remains. He circles the object, bemusedly or lovingly or angrily.

He is a realist, not an abstract thinker, and his respect for reality is positive. Reality cannot be impaled like a butterfly on a pin and filed for future study. Reality is a living, changing, growing thing. The best you can do is circle it and circle it again. Maybe at last you will get the general outline, the feel, the color, perhaps even something of the density.

This is the method of the poet rather than the scientist; concrete, not abstract, and not very popular in the modern world. It was the method of a great Southern writer like William Faulkner, who, it has been said, circled his subject like one of his bird dogs circling a covey, closing in slowly so as not to flush the birds too soon. The fault of the South was not that it pursued this method, but that it did not pursue it intelligently and assiduously enough. Circle with intense concern, circle wide enough, and you enclose the world, as Blake said, in a grain of sand.

Let us consider more closely this absence of the direct approach, this circling movement, without, however, losing sight of an apparently opposing characteristic—the capacity for wholehearted, swift, and sometimes terrible action.

According to the psychologist Erik Erikson,[2] any culture contains a number of tensions or inner strains. These exist primarily because the members of the society, both within and among themselves, desire goods that, to some degree, oppose one another. The style of the culture depends upon its balancing of these opposites. If for any reason the tensions become so strong that conflict results, the society may destroy itself. If the tensions can be maintained, but at a level below conflict, the culture thrives.

This, I think, is but the social expression of what Thomas and Znaniecki call the two permanent tendencies of human nature, "desire for new experience" and "desire for stability." Each of us has both of these desires, but in each of us the relative strength of the desires differs. No one can live without stability; no one can live without change.

Since the Southern character is a variant of the American, let me review here Erikson's view of the American character. In his view, two basic forces produced the American: Puritanism and the tension between home and frontier. In regard to the home-frontier tension, Erikson points out that, until recently, all Americans faced two opposed possibilities of life: to remain at home or to go to the frontier. Some would remain where they had been born, others would go to the frontier. Therefore, these two opposed possibilities existed in the inner life of all Americans.

Puritanism also, though its influence has greatly decreased, still dominates American character. Though Erikson doesn't say this, Puritanism is closely tied in with the home-frontier tension and reinforces the pull of the frontier. It is a "stripped" religion, and suited to the "stripped" frontier life. It is significant that the chief influx of Puritanism came into the South in the eighteenth century with the Scotch-Irish, who even then were known as "the Yankees of the South" and "the Puritans of the South." James G. Leyburn, in his book *The Scotch-Irish,* calls them typical frontiersmen. If they had not been modified by the earlier Southern settlers, who were predominantly English, they would have made the South almost indistinguishable from the Puritan-dominated North. Using Erikson's thesis that the American character has been formed about the opposing poles of "home" and "frontier," I maintain that the distinctiveness of the Southern character lies in the fact that these opposing poles are more closely tied together than is usually so in the American character. It is the nature of any tension that each pole implies the other. In the South, more than in the rest of America, and for reasons we shall examine, home has implied the frontier, and the frontier, home. The Southerner, therefore, carries more of himself into each of these situations than does the typical American. Why and how has this happened?

It began with the deeper sense of home that the Southern settler brought to the New World. He didn't wish, like the New England Puritan, to change the heart of England. Rather he wished to extend, for each man's benefit and for England's, the body of England. Though Virginia was superficially strange and dangerous, and indeed often destroyed men through famine, disease, and Indian warfare, it was not really strange—except in the sense of being wonderful—to the transplanted Englishman. He saw it as still a part of the world which, up to then, had been best represented by "Merrie England," and so it was more homelike than the wintry woods of Massachusetts were to the Puritan.

But perhaps more important than this quality of the land was the basic attitude of the settler. He was less frightened of it, less withdrawn from it, less inclined to whip it into safer form. Therefore, he was more at home even on those first Atlantic seaboard frontiers than was his New England contemporary. It is true, the lure of tobacco soon made him feel increasingly at home, even on his isolated farm along the Virginia rivers, but he went there partly because he felt at home already.

A word here as to the successive American frontiers. As soon as the seaboard was settled, the frontier moved inland. For the first half of the eighteenth century the effective frontier in the South was the Piedmont stretching southwesterly in a fairly wide band from Virginia to Georgia. This was the upcountry or the back country; and its settlement during the mid-eighteenth century predominantly by the Scotch-Irish affected the entire culture of the South. In 1763, the British, having won the French and Indian War, and made a treaty with France, forbade settlement beyond the Alleghenies to avoid further conflict. This outlawing of transmontane settlement hardly stopped it. Nevertheless, until the colonies won their independence, such settlements were both hazardous and uncertain, not only because of the Indians, still incited by the French, but also because of the lack of any legal title to land. With the Revolution accomplished, the bars went down, and by 1800 the westward tide was running, and was not to cease until it had reached the Pacific and covered all available land between. It was during the nineteenth century especially that the frontier assumed that compelling place in American history that was noted first by the historian Frederick Jackson Turner.

There was, of course, a frontier from 1607 on, but the colonial attitude toward it was very different from that of the nineteenth century. During the colonial period, Americans were still Englishmen though living outside of England. Especially was this true in the South. But with independence, Americans turned their backs on England, looked unhesitantly beyond the Alleghenies into the dim forests of the interior, and began a total movement toward the distant Pacific.

It is clear that this large out-migration threatened the position of the entire seaboard. The South, however, seems to have felt this threat less deeply and intimately than the North. Doubtless, this was in part due to the fact that the South was less self-conscious than New England. It had always been less concerned about intellectual and spiritual matters, and had therefore not produced, as New England had by 1840, a group of writers who were able to express these doubts and assurances. What we see taking place is this: During the westward rush of the first half of the nineteenth century the young American from the North went abroad far more frequently to study and to take the European tour than the young Southerner did, and one of his purposes, as he admitted, was to discover what connections, if any, he had with the Old World past. For he was disturbed about the great expansion of the seaboard into the barbaric West. It raised the question of whether the Northeast could maintain its identity, its culture, against such an outflow of human resources.

The Southern seaboard, in contrast to this, had maintained more of England in the New World, had rooted the English culture more deeply here, and was less fearful, therefore, that it might be undermined by the westward movement. Having incorporated more of the past, it could accept more calmly the future. During the colonial period, many young Southerners had been educated in England. This may have been partly due to the fact that the South did not have enough colleges. The result, however, was the rather complete transference of Old World culture to the New. The consequent strength of the Southern seaboard culture prevented it from being unduly disturbed by the westward movement.

I am not saying that the Southerner was not disturbed. He was. Not, I think, because the identity of the seaboard was being threatened, but because its power was being drained off to the West. This naturally disturbed those who had large investments, economic, political, personal, along the seaboard. Virginians, moving westward, established in the richer soil of Kentucky a competitive tobacco industry; Carolinians set up more productive cotton plantations in Alabama and Mississippi. Tidewater South Carolina had already had some experience with this outward flow of political power from the coast into its own piedmont. Even from the earliest settlement of its piedmont, beginning about 1750, there had been a growing demand there for political representation. But Charleston and the tidewater did not yield power to its own piedmont except as that region, through the adoption of the cotton plantation, became sympathetic to the political interests of the South Carolina tidewater. In brief, the sense of regional indentity was too deeply rooted in the earlier tidewater settlements for their people to be overly concerned about its submergence in the westward movement; they were primarily concerned to retain their political power.

Deep down, and half-consciously, however, the Southerner was also concerned about identity. Though the South attained, and is still in process of attaining, an identity more clearly delineated than that attained by any other American region, even the South has never been deeply sure of itself. In the beginning it built wisely. It sought in its future the best of its past. But it was confused, especially by slavery, and made unwise choices. It understood the basic wisdom of combining the past and the future, the attained and the unattained, the tame and the wild, home and the frontier; but it has never known just how to do it.

With the nineteenth-century increase in the pull of the frontier, there was a corresponding decrease, even in the South, in attachment to the earlier settlements, whether these were along the seaboard or in the piedmont. It is significant that perhaps most numerous among the frontiersmen were the Scotch-Irish, who, generally speaking, had never known the appeal of the seacoast. Doubtless also, the more men turned their minds to the frontier and the future, the less they lingered on the past. But in the South, in addition to the temper of the Southern settler, certain facts bound the frontier and the old settlements more closely together than they were bound in the North. The most basic of these was the continuing agricultural nature of the South in contrast to the growing industrial nature of the Northeast.

The westward-moving frontier in the North, turning forest and prairie into farms, was not backed up by continuing farms in the older settlements; it was backed up by villages becoming towns, and towns becoming industrial cities. The countryman who, during the nineteenth century, looked back upon his old home saw it displaced by the industrial city. Being mainly of Puritan stock, he tended less to look back; nor did the changing landscape of his childhood encourage such sentimental ties. As he moved farther westward, therefore, he increasingly cut his ties with the past. It is significant that in creating an industrial world, he created a world from which he increasingly fled. Increasingly but with increasing futility, until, by 1890, as Hamlin Garland points out in *Main-Traveled Roads,* the bank and the railroad had overrun him. The early Puritan thought of himself as being sent on "an errand into the wilderness" to find God. He was to make of the wilds another kind of wilderness: the wilderness of bankrupt Midwestern farms of the 1890's and of the Dust Bowl of the 1930's, and the general industrial wilderness in which modern man now wanders.

Not that the Southerner didn't create a wilderness as well. We, too, raped the land, as certain great gullies in Georgia attest. We stole its wealth through the roots of tobacco and cotton, and then fled westward, leaving broomsedge and old-field pines behind us. But we could always look back to a past that was similar to our present. Or, more accurately, to an earlier place, the home site, that did not change materially with the years. The agricultural seaboard and piedmont, out of which the Old Southwest of Alabama and Mississippi grew, did not become urban and industrial. In spite of all the contrasts between the southeast and what we now call the Old Southwest—and there were many—they were both agricultural sections, and were far more closely bound together through ties of sentiment and of interest than were the frontiers and the older settlements of the North. Economically and politically, the ante-bellum South tried to take advantage of this agricultural unity as against the industrial-agricultural duality of the North. One of the main political concerns of the South, from the Missouri Compromise in 1820 to the Civil War, was to drive a wedge between the industrial East and the agricultural West and to cement the West to the South. The great tie was supposed to be the Mississippi River, running down from the Old Northwest to the Old Southwest; but there were also hopes and plans for railroads running from the Northwest southeasterly to the Atlantic and tying the two sections closer together. The South, however, could never agree with itself, the Northwest was always skeptical of slave labor, the East built railroads and canals tying East and West together, and the Southern agricultural cause was lost to the combined agricultural-industrial cause of the North and West. (Ironically, of course, the agricultural West had also lost to the industrial East by 1890.)

Not only were the agricultural frontiers of the South supported both psychologically and economically by the continuing agricultural economy of the old southeastern tidewater and piedmont, the very ideal of frontier agriculture itself was the Southern plantation. Thus, the continuing ideal of the South was an economic and social institution that perhaps reached its height in the Virginia and Carolina plantations of the eighteenth century.

Furthermore, not only prestige but also political power lay chiefly with the plantation owner. He did not grab this power from yeoman farmers and merchants; for the most part he was granted it as his right, a right that rested upon the fact that his wealth and leisure had enabled him to prepare himself for political responsibilities. It is undoubtedly true that the newness of the frontier and the presence of free land made for the loosening of old ties, including the ties of respect for a landed aristocracy. Men still strove for large acreages and the leadership that such possession would give them. They were still eager to create a new aristocracy in Alabama and Mississippi. It was pointed out by the Alabama writer, Joseph Baldwin, in *Flush Times in Alabama and Mississippi,* that the seaboard aristocrat, whom Baldwin called the Virginian, was too nice and restrained to thrive, sometimes even to exist, in the Old Southwest; but, even so, a less restrained, more rambunctious, more democratic aristocrat was always in the making. So the Southern frontier looked back to and copied, the seaboard plantation home.

One must recognize, too, that the nature of Southern economic and social life kept certain aspects of the frontier closer to the Southeastern plantations than the Northern frontier was to the farms and towns of New England. If the plantations of the South were large and spacious, so were the untouched forests and swamps lying between them. Indeed, the relatively large areas of untouched woods and swamps that stretch across the lower South even today are a surprise to those Americans who have known only the thickly settled cities and countrysides of the East and much of the North. By this time these vast wooded areas have been mostly deforested, sometimes more than once, and the trees that grow so abundantly are usually second growth. But during the antebellum period these woods and swamps had hardly been touched, and like those on the frontier, they were inhabited by many of the original wild animals. Thus, despite the sedate and orderly plantations, these surrounding stretches of forest gave a continuing sense of the frontier. So that what we had scattered over the South, and expressing its chief economic ideal, was the plantation, essentially orderly and rational, established in a natural world still heavily touched by frontier wildness. Through most of the history of the South, then, wherever the Southerner was, he could feel within himself the tension between settlement and frontier, the tame and the wild, order and chaos, culture and nature. Thus, the economic system of the South encouraged that sense of life as rooted in the past and growing into the future that Englishmen originally brought to Southern shores.

CHAPTER 5

BASIC ERROR

Inclined to accept the world as good, or to accept the evil of life as a part of the goodness of life, the Southern settler embraced the hospitable land. In the same spirit, unfortunately, he accepted the institution of slavery. The first Negroes were sold in Virginia in 1619, but they were probably bought as indentured servants, under the same kind of arrangement made with white indentured servants, that is, to work for a contracted number of years. For decades there was confusion about the status of these Negro servants; but by 1662, Virginia law made it clear that Negro servants were servants for life, that is, slaves. The growth of slavery, however, was at first very slow. It had been adopted partly because of the insufficiency of indentured labor, and as the flow of this labor tended to slow down because of improved conditions in England, the need for slave labor became greater. The need for labor in new settlements, where life has to be built from the bottom, is always greater than the supply.

It may be asked what made the Americans fall back upon slave labor. Wasn't such labor already an anachronism in the European homeland? In general, yes. The earlier slaves, or serfs, had largely become peasants. The few remaining slaves were largely household servants, used to cater to the ease and pleasure of their owners, not as productive workers. There was a reasonably large slave population in Spain and Portugal, but this was largely composed of Moors, whom the Spaniards had been slowly forcing from the peninsula for the eight hundred years preceding the discovery of America. This Spanish-Moorish situation provided the main justification for such slavery as existed: Christians could not enslave fellow Christians but they could enslave pagans. Since the Negroes of Africa were also pagans, there was nothing to hinder the Portuguese, using the new shipping that helped to bring in the modern world, from importing Negroes from Africa and selling them as slaves in Europe. In the New World, chiefly in Central and South America, the Spanish and Portuguese continued and expanded the practice of slavery that they had known in the Iberian peninsula. First, Indian slaves, and then Negroes, mainly because the Negroes were more docile.

But the religious note was strong in this Spanish and Portuguese slavery. Slavery was a fit fate for pagans; but suppose the enslaved pagans became Christians? What then? At first it seemed as if they must then be freed; but this was too drastic a measure. So what happened was simply an amelioration of slavery itself in South America. The Catholic Church taught that freedom was the proper estate of man; that to be a slave was a most unhappy fate; and that society should take what measures it could to make this fate easier, and whenever possible to free men from it.

When the early English colonists adopted slavery, more than a hundred years after the discovery of America, and after the Spanish and Portuguese had settled colonies, most of which were in South America, they were in part but following the Spanish and Portuguese example. They, too, were concerned about the fate of the slave who became a Christian. Should he be freed or not? In 1667, Virginia decided he need not be freed; but then, in sharp contrast to the general attitude toward slavery cultivated by the Catholic Church in South America, the predominantly Protestant English settlers slowly came to the conviction that slavery, not freedom, was the natural condition of the Negro. Eventually this attitude became so strong that free Negroes in the South were always in some danger of being thrown into slavery.

This was an ironic development in a land devoted to freedom. The Roman Catholic settlers of South America were closer to the community sense, the inclusive Christian and Catholic sense, of the Middle Ages than were the Protestant settlers of the English colonies. Therefore, they were inclined to feel that the Negroes—or Indians—in their midst, though slaves, were also members of the community, and that if for any reason freed, they could move directly into the full life of the community. The English colonists had moved further from the sense of medieval community into the individualistic freedom of the modern world, and though they cherished their own freedom more, they were less concerned about the freedom of others, especially if these others were distinguished by color from the dominant whites. Paradoxically, the presence in large numbers of the enslaved Negro was to make the white Southerner more insistent than any other American upon his own individual freedom.

To recapitulate, the colonists took up slavery because of the nature of the land—level or lightly rolling, with many rivers available for easy transportation between distant plantations, with its soil and climate suitable for staple crops (tobacco first, then indigo, rice, cotton, sugar cane, hemp)—because there was a demand for these crops in other parts of the world, and because of the ease with which they could be cultivated by generally untrained labor. They were also propelled toward the use of slave labor because they, too, harbored the modern desire to use, to manipulate, to exploit the world. Remember that the land policy of Virginia, and later of Carolina, permitted vast acreages to be granted to men who had the influence or the wealth to demand them. With the vast estates went the need to cultivate them, and this need was met by the use of slaves.

Some slavery existed in all the American colonies, but only in the South were the material conditions such as to make it highly profitable. Had it been as profitable in the Northern colonies as in the Southern, undoubtedly it would have taken root there also, for the Puritans were moving more drastically and rapidly into the modern world than were the Virginians, and the massive exploitation of slave labor would have been an excellent means to that end. It is true that that crusty old Puritan, Cotton Mather, commenting, about 1715, upon the disastrous Yemassee Indian War in South Carolina, said that the province "is newly destroy'd by the dreadful Judgments of God, for which an uncommon measure of Iniquities had ripened it." And one of the obvious iniquities, as we see it now, was the proneness of South Carolina traders to foment Indian internecine wars in order to buy up the captives as slaves. But this same Cotton Mather was hardly opposed to slavery itself, for only fifteen years earlier, upon the occasion of the gift of a slave, he thanked God for the comfort that this gift would bring. Indeed, the sinfulness of slavery, as the early Puritan saw it, was not what it did to the slave but what it did to the owner. The slave would be taught, and forced, to work, and all work was for the glory of God; the owner would be taught to be idle, and "the devil finds work for idle hands" and sin for idle minds to ponder.

We can make a rough guess at what might have happened if the soil and climate of Massachusetts had suited slave labor. The overseers on Southern plantations were often Yankees; the most famous of them all, the legendary Simon Legree, of *Uncle Tom's Cabin,* was a Yankee; and their reputation for harsh driving and cruelty agrees with his. Of course, the overseers were in a tight situation, caught between the owner's desire for profit and the slave's skill in malingering. But there is also the record of Southern plantations after the Civl War in the hands of Yankee owners, who drove the free Negroes as most of them had never, even as slaves, been driven before. With the Puritan and later Yankee emphasis upon the holiness of work and profit, we may conclude that the slaves the Puritan owners did not work to death would have been freed without the expense of a Civil War because slavery would have been found unprofitable. The British geologist Sir Charles Lyell, traveling in the South, made a common observation: "It is notorious, that the hardest task-masters to the slaves are those who come from the Northern free states."[1]

The non-Puritan settlers of the South cared little about the holiness of work and not everything about the profits that might accrue. Carrying much of the Middle Ages with them, where truth was attained through contemplation rather than action, they were less interested than the Puritans in work, more interested in the periods of leisure that could be gained either through work or without it. So they accepted slavery as a way to obtain leisure for themselves—and indeed prestige and power also. (It is only fair to say that over the years they handled slavery more humanely than, with a different attitude, they might have.) In the Modern World, with its emphasis upon work and production, this appreciation of leisure is a true value, however evil the means which lead to it. The basic error was that in adopting slavery the South adopted a means which was so sharply opposed to the ends it sought that it would finally make the attainment of those ends impossible.

Yet, if we would get the exact picture, we must remember that these Southern slaveowners were predominantly North American Protestants, not South American Catholics. They did not really believe, as strict Puritans might have believed, that they were benefiting the slaves by making them work, but neither did they see the Negro slaves as essentially members of the total community only temporarily debarred because of the unhappy and inhuman fate of slavery. These Southerners were going into the Modern World on the backs of these strange, incompletely human beings; but they did not think they were going to heaven or taking the slaves to heaven because of any gospel of work. It is true that in later years, under severe moral and political attack from the Puritans, they did say that by revealing Christ's mercy to the heathen Negroes they were making them candidates for heaven; but by this time, under the influence of the nineteenth-century revivalism, they had become sentimental Puritans themselves.

The South was nominally Christian. When it adopted slavery, Christianity had existed for some sixteen hundred years, in societies marked by slave, serf, and other class divisions. With the Reformation, however, the dynamic Christian movement in Europe began to demand individual freedom—religious, political, economic. This European desire for freedom was accentuated in the New World by the actual freedom possible to, and demanded by the settlers. The South was therefore enslaving one class of men to make another class more free in a world in which freedom was a primary demand. Such a contradictory attitude would sooner or later break down.

In seeking economic freedom, freedom to exploit the world, men would inevitably seek to exploit other men; for the exploitative attitude includes man as well as nature, includes indeed the very ability of the exploiter himself. At this point the South was misled by its land and climate. Westward from all American settlements, North and South, stretched vast, rich lands for exploitation. Largely by necessity, the

North, unable to use slave labor successfully in this exploitation, made the earth exploit itself by inventing tools and machines that could be used in place of human hands. This method proved far more effective than the chattel slavery of the South in realizing the dream of controlling the earth. Granted that the new machines also exploited their operators, this was an indirect exploitation; unlike chattel slavery, the machine society was not in flagrant opposition to modern man's desire for freedom and to the growing sense of democracy connected with this desire. In choosing slavery, the South chose for the long run a relatively ineffectual method of exploiting the earth and, because of its own concern for freedom and its growing concern for democracy, a self-destructive method of exploiting men. What made it in a sense more self-destructive than it had to be was the fact that the South retained a richer heritage of the Middle Ages than the North did. Though men have always exploited others, the Middle Ages not excepted, the Modern World has frankly extended this practice further than it has ever been carried before. The Middle Ages were, at least theoretically, against it. This theoretical opposition, lingering in the mind of the Southerner, touched his conscience, made him an uneasy adherent of slavery, and slowed down the South's advance into the highly exploitative modern world.

We today judge slavery in the abstract: it was, and is, wrong. Even the historical fact (which the South called to its defense) that upon the base of slavery Greece reached a pinnacle of intellectual achievement unattained elsewhere in the world does not persuade us today that slavery can ever be justified. Even granting that it was right for the ancient Greeks is not to grant that it was right for the Southerner. For the Greeks were pre-Christian and had never heard of the Modern World. The South was trying to defend itself, as it did too often, with words that did not match reality. Southerners were not the men, nor was the land the land, to bring forth the intellectual life of the Greeks. The Southerner never really desired such a divisive, individualistic life. Nor could the life he did desire be successfully based upon slavery. This was the Southerner's basic error. He tried to do what neither he himself nor his times permitted.

CHAPTER 6

"GO TO THE ANT"

This was the advice of the writer of *Proverbs,* and was addressed to the "sluggard," who, it was suggested, would find wisdom in considering the busyness of the ant. We in the Modern World, especially we in the South who retain some sense of the value of leisure, have seen too much of antlike busyness. Bertrand Russell said years ago that if modern man would quit working so hard and simply rest awhile, things would be better. Since the development of the hydrogen bomb, Russell has become tragically aware of the truth of his early view. It is true that the Southerner has never been inclined to leisureliness in his use of weapons; "shoot first and investigate afterward" has often been the motto. But, in general, leisure has been considered a value, and the lack of intensity associated with leisure has been a mark of Southern life. It is this lesser intensity that distinguishes the Southerner from the Puritan or Yankee. Herein lies the strength of the South, as also its weakness.

Undoubtedly, one cause of the high valuation the South has put upon leisure was the existence of slavery. For certain whites, slavery made leisure possible. But even had there been no slavery, a slower pace, and less work—that is, more leisure—would have been suggested by the climate of most of the South. I remember my first reaction as a young man—and, as I came to realize, young Confederate—to Northern energy and a Massachusetts winter: "You people move fast because you have to to keep from freezing. But try this in a South Carolina summer and you'd have sunstroke." I realize now that there is more to Yankee drive than I thought then, but a part of its cause, and a part of the cause of the leisurely Southern pace, is the climate. Even within the limits of one state, South Carolina, you can feel the pace slow down, the tension relax, as you move from the Scotch-Irish piedmont toward the English coast. And as one approaches this coast, with its many rivers and streams, along which innumerable fish swim, almost begging to be caught for breakfast, the question arises, why should any man exert himself greatly? God will take care of him.

Regardless of whether he worked hard or not, the Southern settler was less inclined than his Northern counterpart to give a religious value to work. Work was a necessity; in a new land rich in raw resources, work was a way to great success. The Southern settler was an early modern who wished to better his condition, and therefore he worked and toiled at conquering the forest. But he was not accustomed to tell himself that he was working for the glory of God. And though he was an early modern, driving into the future, it was a future not too unlike the best of the past, only richer and more expansive. Certainly when the landed aristocracy developed, it made a conscious attempt to bring the sense of English scenes to America, and this meant a frequent pause for reflection as one drove ahead. As this landed aristocracy supplied the social and political leaders, their attitudes affected the entire society.

The struggle, expecially on the frontier, was hard, the hours long. Yet, observing their leaders, men came to value leisure. Even poor men valued leisure—and I'm not referring to that actually small group, the poor whites, who play such a large part in the stories about the South. For them, leisure—the absence of work—was the greatest need after a mouthful of food. I'm thinking of small but independent farmers. They couldn't ride to hounds with the rich gentry, but they had their own coon and possum dogs. They couldn't sit on the front piazza and sip mint juleps, but the men could sit in the breezeway and chew tobacco, while the women, if they wished, could smoke. And this generally in considerable peace and without much envy of their more successful neighbor. For they were free men, made more independent in fact and in attitude by the vast untouched land in which they lived; but they still carried with them a strong sense of each man in his place. They felt themselves members of the community of which the gentleman on his broad piazza was the leader.

There remained the Negro slaves. The bitter abolitionist who visualized them as being driven to death suggests that they who were so important in providing the leisure for the whites had none for themselves. It must be admitted that some slaves were driven to death. Everything that happened in *Uncle Tom's Cabin* probably happened in the South. But the picture of the Negro slave being driven to death is no more true to the total picture than *Uncle Tom's Cabin* is. For one thing, it does not give sufficient weight to the power that the Negro has always exerted in the South. Though highly discriminated against, he yet made his weight felt in all the operations of the plantation. Planters soon found it was easier to persaude him than to make him work. If he felt too driven, he would move at the very lowest limit of the overseer's endurance. In general, the slave moved at his own pace, and it was a common observation of Northern travelers that this was but a fraction of the pace observed by free Northern labor.

In this connection, William Cullen Bryant made the following observation: "It is, of course, the desire of the master that his slaves should be laborious; on the other hand, it is the determination of the slave to lead as easy a life as he can. . . . The result is a compromise in which each party yields something, and a good-natured though imperfect and slovenly obedience on one side, is purchased by good treatment on the other."[1]

This refusal to work fast, this leisurely pace, does not mean the presence of any great degree of artistic creation among the slaves. Indeed, one of the matters we shall have to consider is the apparent lack of artistic creation among even those whites who had leisure. But at the moment I am not discussing what the South did with its leisure; I am simply saying that, from the top to the bottom, Southerners had more or less of it, and they valued it. To suggest, as I have done, that the gentry set the pattern and the others followed is probably an oversimplification. For that pattern the gentry set was in part the pattern set by the slaves. Since it was apparently impossible for the master to make the slave take life too seriously, it hardly seemed worthwhile to take it too seriously himself. One of my neighbors, a hardheaded farmer, certainly no sentimentalist in his treatment of his Negro labor, said to me once, "There's one thing sure. You've just got to let them take their time; you can't hurry them." Did the slave move slowly because he saw his master sitting on the piazza, or did the master sit long hours on the piazza because his slave moved slowly? Whatever the cause and effect, Southern whites and Negroes accommodated themselves to one another remarkably well.

Another way of describing the sense of leisure in Southern life is to say that there was more play here. More emphasis upon entertainment, shows, storytelling, practical jokes, even theater. Though formal theater never occupied a large place in the total life, chiefly because of the scarcity of large cities. Charleston had the first real theater in America; and there, as well as in a few other cities, such as Savannah, Nashville, and New Orleans, excellent shows were given from time to time. Amateur theatricals, parties, and balls became identified with Southern life. Visitors sometimes ascribed this to the boredom of life on the isolated plantations. Rollin G. Osterweis, in *Romanticism and Nationalism in the Old South,* speaks of Southerners as an agrarian people "over whom the shadow of boredom and monotony hung constantly."[2] In fact, Osterweis sees the entire cult of chivalry, and other related interests, as the result of boredom. "Color was supplied by romantic literature, by the military cult, the adoration of women, flamboyant oratory." A. DePuy Van Buren, a Northerner who taught in the South in the ante-bellum period, also saw the emphasis upon amusement as stemming from boredom; but he found the life boring because it seemed to have no purpose.[3] The doubtful word is *purpose.* To Van Buren, *purpose* may have meant the intention of changing and improving life, both one's own and that of others. The Southerners he observed may have been more concerned than he was with living itself as the purpose of life. If so, and if they felt they were living, they would not have felt life purposeless, and therefore boring.

As for the storytelling propensity of the Southerner, this resulted from his possession of leisure and from his rather large interest in the mere passage of life as distinct from what profit he could get out of it. Being generally interested in life itself in its varied, concrete expressions, and finding time to recall such actions, he naturally made stories out of them. His interest in practical jokes, although in part the influence of the frontier, was also due to his interest in the public expression of an easy and relaxed nature.

The place of play in Southern life is similar to that of the play in a machine. Machine play, or tolerance, is the degree of looseness with which the moving parts of a machine are interrelated. There is a sense in which the play of Southern life is a part of its relatively uninstitutionalized life, its emphasis upon the person and upon personal, organic relations. Typically and historically a nonspecialist, the Southerner is less closely bound to others than the more abstract and specialized members of an industrial order. In his type of society, he demands more leeway, more tolerance, more play. Having more play, he is basically more tolerant. (I do not forget the white's lack of tolerance toward the Negro.) "A man has a right to make a fool of himself," he says. No tightly structured society can permit this; the wheels mesh too closely; looseness at any point endangers the machine.

But why this relative looseness of social structure in the South, this tolerance? What is there within the individual that allows this social play? It can be explained, I would say, as the reasonably healthy tension between the two main poles of his life—home and frontier—which is perhaps only another form of the past-future tension. He has play within himself and can allow play in society because the basic tension of his life is not too taut and because he is not stretched too tightly. This relative slackness is due to the fact that each of the two basic poles of the Southerner's life includes, like a shadow, the other. The strangeness of the frontier lies close to home, the security of home touches the frontier. This attitude at its best makes the Southerner at home in a strange world.

It is this subsoil that sustains Southern culture. The two poles, the home and the frontier, become one. This is another way of saying that God is in the world. The inner tension is not, as in strict Puritanism, between God and the world. Such a tension will drive the poles apart and split life in two, with an ideal half-world for the Puritan and a material half-world for the Yankee. A true culture rests upon wholeness and is deeply religious. All its details, all its aspects, have meaning; point to a center; imply God.

It is probable that Southerners had too much leisure, played too much, were too tolerant of themselves, of other fools, and of the world. It is probable they accepted life too easily, became therefore too closely involved with it, and were swallowed up by it. God was so much a part of the world that the world was God. Whatever was, was right. It is only safe to love the world in God; to love each detail in its infinite meaning, under an eternal light, not merely in its immediate pressure.

Yet it was the extreme and fatal acceptance of slavery that at long last has brought the South to the verge of a deeper realization of God's presence in the world. The South played, played fast and loose, and lost all. It may now win what it never even bet on. This is the way of life, and this is the story we're unfolding.

CHAPTER 7

TIGHTENING BOW

Sidney Mead, in *The Lively Experiment,* makes the interesting observation that "Americans have never had time to spare"; and he quotes the lines from Stephen Vincent Benét:

> *There is no time to grieve now, there is no time.*
> *There is only time for the labor in the cold.*

He says further: "What they did have during all their formative years was space—organic, pragmatic space—the space of action." They also had social space: a considerable freedom from the bondage of habit, class, and custom. "It is not too much to say that in America space has played the part that time has played in the older cultures of the world," where men have matured slowly and patiently through time under the endless flow and flux of events.[1]

But the Southerner has had time—at least more time than the typical American. He brought more of it with him; he brought more of the past. Partly because of this, but also because of the economy he developed, he had more time here, and valued time more for itself and less for what might be produced through it. Having more time, he was less determined and ruthless in his handling of space. Admittedly, he, too, was fascinated by the great open spaces, and often ruthless in his handling of them. But he carried more of the past into them than did his Northern counterpart, though some of what he carried was a burden of guilt unrecognized by the more youthful and time-lacking Northerner.

The essential quality of the Southerner is a true conservatism, expressed in a healthy tension between past and future, between the place already occupied and unoccupied space, between home and frontier, between the already achieved and the still-to-be achieved.

But tensions, within an individual or a society, may become too strong, and instead of serving to keep the organism toned up may cause it to fly to pieces. This is what happened in the South, and slavery seems to have been the cause. For slavery confused the South in its poised movement from the past into the future.

Though the early Southern settler was different from the early Northern settler, and though the land and climate tended to increase this difference, it is highly improbable that without slavery the two sections would have come to civil strife. For, without slavery, the South would have held less strongly to the past; without slave-produced staples, the manufacturing and commercial North would have moved less swiftly ahead. The two sections, therefore, would have remained closer together, and would probably never have found sufficient cause for armed conflict. But slavery confused and embittered both North and South as they moved side by side, but at different speeds, into the Modern World.

For slavery looked strongly both backward and forward. Why, then, did it not suit the Southern mind, which we have described as a balanced concern for both past and future? Because slavery was too opposed to the increasingly democratic spirit of the Modern World, and the attempt to hold them both together resulted not in creative tension but in disastrous conflict.

In its inception, slavery looked mainly forward. For it was the result of the invasion of European man into the vast, unexploited spaces of a new world, whose peoples were so different in appearance, culture, and religion that they could be considered objects of exploitation, like the land itself. Since Indian slaves proved relatively inefficient, Negro slaves were increasingly imported from Africa.

Slavery, then, was a part of Western man's capitalistic, exploitative thrust into the Modern World. The Southern slaveowner of the nineteenth century was aiming at profits on his capital in much the same way the Northern millowner was. But he was less rational about it, and therefore less successful. He was less rational because he was more deeply imbued with the Renaissance ideal of the complete man, for whom rational work was not of supreme importance. According to Max Weber, the basic force that created modern capitalism was the acceptance by workers generally of the Calvinistic thesis that all work is for the glory of God. Imbued with this idea, a nominally free worker could keep going just above the edge of starvation. It was more than even a Calvinist could do to sell such an idea to Negro slaves. About as far as the slaveowners got in their use of religion was to try to persuade the slaves to follow Paul's injunction, and "obey their masters."

The Southerner, therefore, adopted slavery because it seemed a faster way into the Modern World. Like the Puritan, he was interested in this world, though not so deeply. Perhaps because he was less passionately interested, he was less intelligently interested, and chose less effective means than those chosen by his Northern counterpart. What was the effect of slavery upon the progress of the South?

William Henry Drayton, in his *History of South Carolina to 1808,* says that, regrettable as slavery was, without it South Carolina could not have made the material advances she had, nor could she have taken a position of leadership among American states. It is doubtless true that the great exports of timber, tobacco, rice, indigo, and, by the time Drayton wrote, cotton, would have been curtailed without slave labor. This would have retarded the material advancement, not only of South Carolina but of the whole South as well as the manufacturing and trading North. Later, when the Southern defense of slavery grew strong, the myth arose that white Southerners could not bear labor in the southern sun, and that therefore Negro labor was necessary for the very life of the South. The truth here seems to have been that Negroes were less subject to malaria than whites and in the watery rice fields malaria was one of the chief enemies. But commercial rice never extended beyond tidewater, twenty or thirty miles inland, and though rice cultivation resulted in great fortunes and resultant social and political influence for a few, the South as a whole got little from it. Meanwhile, giving the lie to the myth, white yeoman farmers all over the South were working in the fields from sunup to sundown, often side by side with the one or two slaves they owned. It was a pleasant myth for a white Southerner to hold, however, as he sat on his broad piazza sipping a mint julep, but few Southerners sat on broad piazzas, and fewer sipped juleps.

Granted, then, that slave labor did temporarily project the South more rapidly into the Modern World than it could have gone without it, in the long run it held it back. There is no exact agreement as to how efficient slave labor was as compared with free labor. There can be no doubt, however, that the South as a whole was in the long run handicapped, both materially and spiritually by slavery. Here we need only mention the fact that until after the Civil War the South generally failed to develop manufacturing, both because of its success with a slave-based agriculture and because of its love of plantation life. The body of its labor force, the Negro slaves, could not handle the delicate processes needed in manufacturing, the South maintained. The truth probably is that the training of the Negroes to handle these processes would have led to an advance not contemplated and perhaps not possible under slavery. Largely because of slavery, therefore, the South remained almost entirely agricultural, and paid tribute to the increasing economic and political power of the North.

But now, having adopted slavery in the hope of speeding its progress into the future—a hope destined to fail—the South had to turn increasingly to the past to find some defense of its "peculiar" obsolescent institution.

It didn't begin by seeking such a defense. But since the Southerner was a man still strongly influenced by the past, he handled slavery not in the relatively pure modern spirit in which the Northern millowner learned to handle free production, but in a mixed spirit touched by the slow-moving, relatively static social order of the past. The Virginia, and later the Carolina, plantation owner was still far from modern individualism. He thought of himself as an English squire living in the provinces. He felt the sense of a man's proper place, of every man in his place, and of a place for every man. He thought of the plantation as a community, and of himself as belonging with his plantation to a larger community. When, in the later days of slavery, he began to refer to the slaves as "our people," he was expressing not only his sense of relationship to family and kin, but also his sense of relationship to the slaves. This sense of a social order rooted in the past was very different from the stripped individualism which, in part under the influence of Puritanism, was to create the Modern World.

But the Southerner did not look increasingly backward solely to find some defense for slavery. With the coming of the nineteenth century, the increasing need for such a defense merged with Romanticism's interest in the Middle Ages. Even without slavery, the South would have been affected by this movement; the North was. But it is highly probable that Romanticism's concern for the past found in the slaveholding South a fertile soil. Romanticism turned away from the immediate past, the rationalistic eighteenth century, toward the Middle Ages, a period concerned with the emotional depths of man's life, in contrast to the eighteenth century that tried to contain life at the shallower level of reason. It was in part the South's nineteenth-century emphasis upon emotion and sentiment as opposed to reason that made it sympathetic to the vague shadowiness of the Middle Ages; but, partly in justification of slavery, it had also begun to think of its social and economic structure as medieval. In this view, the masters were feudal lords and the slaves their retainers. This identification was made possible by the preeminence in the South of personal life and personal loyalty as opposed to institutionalism, by the aristocratic emphasis upon family, and by the large influence of the eighteenth-century Scotch-Irish settlers, who had brought with them some memory of Scottish feudalism out of their not distant past. The popularity of the romances of Sir Walter Scott during the second quarter of the nineteenth century is a part of this same identification. Southerners were sympathetic to Scott's attitude, though as we shall see they probably misinterpreted it.

But the effect of the Romantic Movement was relatively limited in the South. Romanticism was predominantly an individualistic rebellion against both the constrictive force of the rising industrial order and the generalizing effect of eighteenth-century rationalism; the individual felt himself increasingly hampered by the abstract mind and by the economic order created by that mind. In the South neither the rationalizing mind of the eighteenth century nor the rational economy of the nineteenth ever became highly important. Therefore, the main effect of the Romantic Movement in the South was to blur with sentiment the fairly clear and rational plantation order of the eighteenth century. A few Southerners may have rebelled against the Southern economy with essentially the spirit of the New England Transcendentalists. Most of them, however, approved of the economy, and were satisfied merely to soften its structure with sentiment. After this economy had been destroyed by the Civil War, the mass of white Southerners became extremely romantic in their attachment to this period of their past; the ante-bellum South became for them the Middle Ages of typical Romanticism.

But though the South before the Civil War regarded the past without obsession, it showed considerable uncertainty about the proper use of the past. Because of the growing conflict within itself, a conflict rooted in the presence of slavery in a modern community but cloaked and submerged both by the authority of a leader like John C. Calhoun and by the general will to present an undivided front to an increasingly unfriendly world, the region was not sure which past it wanted to model itself upon. For while the sentimental South was reading Scott and holding medieval tournaments, complete with gallant knights and fair ladies, the more sober South of the educated planter and the politician was steeping itself in Roman history. What appealed to them there was the dogmatic assurance of the Romans, their political ability, their excellence in fashioning laws and maintaining a peaceful social order. There was little similarity between the clear and ordered mental processes of the Romans and the vague but hell-deep and heaven-high hopes of medieval man. Yet the South was trying to interpret its life as both medieval and Roman. (Roman names were commonly given to slaves.) It may be that the lighter, the recreational, side of Southern life supported chiefly the medieval pattern; the ladies read Scott and participated with the young men in medieval tournaments. The more serious side, represented by planters, professional men, and politicians, looked back to Rome; and the young men and young ladies, as they grew up, passed into the more exact and orderly ante-bellum world of plantation and legislative hall. But I doubt if it can be successfully argued that anything like a complete integration was attained between these two so dissimilar earlier worlds. Rather I think what we have here is one indication of the split within the Southern mind as it moved unsteadily out of the past into the future. The Southerner wanted to take the past with him; he wasn't willing to make such a clean break as the Puritan had made; but because his mind was infected with the individualistic virus of the future, and because he had chosen slavery as a means of attaining that future, he simply could not decide which past was most suitable to his purpose.

A few Southern leaders, Calhoun among them, even sought their model in Greece, and said that the South was trying to attain a Greek democracy. This would be a democracy—or perhaps aristocracy—of whites resting, as Greece rested, upon slave labor. But when we consider what the individualistic Greeks made of the leisure provided them by slave labor, the towering philosophical edifices they created, the clear, intellectual light of that sunny land, we see how far off the social-minded South was, how much closer it was to Rome with its emphasis on law and order. And when, as I said, we add the romantic Middle Ages to the models, we wonder what the South really wanted to be.

Of course, it didn't know. In this it was different only in degree from the North. They were both moving out of the medieval world into the modern; they both knew better—because more concretely—what they disliked in the past than what they hoped for in the future. The North, disliking the past more, was more detached from it. Instead of looking for models to imitate, it analyzed life and the world in the attempt to attain its hopes rationally. This rational attitude carried the North—and with it the nation—more rapidly into the future and the Modern World; whether it brought a deeper fulfillment is another question.

It is significant not only that the South was confused about which historical model to adopt, but also that it looked for any model at all. For this, as we shall see—and I think there was no confusion here—was basic in the nature of the South. It tended to live, not by analysis, but by contemplation: of things that had existed in the past, of things that existed in the present. This is to say, it tended to live in an extended, a spatial world. Even at the deepest level, the religious, it tended to contemplate images, not to analyze relations. It is this tendency toward contemplation that both relates the South more closely than the rest of the nation to the slow-moving Middle Ages and underlies that quality of leisure and relaxation that marks the life of the South.

This same tendency also relates the South to ancient Greece (Calhoun had his point): the frequent pauses for discussion, the wide interest in conversation, and, among its leaders, the loving handling of space in grounds and mansions, wherein these reflective pauses could occur. The Southerner, however, unlike the Greek, was both too social and too unintellectual to push these reflections to their metaphysical limit. He let them trail off into moods, sentiments, and the blue haze of romantic distance. The base and the tempo of his life may have reminded him of Greece but the culture he created was the proper expression of his own humid atmosphere, now lurid and stormy, now touched by the romantic miasmas of his swamps. So close together, so interfused, are the romantic and classic attitudes in the South. Considered abstractly, this balance of the opposing qualities should be a source of strength. Under pressure, it may become a weakness, producing inner conflict where strict unity is needed. In the South it tended toward weakness because it rested upon the system of slavery, which the South was increasingly unable to defend.

The career of John C. Calhoun illustrates beautifully how the South, beginning with a balanced attitude toward past and future, was, by the adoption of its "peculiar institution," led into an impasse. That was Calhoun's phrase, the "peculiar institution," and it was he who formed, with Clay and Webster, the great triumvirate which, from 1825 to 1850, dominated American politics. But however brilliant his mind, his thought illustrates the South's confusion in regard to past and future. For in defense of its economic and social order, he presented the South in essentially medieval terms, as a feudalistic, aristocratic society, which was simply what it had grown to be; that is, as an organism. As such, it had its own slow laws of growth and change, subject to its own inner forces, and not to be manipulated by political maneuvers. Yet in his defense of this organic South, Calhoun not only called into play all the political ideas of the eighteenth century but, in his plea for the device of the concurrent majority, carried a step further the eighteenth century's attempt to protect the individual against society and a minority group against the majority. The irony of this is that the politics of the eighteenth century had been conceived and elaborated primarily to destroy the lingering feudal powers of the Middle Ages. Calhoun, therefore, was trying to protect an American feudalism with the weapons that had been created to destroy a European feudalism; in other words, he was trying to use the future to protect that very past the future was bent on destroying. He was using the modern weapon of reason to protect the larger, nonrational life that had preceded it. It may be possible through reason to defend a life prior to and larger than reason, but Calhoun was unable to do it.

In its final desperate search for models, the ante-bellum South plunged deep into history, past the Middle Ages, past Rome, past Greece, until it came to Yahweh, the God of the ancient Hebrews. Even Calhoun made this step, but somewhat tentatively; primarily it was a retreat of the religious leaders. But it will be easier to follow this retreat if we postpone its consideration. Let us see now what effect the presence of Negro slavery had upon the South's sense of space, that is, upon the spatial tensions of the Southerner.

At the opening of this chapter it is stated that spatial tensions are closely related to temporal. This is evident. No matter where we are in space, we are also in time, and our leaning toward the past or the future is necessarily a leaning toward a place remembered (and perhaps in part imagined) or a future place solely imagined. Erikson describes the basic spatial tension in the American as that between home and frontier.

I shall use the terms *place* and *space,* the former to mean the already achieved and settled, the home, the latter to mean the unachieved and as yet unsettled. Place therefore implies the past as it has been shaped into the present; space, the future. There is also, as we shall see, social place, which implies social rank already achieved and relatively static, in contrast to the future-oriented and dynamic idea of democracy. Let us consider first physical place and space.

Just as all men sense some tension between the past and the future, so they sense some tension between a particular place and space. The degree of this tension varies, both among individuals and among peoples; the pull of either pole varies. A nomadic people is less attached to a particular place than an agricultural. This may also be said, though with reservations, of a trading and manufacturing people. A part of the South's strong sense of place is a result of its agricultural history.

Though there are rolling stones and pillars of society, adventurers and stay-at-homes, there is in every man something of both; even the adventurer grows nostalgic at times and the stay-at-home grows wistful. The health of a people probably depends upon some balance between these opposing interests. To wander in complete forgetfulness of a center makes no sense; to remain fixed in one place with no thought of surrounding space makes no sense either. The end result of both attitudes is boredom. In any healthy society, men look both in toward some particular place and out toward infinite space.

We may further describe this balance of interests between place and space, this tension, as follows. Place is here, space is there; place is now, space not yet. Place is home, space the frontier; place is human, space the more than human; place is the kindly and comfortable, space the powerful and terrible; place is the tame, space the wild. Thoreau, speaking out of an orderly, successful New England, maintained that men are saved only by a continued intrusion of the wild either from nature or from their own hearts. He wrote at a time when Americans were driving westward and Mungo Park was shooting game in Darkest Africa. It would be better, he said, if men would plunge deep inward and shoot themslves! Become aware, that is, of the wildness within their hearts, of the unexplored spaces within the little place called home.

It is only by attachment to a place that a man is able to imagine attachment to other places and perhaps at last to the infinite expanse of space itself. And place is not only physical but also social—place in a human community. Only by the handle of a community, says Yeats, can we pick up the world. If we can find our place in the world of nature and of men, we are on the way to finding our place in space, we are on the way to humanizing the universe. The fundamental problem of man, says Nicholas Berdyaev, the Russian philosopher and early Marxist, is the humanization of God.

This does not mean bringing God down to our level; it means, somehow, meeting him. The doctrine of the Incarnation, which deals with this problem, maintains that the spirit of infinite space is here, and that the best we know here, in this place, also exists there, in infinite space. Thus man is raised to God; God descends to man.

This is surely to put on high enough ground the importance of a balanced relationship to place and space. To what degree did the South possess originally such balance and to what degree was this upset by slavery?

The South in its beginnings tended to transfer to the New World the English sense of place: the tight little isle, the estates of the landed gentry. This was balanced by the spacious, westward-running mind of the Southern frontiersman. We have spoken already of the wide-sprawling land. We have noted that the Virginia settlers brought the tendency to take this land at its face value, to sprawl across it and relax within it. Actually, their acceptance was more positive than this. For these men lived in the afterglow of the Elizabethan period. The very first settlers, Raleigh's ill-fated "Lost Colony," had come during the spacious days of Elizabeth herself. They had failed partly because in the New World courage was not enough. Their failure taught the next generation how to form, in the London Company, a prototype of the modern corporation, but the tide of Elizabethan adventure still ran strong. Many a man, indeed many a common man, crossed the wide ocean and landed on these strange shores partly for the glory of England. The adventure may have been mainly for gold, but the sense of the strange, the new, the undiscovered, was also there, though it was to be a hundred years before this sense found its proper image in the journey of Governor Spotswood and his sixty gentlemen westward through Virginia to the summit of the Blue Ridge to stare across the fabulous valley of the Shenandoah beyond. In fitting commemoration of this ride, Spotswood had golden horseshoes struck and presented them to the company. A mere gesture? Yes, but a spacious Southern gesture, matched and to be matched again by the frontiersmen of the South. Southward in Carolina, explorers, unsurpassed in the annals of the English in America, drove westward from Charles Town settled in 1670, and within a dozen years were trading along the Coosa River seven hundred miles to the west, and by 1705 had reached and crossed the Mississippi. In the last half of the eighteenth century came Daniel Boone, born indeed in Pennsylvania, but at sixteen migrating down the valley of the Shenandoah to North Carolina, a pioneer so important in the early rush across the mountains into the "bloody ground" of Kentucky that he has become for all Americans the image of the perfect frontiersman. It seems now that Boone was largely a myth, but the myth grew in Southern soil. From the earliest days, and continuing for a long time, the Southerner moved easily in space, seeking richer and broader fields, but seeking also wider vistas, and whatever it was that lay within the forests and beyond the hills.

The introduction and development of slavery affected both positively and negatively this large and generous, indeed this spacious attitude. As Drayton argued, it probably increased, at least temporarily, the progress of the South. But if we look at the South two hundred and fifty years after it had been settled, at the opening of the Civil War, we see that this early largeness had given way to narrowness and intensity. It may be said that this change was due not to slavery but to the general development of the American mind, from the adventurous spirit of the Elizabethans to the calculating mind of the nineteenth century. Undoubtedly there was such a mental development, but it is part of the thesis of this book that slavery was the most important factor in shortening, narrowing, and warping the outlook of the South. It may also have deepened it, as we shall see.

Beginning about 1820, the year of the Missouri Compromise, the South became increasingly aware of forces forming against it and of the lines tightening around it. It was during this period that the North thought of the West as boundless space: innocent, untouched by time, free of the evils of the great cities, of the past, of Europe. In these vast expanses, men would become men again, beginning anew like Adam in the Garden, sounding, like Whitman, their "barbaric yawp over the roofs of the world." Cooper's famous scout, "Leatherstocking" was such a man, untouched by the evils of time and civilization, living on the edge of boundless space, in a perpetual and innocent dawn.

It is clear that this view could not be held to any great extent in the South. Any Northerner, even after the Missouri Compromise, could pick up his belongings, lock, stock, and barrel, and move into any area of the United States in which he could find land, but no slaveowning Southerner, or no Southerner who hoped to own slaves, could do this. The region to which slavery was limited may have been wide enough, but it certainly was not the boundless West open to the Northern settler. True, the Northern settler might not wish to move into slave territory, or into territory that might become so, but he could if he wished to, and take all his property with him. True, also, that only a minority of Southerners owned slaves, and nonslaveowners had before them as spacious a frontier as any Northerner. A few Southerners were so opposed to slavery that they left the South for free states (the Quakers are the most notable example). But slaveowning was a basic fact in the South, and the slave-operated plantation its ideal. The general mind of the South was not opposed, and this general mind resented the limits drawn about the frontier by the will of the North.

This limitation within the nation drove the South finally to its excessive dreams of a frontier in Mexico, in South America, in Cuba. It would create a slave-empire, whose inland sea would be the Gulf of Mexico. This may seem to indicate a sense of spaciousness far greater than the Elizabethans had had. It was not, however, the natural, easy expression of men seeking to explore a great world in which they felt at home, but rather the tight, aggressive drive of men feeling space tightening about them and trying to break out before it was too late. This is an indication of the extremism that overtook the moderate Englishmen who settled the South. Its cause lay in slavery and the struggles incident to it, though also, it should be added, in the extensive influence of the more aggressive Scotch-Irish from the mid-eighteenth century on.

The early Southern settler brought to the New World a relatively high degree of at-homeness in the Old: rich memories of the past to mix with great dreams of the future; the determination to create from New World spaces not merely desirable material products, but places to which he could attach himself as he had been attached to places in England. For a while the struggle was too hard for him to be able to realize this ideal more than slightly; many Southerners never realized very much of it. But because of the land and climate, and because of the English ideal, a land-based aristocracy came into being. Here, in the spacious estate, was expressed the balanced interest in place and space. It was a fluid aristocracy, over the generations rising and sometimes falling. It expressed the dominant ideal of the South, and those who composed it had a clear sense of both geographical and social place. But slavery, which was the almost inevitable accompaniment of these plantations, ended by contracting severely the spacious mind of the South and limiting its geographical reach to a certain confined area. It contracted also its social reach from the spacious sweep of democracy to an order in which the Negro slave had an unalterable place and the white freeman, so-called, was bound to consider first of all how to keep him in it.

The sense of social place is merely an extension of the sense of physical place we have been discussing. Furthermore, the ties that bind us to social place, like those that bind us to physical place, are both economic and sentimental. Just as we need to belong to a physical place, to have a niche in the world of nature, so we need to have a social place. Or, more simply, as we need to belong to nature so we need to belong to man. Indeed, it is simpler than this. We need to belong to the world which immediately surrounds us and which also stretches infinitely far away; and the world is things and people. At the deepest level, said St. Augustine, we need to belong to God.

The South possessed from the beginning, and kept, a strong sense of social place. Though the existence of the frontier continually weakened this sense—as indicated by the roistering democracy of the Jacksonian era—and though the Civil War, and its long aftermath, almost destroyed it, even today it isn't quite gone.

Without slavery, then, there might have remained a healthy, creative tension between aristocracy and democracy, between past and future, between filled places and empty space. Without slavery, the Southerner might have been balanced between frontier and home, lured on by the natural wildness that has never been eliminated from the South, held back by the memory of earlier homes that would shape into place even the wildest frontier. But with the coming of the Negro slave, place, both physical and social, but especially social, became too important. For here, at the base of society, was a large group that had been frozen into place, regardless of its own wishes or needs. And this occurred while the South was undergoing its natural swing into the future, swayed forward by both the pull of the rich land and the eager, modern, worldly desires of Southerners, swayed backward by the memory of a past too attractive to be dismissed or, even worse, denied. With the Negro slave fixed irrevocably in place, without past or future, the South slowed down, stopped, and even turned backward in the vain attempt to defend before the world its "peculiar institution." All white men were free to change their places as desire and native ability suggested, and they did change. Nevertheless, in the long run, and under the dangerous pressure of the ever more critical North, even the white man began to lose the right to change the economic base of his life and the desire even to suggest such a change, almost to think about it. So, in the years before the Civil War—and in much of the period since—the South, which had never emphasized thought because it felt no urgent need of it to defend the kind of life it preferred, found itself almost unable to think at all. This has been, and perhaps still is, one of its basic lacks. Slavery did not cause it, but it so intensified a native tendency to resist change that inner conflict and outer pressure combined to shatter the region. To attempt to keep one element of a dynamic Western society in a changeless place is eventually to destroy the society.

So slavery stretched to the breaking-point the originally creative tension between the future and the past, between space and place, between the potential and the actual. If the South had been left alone, it would in time have had to rid itself of the incubus of the past as represented by slavery with its law of immutable place; for, after all, the South was a part of that modern civilization that has now spread to the ends of the world. But it was too closely bound to the North, geographically, economically, politically, to be left alone. Even while it was maintaining a type of man clearly marked by feudal characteristics, the North was evolving the stripped and abstract modern, intent almost entirely upon the future and the mathematical enclosure of mathematical space. The South, lying next door, was so much space that might be profitably enclosed. Furthermore, this modern Yankee, because of his Puritan ancestry, was both a democrat and a humanitarian; and the South gave him an opportunity for profitable good works that could not be resisted. In the ensuing struggle, it was inevitable that the South be defeated, both because it was really pitting itself against the modern world represented by the North, and because the modern tendencies it carried within itself sympathized with the North and struggled against its own backward-looking desires.

In the years immediately preceding the actual conflict, however, these forward-looking national tendencies were driven deep underground. The Southern mind that, during the first two centuries of its existence had been the most expansive mind in America, creating first the far-ranging traders and the scout Daniel Boone, and then that galaxy of world-statesmen centered in Virginia, now shortened its range, narrowed and intensified its focus, and became provincial and indeed chauvinistic. From having brooded with Raleigh upon the star-filled glory of the world, it came to a gossipy analysis of its neighbor's thoughts and intentions. From an image of place as centered here but running endlessly outward, and sacred because belonging to the whole, it came to an image of place limited to the boundaries of the South, loved too intensely because threatened by a dangerous world beyond the Potomac, and defended blindly and fiercely because in mortal danger. The Southerner became inordinately proud of a land cherished beyond reason. The level-headed South Carolinian of 1800, following Calhoun not wisely but too well, became the Hotspur of 1860.

CHAPTER 8

"PURITANS OF THE SOUTH"

The damage wrought by slavery, however, was not wrought mainly in the somewhat simple, predominantly English, South of the first century of settlement, but in the complex English-Scotch-Irish South of, say, 1750–1860. Before we consider this damage further, therefore, we must ask how the coming of the Scotch-Irish modified the temper of the earlier South.*

The Scotch-Irish, who were strict puritans, had been preceded by another group of "puritans," the French Huguenots. These had come mainly around 1700, following the revocation of the Edict of Nantes in 1685, and had settled rather numerously in South Carolina. There they tended to become successful planters and merchants, and to unite easily with the rising English aristocracy of that province. Doubtless they brought to the ruling class in South Carolina a certain soberness and strictness, but they were neither sufficiently numerous nor sufficiently extreme to modify the typically English South as the Scotch-Irish did.

Some two hundred or more thousand of these came to

* I am indebted for the materials of this chapter especially to James G. Leyburn, *The Scotch-Irish: A Social History*, Chapel Hill, 1962. The attempt to weigh the Scotch-Irish contribution to the Southern character is, however, my own.

America in the great migrations between 1717 and 1775, and most of them settled in the South. There had been a few before this period and they continued to come after it, but during these years they came almost by communities and settled in communities. Who were they and why did they come?

They were originally Lowland Scots, who had emigrated to northern Ireland during the seventeenth century, in what was basically a political migration, set in motion by James I of England—and VI of Scotland—in 1610, and carried on by his successors. Its purpose was to settle the King's Ulster Plantation, that ravaged stretch of northern Ireland from which the Irish had been driven by English arms or in which scatteringly they remained under English domination.

Though others besides the Lowland Scots settled in Ulster, especially some dissenters from London, the Scots formed the great majority, and set the tone of the settlement. In a sense it was a movement of frontiersmen to a new frontier. For the Lowland Scots had lived for centuries on the border between England and Scotland; and when in Ulster they were forced to defend themselves against the outraged Irish, they were doing little more than they had done intermittently against the English for some four centuries. They would carry this same readiness for defense and attack to the American frontier of the eighteenth and nineteenth centuries.

As Lowland Scots they had found life hard. A poor soil, a poor and backward country, beyond the stream of the European Renaissance, but, through John Knox, fired by the zeal of the Reformation. In 1561, they revolted against Rome and established the Scottish Kirk. Then, with marvelous speed, they turned from widespread ignorance and irreligion to an unheard-of passion for knowledge and the church.

Those who went to Ulster did so primarily because the economic outlook was better there. They still had the Irish to contend with, as once they had had the English; but as they had long ago learned to rebuild hastily their clay huts destroyed by English raids, so now they learned to build stone houses and walls against the marauding Irish. Again, though they did not know it, they were fitting themselves for the dangerous and mobile life on the American frontier.

Why, between 1771 and 1775 did they leave Ulster in such numbers for America? Religion had something to do with it, economics—and politics—more. Religiously, what galled them most was the 1703 Test Act of Queen Anne, which required all officeholders to take the sacraments according to the prescriptions of the Established Church. Queen Anne was High Church, the Ulstermen Presbyterians, their lives wrapped up in their theology and their church. As for economics, it was in part the very success of the Ulstermen that got them into trouble. Having a climate admirably fitted to sheep-raising, they raised sheep, and soon manufactured so much woolen goods that the English manufacturers had the production outlawed. The same thing happened when Ulster turned to flax and the manufacture of linen. The truth was, northern Ireland was an English plantation, and the English didn't know what to do with it. Added to this costly uncertainty were the drought-ridden years from 1714 to 1719. Finally, there was the suffering caused by "rack-renting," the raising of rent upon the expiration of a lease, many of which expired about this time. By 1717 the great migration to America had begun. Sometimes whole communities went together, taking their pastor with them. These migrations continued until the American Revolution. They increased during periods of economic disaster in Ulster.

Where did they settle in America? At first, as a rule, they steered clear of the South, since this was already the land of plantations and they were for the most part small farmers. They tried New England, where, as strict Presbyterians, they should have found the puritan atmosphere congenial. But by that time the early New England settlers had become New Englanders, disposed to view with condescension or even disapproval all outsiders, especially such outsiders as these, in the New England view uncultured, rough, and dirty. In such an atmosphere, the Scotch-Irish did not feel at home. They had heard that New York was harsh on dissenters; they had also heard of the immense plantations along the Hudson. This left as a possibility the Middle Colonies, with Philadelphia the largest city. Therefore, most of them headed for that area, eventually spreading out westward and occupying the open land in the Great Valley. Succeeding groups settled this valley westward until it reached the mountains; then they turned southward down the Valley of Virginia. They followed this to the end, and, facing the choice of crossing the mountains to the west or fanning out southward through the hills into the North Carolina piedmont, they generally chose the latter. This was during the 1740's and '50's. During the 1760's, they were filling the South Carolina piedmont, and, before the Revolution, had passed into the Georgia piedmont.

In thus settling the back country of the southeastern states, the Scotch-Irish were the first, the largest, and the most effective group of American pioneers. The historians of the American frontier, chief among them Frederick Jackson Turner, have usually taken the position that the frontier began to assert its power in American history after the Revolution. It was then that the Appalachians were crossed by numerous settlers, and the wave of the frontier began to sweep toward the Pacific. It was Turner's theory that the growth of American democracy depended upon the free land that bounded on the west each successive frontier.

But this same growth may be seen in the Scotch-Irish who, during the middle of the eighteenth century, flowed southward through the lower valleys and the foothills of the Appalachians. These people had left, a hundred years before, the poor soil of Lowland Scotland for the better land and climate of northern Ireland. They were still seeking land—more land and better land—in the southern piedmont. Driven by this desire, and by an unaccountable restlessness, they poured southward in a stream down the Valley of Virginia, and, reaching its end, inundated the Carolina piedmont. In Scotland, they had lived under feudalism—they had once been clansmen, but that was gone now some hundreds of years—proud though poor followers of their lairds and lords. In Ulster they had moved away from feudalism, toward the free, contractual position of modern man. They were still closely bound together, however, by their most important institution, the church, and by their general acceptance of a class society, in which men of position rightfully held influence and power and other men followed their lead. When they left Ulster, they had no intention of leaving this kind of society behind; they were not seeking what we know as democratic freedom. They came with the intention of setting up in America the same kind of social structure they had had in Ulster, with the exception, perhaps, that they would be less under the thumbs of the English manufacturers and the Established Church. They brought with them a class structure and the Presbyterian Church, and as conditions permitted, they preserved these institutions. The first desire of every newly settled community was a church, with a minister who would, if possible, also conduct a school; the next was a store, with perhaps a tavern; third, a court, with a judge and lawyers to plead cases. But, inevitably, as they continued to move, land-hungry and restless—in sharp contrast to the Germans who were trickling into the South at the same time—they became more individualistic, the old structure of class and family weakened, the church could not always keep up with the advance, and wildness and impetuosity increased.

Without really intending it, they began to develop a democratic independence, and to value a man, not for what his family had been but for what he was.

From the very beginning, the predominantly English settlers of the seaboard, perhaps more conservative originally, and certainly made more conservative by the experience of a hundred years of settlement and by the establishment of a great plantation system, viewed them with concern. It is true, Penn had welcomed them; it is also true that Virginia made large grants in the Valley in the 1730's upon condition that they be settled, especially for purposes of defense, and the Scotch-Irish were the chief settlers. But these Scotch-Irish, in contrast to the generally peaceful and patient Pennsylvanians, wanted land and cared little about the Indians from whom they took it. They had spent a hundred years in Ulster holding the land they had in effect stolen from the Irish, and they probably felt that since they could make more out of Pennsylvania land than the Indians could, it belonged to them.

They were not only quick to take and fierce to hold, they insisted upon being treated fairly by the tidewater governments. In Pennsylvania, they got up a remonstrance against the government, and then, with arms and a great show of force, presented it. In the piedmont of North Carolina, they were the backbone of the Regulators, who fought Governor Tryon because they felt they were being unjustly taxed; in South Carolina they were also the backbone of the Regulators, who, angered because Charleston would not give them courts, drove out by themselves the murderers and other desperadoes that infested the back country. Whether they thought they had too much government or too little, they were quick to act, and if necessary violently, to change the situation.

All this raises the question as to how this great group of

Scotch-Irish, after the English by far the largest group in the South, were balanced against or mixed with the earlier English in the formation of the Southern character.

As to the physical mixing of the two groups, we know generally what happened. Until the Revolution, the Scotch-Irish settled in loose communities, down the valley of Virginia and through the piedmont of North Carolina, South Carolina, and northeastern Georgia. Between them and the earlier coastal settlers, mainly English, there was a fairly clear division, which in North Carolina was marked by a broad belt of unsettled land. There was also a rather marked opposition: the English felt that, though the Scotch-Irish were excellent frontiersmen, they were wild and lawless; the Scotch-Irish felt that the English were dictatorial and oppressive. But, after the Revolution, with the frontier now beyond the Appalachians, the Scotch-Irish frontiersmen generally moved as individuals, settled at random among other westward-moving individuals, and undoubtedly intermarried with them. Now they began to think of themselves, not as "Irishmen" (which they had called themselves before) but as pioneering Virginians or Carolinians.

Leyburn calls them typical frontiersmen. They were self-reliant individualists and hardy fighters, sustained in their unrelenting struggle against Indians, woods, and weather by their Calvinistic conviction that they had been called by the Lord to subdue the earth. They were not, says Abernethy, "impoverished drifters; they were fighting for empire and they knew it. Of Celtic blood, they were a sturdy breed: they blazed trails, fought Indians, established governments, founded churches and schools, speculated in lands, and dabbled in politics."[1] We have noted their preparation for the frontier role, both in Ulster and in the Southern piedmont. It may well be that families of Scotch-Irish descent carried into the Mississippi Valley and the Gulf region more of the pioneer spirit than did the men who came from coastal and plantation areas. So far as we know, however, these two groups mixed on the successive ante-bellum frontiers, and together created the Southern type, especially in its western expression. The question that is still unanswered is this: To what degree did the old seaboard and early-plantation South remain one, opposed by, balanced by, cooperating with that newer South, the Old Southwest? To what degree did these two regions dissolve and fuse and the basic attitudes of the early South extend into the Southwest to modify the typical Scotch-Irish frontier attitudes, while these extended backward to modify the Atlantic seaboard attitudes? To phrase this question differently: To what degree was the ante-bellum South one, a compound of plantation and farm, of settled seaboard and moving frontier? To what degree was it two, with the conservative forces lying mainly in the southeast, the progressive forces in the Old Southwest?

The question raised here is really a question as to when the Southerner came into being. Was he in existence before the Civil War? Did that war only stamp deeply into his nature what he already was? Or did it create him? Certainly the Civil War and the hundred years since have been tremendously important in producing the Southerner we know today. But did he already exist before that war only to be made more clearly distinguishable and more definitely himself by that conflict and the hundred years since?

Of this much we can be sure: The materials that were to form his character were in existence before the Civil War, whether fused together to form that character or not. Out of the furnace of war and reconstruction the white Southerner appeared. I think we can show also that out of the pressures and lures of all his history, the Southerner is appearing today.

Let us consider how the Scotch-Irish, either singly or in

groups, modified and were modified by the earlier settlers, who were predominantly English.

In the first place, the plantation was the most important economic institution among the English, the farm among the Scotch-Irish. The Scotch-Irish, however, were notoriously land-hungry, and, therefore, wherever conditions permitted, they enlarged their farms to plantations and employed slave labor. Through much of the Southern piedmont, physical conditions were not highly favorable to the establishment of plantations, which demand a staple crop easily cultivatable by untrained labor. But, following the Revolution, the invention of the cotton gin, and the expansion of the Scotch-Irish—and others—into the Nashville basin, western Tennessee, and the broad-lying fertile lands of Alabama and Mississippi, the Scotch-Irish were as quick as others to develop plantations. Their Presbyterianism—or the Baptist or Methodist faith that many of them adopted on the frontier—was no bar to slave-ownership. Indeed, with their strong feeling that land belonged to those who could use it best, a feeling that had developed both in Ulster and on the early Indian frontier, went naturally the feeling that the labor of other men belonged to those who could use it. Except among the Quakers, there was little feeling against slavery before the American Revolution. It had been legal in all the colonies, and even the foreign slave trade was not prohibited until 1808. It was the Revolution that spread the flame of freedom.

Furthermore, though the plantation did not become the dream and legend of the South until the second quarter of the nineteenth century, its ownership had become very early the mark of those who directed and controlled society; of the elite, the aristocrats. Though the Scotch-Irish had little aristocracy, they had brought to this country, and had long maintained, the sense of a graded society with the best people at the top. The best people, in America, would soon have wide acres, "hands" to work them, leisure, and other evidences of culture as yet unattained by the many below them. Piedmont South Carolina, for instance, was settled almost entirely by Scotch-Irish. Yet, during the first years of the nineteenth century, the plantation system swept northwestward across the piedmont to the very foot of the Blue Ridge.

Along with this spread of the plantation across the South went some sense of order and stability, a necessary characteristic of the plantation economy. The larger the plantation, the better it had to be organized to insure success; also, as a rule, the larger the plantation, the more settled and stable. It was a much simpler task to pick up a farm, lock, stock, and barrel, and move it a hundred or five hundred miles west than it was to pick up a plantation. As a result, the restlessness and impetuosity of the Scotch-Irish were to some degree modified and restrained by the possession of plantations. At the same time, the plantation economy, moving westward to successive frontiers, was continually made less stable and more fluid, as the individualism of the frontier, and the swift rise and fall of fortunes there, affected it. This had now become the dynamic, westward-surging nineteenth-century America, entirely different in tone from the established, stable plantation economy of the Atlantic seaboard during much of the eighteenth century.

With the advent of both the Scotch-Irish and the urgent frontier, education and religion would change. The education of the seaboard had been humane and aristocratic. Its ideal was the Renaissance gentleman, the well-rounded man of outdoor sports, of business, of culture. Few could aspire to such an education. The mass of men got along without it; indeed, without much education of any kind, since the broad, open, practical life of the South seemed to demand little. The simple farmer, the artisan, secure in his own position, observed for the most part without envy, and often with admiration, the power and the privilege of the great.

But the Scotch-Irish brought to America an entirely different ideal. From being among the most ignorant people of Europe, their Lowland Scots ancestors had, with the establishment of the Scotch Kirk in 1561, become most passionately concerned about education. But this was an education connected with the church, essentially a religious and moral education, of the type fostered by the schoolmen of the Middle Ages, not the humanism of the Renaissance, the aim of the Southern aristocrat. It was also an education for every man. The governor of Massachussets, in 1718, commenting upon a petition signed by an Ulster community requesting permission to settle in Massachusetts, said that "It may well be questioned, whether in any part of the United Kingdom at that time . . . so large a proportion as ninety-six percent of promiscuous householders in the common walks of life could have written their own names."[2] As these Scotch-Irish moved southwestward and westward in America, they carried with them wherever they could the community church and, connected with it, the church school, conducted, if possible, by the minister.

The effect of this strict and limited moral and theological education, given both in school and in the logical Calvinistic sermon, was to increase the dogmatism and pride of a people already stern, hard, and proud. Such an education was also in strong contrast to the richer and more humane education of the coastal aristocracy, and to the unpretentious lack of education of the yeoman farmer and artisan of that region.

The humanist education of the coastal aristocracy assumed that character and moral integrity were an essential part of the gentleman. But only a part. Beyond this was his administrative ability, his physical prowess in war and peace, his religious decorum and piety, his personal charm—that is, his total manner. Among the Scotch-Irish and their mixed descendants on the moving frontier, as long as the church was strong enough to control them, there was a certain restraint and softening exerted by the community. But as they moved rapidly westward, out of reach of the church, or, in their native restlessness and impetuosity, refused to obey the church, the hard, dogmatic character induced by their life and theology tended to become violent and corrupt, even while retaining a sense of its own rightness.

In the late eighteenth and early nineteenth centuries, the Methodists and the Baptists generally captured the frontier from the Presbyterians. The Baptists did this by not insisting, as the Presbyterians did, upon educated preachers; the Methodists, by the same means, and also through their circuit riders, who could cover, however sketchily, large areas. In this way, but originally through the influence of the Scotch-Irish, the puritanism of the South developed. It was different from that of New England more than a century earlier. The deeply passionate introspection of the New England Puritan and his wide interest in humanist education were both lacking. The Scotch-Irish were not interested in humanist education, and their introspection was dogmatic and logical, not spiritual. As their passage through successive frontiers lessened their education and increased their individualism, they became increasingly moralistic; also, as part of the effect of the lonely, violent, and boring frontier upon their restless and impetuous nature, they became increasingly emotional.

Thus, at the time when the original American puritanism had practically played out in New England, there came to the South a puritanism stripped of most of its social and intellectual interests down to the bare bones of an individual morality and the vacuity of a highly emotional religion.

We know that during the nineteenth century this religion of the frontier washed backward and affected the seaboard states. Even the leaders moved from the quiet deism of the eighteenth century to the evangelical theism of the nineteenth. The change is illustrated by a fact in the history of South Carolina. Dr. Thomas Cooper was president of the South Carolina College from 1821 until 1834; he was either a deist or an atheist. But he was fighting a rear-guard action. "By 1830 the Southern people had become thoroughly converted to religion; the scepticism that existed among the gentry, the age of reason, had virtually disappeared. The last great outspoken sceptic was Dr. Thomas Cooper."[3] Twenty years after Cooper resigned, Dr. James Thornwell, Presbyterian preacher, defender of God, slavery, and the Southern way of life, had become president of the college. As late as 1912, when the name of Thomas Cooper had been almost forgotten, I, a high school senior, was asked if I intended to enroll at "that hotbed of atheism."

The Scotch-Irish and the frontier—perhaps we may say the frontier Scotch-Irish—together with the advance of the nineteenth century sharpened and intensified the religion of the South. It had been, if anything at all, a somewhat urbane Episcopalianism, supported largely by liturgical form; it became individual, emotional, moralistic, and creedally inflexible. There had been no strong intellectual structure in the eighteenth-century church; there was no strong intellectual structure in the nineteenth, though the nineteenth-century dogmatic emphasis upon creed gave the appearance of an intellectual structure. In its slight regard for intellectual training, the South had not changed. It still did not believe that one had to think hard, perhaps passionately, either to live in this world or to prepare for another. It had become emotionally more intense without becoming intellectually stronger. It was inclined to substitute for the more genial acceptance of earlier days a dogmatic and generally negative assurance. Southerners were beginning to be more certain of what they were against than of what they were for. Of course, this dogmatism, though rooted in the emotional puritanism of the Scotch-Irish, was nourished by national events that limited the vision of the South and put it on the defensive.

But, balancing this unfortunate weakness of intellectual concern was a positive force that the English South had possessed and that was not diminished by the coming of the Scotch-Irish. This was the deep, essentially religious feeling that life is not explainable, that the very existence of man is a mystery, and that he lives out his brief day against a dark, incomprehensible background. The typical Southerner has never thought, either in the earlier, more complacent period or in the later more intense one, that he could think his way out. The quality of his religion has changed, but he has not become irreligious. He has not explained the mystery away. This is a result of his closeness to the concrete, inexplicable fact, the grain of sand that contains the world. If, through the poverty of his abstract thinking, he has moved slowly into the modern world, through this same poverty he has succeeded in keeping his religion. But he would have done better—indeed, he would do better—if he thought more poetically, that is, more imaginatively, about that religion.

The one thing that the Scotch-Irish surely brought to the South was an inwardness and intensity. We have already spoken of the open, public character of the early Southerner, his lack of inner doubt and questioning, his social nature, his rather simple and relaxed acceptance of the world and of himself. The Scotch-Irish came from a harsher world, of Lowland Scotland and Ulster, and brought with them a harsher attitude toward the world and men, including themselves. They took the land they wanted and, in contrast to their fellow German settlers of Pennsylvania and Virginia, defended it with their lives; they were hard upon others and upon themselves. Their theology, properly, was more world-denying and self-denying than that of the earlier English settlers. It had to be: they were more wild and impulsive, and strayed further from the fold; they had to be brought back and kept there by the stern measures of the community institution they valued most, the church. In their acceptance of such restraint, however formal it may often have been, they indicated their realization of their need of it. In spite of their individualism and their inwardness, the church was a public, community force they generally recognized.

Yet they never denied this world with the passionate intensity of the New England Puritans. Though religion did have something to do with their coming to America, it was not the important factor. They were opposed only, though of course strongly, to certain matters of form and polity insisted upon by the Established Church. Their quarrel was primarily over church government, not over the basic question of man's relation to God. Insofar as religion motivated their coming to America, they came not to be bothered; they had no thought of finding God in the wilderness and establishing his true kingdom there. Mainly they wanted more land and better crops. They injected into the bloodstream of the South, therefore, a puritanism more limited and moderate, except for its emotionalism, than that of New England; a puritanism much closer to the general religious attitude of the English settlers of the South. Though they were called, even during the eighteenth century, "the Puritans of the South," and "the Yankees of the South," they were Puritans and Yankees with a difference, a difference so great that they themselves both absorbed and were absorbed into the earlier life of the South. As a result we have now in the South a mixture that it is almost impossible to define, a mixture of inwardness and outwardness, of individual and community, of satisfaction in the present and drive into the future, of this world and another, of acceptance of life and sharp rejection, and, in regard to the racial problem every white Southerner faces, a mixture of shame and guilt.

In the nonintrospective world of the early South, and in whatever twilight of that world lingered in the older states even until the Civil War and afterward, the slaveowner was probably moved more by a sense of shame if he mistreated a Negro slave than by a sense of guilt that he kept him in slavery. There was a code about the treatment of slaves, as about most other things, and a man was shamed if he failed to keep it. But later the code of the gentleman, the code of the community, began to break down and to be replaced by an inward sense of guilt and sin. This occurred with the movement of the plantation westward and the coming of the more inward-looking Scotch-Irish Presbyterians (and their successors, the Baptists and Methodists), and with the passage of time into the more materialistic—and also more idealistic and emotional—nineteenth century.

In that post-Revolutionary, humanitarian century, it became hard for men to avoid a sense of guilt over keeping other men in slavery, regardless of how humane the treatment of the slave might be. The desperate effort the South made to justify slavery by involved religious arguments in the decade preceding the Civil War suggests how deep the sense of guilt was. This generally unrecognized and unadmitted guilt in regard to the Negro inevitably increased the distance between white and Negro, and produced in many whites a bitterness toward the Negro that had not existed before. Among those who had the power, this bitterness expressed itself in harsh treatment. So on the very deepest level, and in regard to the South's greatest problem, the coming of the Scotch-Irish, especially in the role of frontiersmen which they naturally assumed, modified the earlier South radically, and, it would seem, unfortunately.

It is generally held to be a social advance for men to transfer right and wrong from the outer to the inner world, and to act from self-approval and condemnation rather than from social approval and condemnation. What has happened in the South, however, is this: during the past two centuries' decline of the plantation ethos, the Negro, never occupying an equal place in the community, has been pushed increasingly onto its outskirts. (We are of course witnessing now his slow integration into the community.) Along with the weakening of his ties with the community went decreasing shame on the part of the community at the mistreatment he received. If this decreasing shame had been balanced by an increasing sense of guilt about the Negro, there would have been a general improvement in his situation. There was indeed an increase in the sense of guilt in the South. It resulted from the growing individualism of the frontier, of the nineteenth century, of the Scotch-Irish and especially of their Calvinistic religion. This guilt had little to do consciously with the South's treatment of the Negro; it had to do with individual sins, especially adultery, drunkenness, gambling. But it is highly probable that the ease with which this guilt could be aroused stemmed from the backlog of unrecognized guilt resulting from the unjust treatment of the Negro. In a region as insistent upon community as the South, this unconscious guilt was increased by every act which tended to push the Negro out of the community. However, not being generally recognized and admitted, it resulted, not in any improvement of the Negro's lot, but in increased bitterness toward the Negro himself. It is for this reason that the shift from shame to guilt may have been unfortunate for the Negro and consequently for the entire South.

I am aware, of course, that not all the hard feeling of whites against Negroes is due to repressed guilt; much has its source in the competition that Negroes have offered white artisans, mechanics, laborers.

There is one other characteristic of the Scotch-Irish mentioned by Leyburn that seems significant in this context; a weak esthetic sense combined with a strong moral sense. Leyburn attributes their lack of esthetic sense to their centuries of hard, mean life in Scotland, followed by a century of struggle in Ulster. Consequently, they built no beautiful dwellings or other buildings, either in the starkly simple style of the New England Puritans or in the more decorated strength of the Germans who settled the piedmont with them. Again, unlike the Germans, they did not linger on their new-found acres, enriching and beautifying them. On the contrary, they were forever hurrying on to richer fields ahead. Apparently they felt but weakly that love of a place one has made one's own; the love so dominant in the earlier, more English South; the love that can encompass infinite horizons. Perhaps, as proud Calvinists, they had already been granted their heavenly places, by God, and therefore felt at liberty to exploit and discard as they pleased the less important places of earth. This disregard for the finer uses of earth and for the slow processes of community growth is a disregard for taste, for esthetic values. They were practical men, who could attain their relatively simple ends more quickly by depending upon a clear, simple, and stern morality.

These especially Scotch-Irish characteristics, together with their tendency to shift the discriminatory treatment of the Negro from the public world of shame to the private world of guilt, were a part of the failure of community, which was the basic flaw in the South: its noblest attempt and its deepest failure. For it no longer believed in a complete human community; it was already too infected by modern individualism; it was using the Negro as a means for the material advancement of certain whites. And the Scotch-Irish, deeply marked by individualism through their stay in Ulster and their frontier experience in America, and supported in this individualism by their logical Presbyterian faith, pushed the Negro even farther out of the community and made him still more both the material resource and the moral problem of the individual white. The more power this Presbyterian gained, the more he was convinced that this was his predestined state, while the state of the poor slave was predestined also; if the mudsill of the community of men, an unanswerable question in the community of God.

The Scotch-Irish did not create this rift in the mind of the South, they only widened and deepened it. In the early nineteenth century, they produced national leaders; later, they led the South more hurriedly down the road it was pursuing anyway. In spite of the rift, or because of it, they threw their great weight into uniting the South passionately in self-defense. Mary Boykin Chesnut, author of that classic *A Diary from Dixie,* praises their spirit in contrast to that of the earlier plantation leaders. On June 5, 1862, she wrote as follows: "With two or three generations of gentlemen planters, how changed has the blood become! Of late, all the active-minded men who have sprung to the front of our government were immediate descendants of Scotch or Scotch-Irish—Calhoun, McDuffie, Cheves, and Petigru, who Huguenotted his name, but could not tie up his Irish. Our planters are nice fellows, but slow to move; impulsive but hard to keep moving. They are wonderful for a spurt, but with all their strength, they like to rest."[4]

Let us notice briefly three of the great Scotch-Irish leaders, the first two outstanding in national affairs, the third in regional, but making a name there acclaimed wherever war is studied: Andrew Jackson, John C. Calhoun, and Thomas J. ("Stonewall") Jackson. All typically Southern, men of the field and the forum. Andrew Jackson, military and political leader; Calhoun, political leader of the South for twenty years; "Stonewall" Jackson, military leader *par excellence.* The first of these in time, Andrew Jackson, "was a typical son of the unadulterated frontier. . . . His most striking traits were those of the frontier—provincialism, self-confidence, energy, persistency, belligerency, insubordination, individualism, honesty, simplicity, ignorance of books, loyalty to friends, and hatred of enemies."[5] As for Calhoun, he ties together in time the hero of New Orleans and the hero of the Valley of Virginia. He was aggressive, individualistic, and logical to a fault. Like many another member of the Scotch-Irish group, he married into the coastal aristocracy. In "Stonewall" Jackson, dead at Chancellorsville at thirty-nine, we find the powerful religious strain of the Scotch-Irish combined with the cool, detached mind of the academician—he was professor of natural science and instructor of military tactics in the Virginia Military Institute. "God has been very good to us this day," he said during the Confederate advance at Sharpsburg.[6] At Chancellorsville: "I feel His hand led me—let us give Him the glory."[7] His hard intensity appears in his reply to the question "Sir, how will you deal with the enemy massed there against you?"——"Kill them, sir, kill them all!"

Far from this Old Testament fury lies the deepest wisdom of the South, a wisdom that may find its partial source in the fusion of the English and the Scotch-Irish. The English had developed the plantation, which had supported a rich culture—too rich perhaps, too much of this world. The Scotch-Irish generally accepted this culture; the plantation with its looseness and its sense of leisure also became their ideal. Yet even while accepting the world, like stern Calvinists they denied it, and their denial modified the South. C. Hugh Holman maintains that "the religious patterns of the region were much more shaped by the Scotch-Irish Presbyterians who settled the back-country and fanned out to encompass the region except for the coastal plain than it was by that plain's essentially Episcopal quality."[8] The Episcopal quality of the plain was itself influenced, as is probably shown by the spirit of William Gilmore Simms, outstanding ante-bellum writer of South Carolina, who belonged to the plantation belt and wanted most of all to be completely accepted into the Charleston aristocracy. Yet he wrote in 1842, "We are–only so many agents and instruments, blind, and scuffling vainly in our blindness"; and in 1859, even while filled with hopes for the establishment of the Confederacy, "We are of those who think we have very little to do with happiness."[9]

This acceptance of the complex social culture of the plantation with skepticism, often indeed denial, of that culture suggests a deeply divided mind, as indeed the mind of the South was: the earthly community could find no unearthly justification. Yet this dual attitude lies very close to wisdom. It approaches the realization that the world is both everything and nothing. In the epigram of Charles Williams, it is possible to say of anything, "This also is Thou; neither is this Thou." The world is to be loved, but with understanding. This demands the "precarious vision," which is a part of wisdom. What the South could not achieve many individual Southerners did. Whether they know it or not, they probably act under the influence of the Scotch-Irish, who both accepted the English culture of the South and condemned it.

CHAPTER 9

EARTH'S CORRUPTION

Having now introduced the Scotch-Irish as sharers in the creation of the culture of the South, we return to the problems created by the introduction of slavery. For one thing, the enslaved Negro tended to separate the white from the earth, and, therefore, from that divinity men have always felt within the earth and have expressed most cogently in the doctrine of the Incarnation.

Allen Tate makes essentially this point in his essay "The Profession of Letters in the South." The Negro, he says, is a barrier between the white and the earth. The situation in Europe stands in contrast to this. There, though the upper orders rest upon the peasant as the white does upon the Negro here, since the culture is the same for all, the earth-supported peasant transmits to the orders above him the strength of earth. Here, since the Negro peasantry is excluded from the culture of the White South, it fails to transmit the strength of the earth to that culture. The Negro is, therefore, a deterrent to the achievement of a true culture, which must rest upon the earth.[1]

Though I agree in the main with this thesis, I think it needs some modification. In the first place, though Negroes have predominantly formed what has been realistically called the mudsill of the South, the majority of whites have also rested directly upon the earth and gained their strength from it. The most important of these formed the large group of yeoman farmers, who with the help of a few slaves or none worked the earth themselves. According to the myth, it was the Negro alone who did the work.

In regard to the claim that the different cultures of the two races prevented the white man from basing himself, through the Negro, upon this earth, this must be said: however different the culture of the Negro and the white man may have been at the beginning, the white stripped from the imported slave as much of his original culture as possible and replaced it with whatever snippets from the white culture would make the Negro a serviceable laborer. This has been the general situation throughout the Negro's life in America. He may have maintained something of an earlier style, some rhythm, some mood, but far more than we realize he has put on the culture of the surrounding whites, and has worn it a generation late, as a poor man wears, a season late, the coat his rich relative wore in its prime, Indeed, he has done more than this. He has worn his rags with such an air that at last, as we shall see, he is setting the style for the South.

Insofar as the Negro has broken the Southern white's contact with the earth, he has weakened his religious sense. For in all religions the earth is preeminently important. The earth itself is feminine: she holds within her womb the seed of life and gives birth to all plants; she nurses animals and men upon her broad bosom. And if the earth itself is not a goddess, it is at least—let us say—a summer home for the gods, who wander here from time to time as men and women. In the Christian view it is more than this: it is the special object of God's delight, where once his Son came to live, and die, and rise again, and where, in the form of the Holy Spirit, he lives until the end of time.

But considering the feminine quality of Southern culture, it might be more accurate to say that the Negro has not caused the white man to lose touch with earth but has confused and corrupted the touch. Consider the Southern settler's view before slavery became widespread. It was not that the earth was innocent. All men still carried enough of the Middle Ages in them to fear, for instance, the witches and devils that might inhabit the dark forests. On the other hand, even the most extreme Puritans felt a love for nature. They felt, however, man's corruption so strongly that they were cautious about yielding to the pleasures and joys of earth: these could too easily feed his corrupt nature and distract him from heaven. The non-Puritan Southern settlers were less conscious of man's danger amid the pleasures of the world; thus they tended to live in the world with considerable relaxation.

But then Negro slavery became widespread. It had been adopted primarily to help white men move more rapidly into the modern world; but for many of these men it brought the possibility of greater relaxation, and for the South generally it helped to create the ideal of leisure. In such a world miscegenation naturally occurred. Historically, the men of a master race have always made free with the women of a servant race. The degree of corruption, however, depends considerably upon what men think of these relationships. They occurred very widely between the Spanish, Indians, and Negroes in South America, as the mixed population of that continent attests. But because of the weakness of the puritanical attitude there, the Spanish master accepted miscegenation, and over the centuries admitted to full social rights, and generally without violence, the slaves and their mixed descendants. The English settlers of North America could not do this. Even without the influence of the Scotch-Irish and other puritan and pietist sects that flowed into the South during the eighteenth century, Southerners could not do it. They were proud Englishmen, young nationalists, too far from the Middle Ages to be moved by its sense of a universal humanity, too sure of themselves as they faced with superior ships and arms the newly discovered Negro and Indian. From the beginning they looked down upon these "lesser breeds without the law." But when to the pride of the imperial Englishman was added the spiritual pride of the God-selected Calvinist living alone or in small enclaves within a corrupt world, the white Southerner inevitably saw the Negro, just snatched from heathendom and barbarism and as yet but lightly washed in the Blood of the Lamb, as himself a part of the corrupt world. That it was the white man who corrupted the black man by making him defenseless in a strange land, the white man was inclined to forget. Though his leaders—for instance, Jefferson—saw that it was slavery that was corrupting the whites, the whites generally saw only the Negro.

What made the white man feel it was the Negro himself, not the institution of slavery, that was corrupting? For one thing, the Negro was himself very close to earth: an earth figure at work or rest, of the same dark color as earth, suited to black lands, deep forests, and mysterious, impenetrable swamps. So that when one mixed his keenest pleasure with these people, he was mixing himself with the dark forces of the world. The white Southerner did not clearly tell himself this but, moved by the physical relaxation of the land, the moral relaxation of slavery, the defenseless position of the Negro, and a predominantly Scotch-Irish puritanism, he felt it. Consequently, the man who had earlier tended to be a moderate accepter of the world now became either an extreme worldling or a fanatical world-denier, or, in changing mood, extreme worldling then fanatical world-denier then extreme worldling again—depending upon what time of the year it was, open season for devilment or revival time.

So the system corrupted the white man and the Negro woman directly (though not equally since the woman had not yet been touched with puritanism) and the white woman and the Negro man indirectly. The indirect effect, especially upon the white, was probably greater than the direct effect. The height of the pedestal for the white woman was equal to the depth of the furrow in the high cotton for the Negro woman. To the degree that sex became the prerogative of the women of the servant race, it became the scandal of the women of the master race. These originally robust Elizabethans tended to forget the words a later Englishman, Browning, put in the mouth of Fra Lippo Lippi:

I always see the garden and God there
A-making man's wife, and, my lesson learned,
The value and significance of flesh,
I can't unlearn ten minutes afterwards.

Of course, by the closing days of the ante-bellum South, the Southerner had Sir Walter Scott and Victorianism and Tennyson's "Dream of Fair Women" to help him forget the significance of flesh. But even without these helps, he had to make the white woman an asexual angel to balance the highly sexed female he sought and found and created among the Negroes.

This attempted divinization of the white woman and brutalization of the Negro woman, this dehumanization of both, weakened the South when it began its fight for independence from the North. It has been said that the martial spirit of the South itself was a woman, for whom each soldier ventured. And truly said. For the quality of Southern culture is essentially feminine. But when the Southerners came to defend that culture in war, though they had all the historic words that have inspired men—altars and fires, God and native land—they had not fitted these together in one indissoluble pattern. For, the *fires*—that is, the homes, that is, finally, the women—the women had been split into two parts through the moral distortion induced by slavery: the white woman, an angelic being, hovering high above the earth, a "beautiful and ineffectual angel"; the Negro woman, so clothed in earth she could hardly be distinguished from it, a being that suggested to the late arrived puritanism of many Southern whites the fascinating diabolism of the earth. Yet the Negro woman was an integral part of this native land the Southerner was fighting for, but, alas, she was divorced from Yahweh, the fighting god of a chosen people; while the white woman, whom he said he was fighting for, hovered too high above the land to represent effectively any earth goddess.

This picture is too heavily drawn. The Negro woman was far more complex, and so was the white woman. She may have been considered in girlhood a Victorian angel, skimming this lovely Southern earth without benefit of ankles, but when she became a housewife she landed with a thud. Though she still remained the arbitrator of culture and the ruling voice in the home, she had to pay for these privileges even in the homes of successful planters—perhaps most of all there—by carrying the heavy keys of the household and managing for twenty-four hours a day a ménage most of whom were but devoted children. Moncure Conway's mother writes to him in 1850 from Virginia: "I am the greatest slave here at any season to the servants of our household, who are raised in such a state of dependence of thought and action that they will not even make an effort to make their own clothing."[2] It may be that the actual life of the South rested chiefly upon the women; but it is very doubtful if the dreams, either good or bad, did. These circled about white disembodied spirits and dark dis-spirited bodies. What I'm saying here is that the South failed to develop the dreams that really expressed its desires. It had neither the poets nor the saints through whom to substantiate its soul.

But the unconscious need for moral justification was not the only need that drove the white Southerner to deify his own women. By its side existed the more clearly conscious need to keep the white woman from interfering with slavery. Uplifted in the home, she gave the final word on domestic and on general cultural and religious matters. She was the divine Athena. But, so deified, she was prevented from raising unhappy questions about the practical surrounding world, the core of which was the slave system. If she had not been, her sensitive, nineteenth-century humanitarian nature might have set the wheels of emancipation turning as well as ameliorated the lot of individual slaves. Feminist leaders had become aware long before the Civil War that discrimination against Negroes and discrimination against women were parts of the same pattern. The Grimké sisters, who left Charleston in 1836, became both abolitionist and feminist leaders.

This willingness to let the white woman rule in the home, but to deny to her any authority in the world, is an indication of the corrupting influence of slavery. It was one of the main forces that split the South, in puritanical fashion driving a wedge between this corrupt world and another of angelic purity.

But now, with the world split in two by the wedge of slavery as interpreted by Calvinism, what became of God? If there are really two worlds, there have to be two gods. Unless, of course, you run the full career of the Puritan-Yankee and split the world into so many fragments that even Puritan-Yankee ingenuity cannot find a god to cover such a chaos, and so gives up—first, any orderly search, then the chaos itself. Which is pretty close to where the typical American stands now.

But not the Southern American. Two gods are not impossible, though they do strain the devotee. The Southerner—I'm still talking about the white Southerner—still worships, but the god he worships depends upon the situation he's in. As we suggested earlier, the increasing future-past tension produced by slavery pushed the nominal god of the South clean back before the Christian era into the form of Yahweh, the early tribal God of the Hebrews. Here was a god of a chosen people fighting for their lives amid aliens. Insofar as the Southerner was changed by Calvinism, he became one of a chosen people, and he was defending at least his way of life, caught between increasingly alien Northerners and barbaric Africans. Yahweh was a suitable leader for such a fight.

But the mood of the Southerner hadn't hardened entirely from the more receptive mood of the early English settler, in which all the world was God's. Indeed, this early mood had been in a way softened by the pervasive humanitarianism of the nineteenth century, itself an indirect expression of the Christian influence and of the doctrine of the Incarnation. Yahweh, therefore, in addition to being a tribal and warlike God, put on at times the garments of his nominal Son, the gentle Jesus, in whose name the white Southerner administered the unjust and tribal system of slavery with considerable kindliness. But for the large issue of justice itself, there was little concern. The institutions of this world, slavery among them, were created by God for life in this world; if they were attacked, Yahweh would defend them; indeed, the Southerner might even look toward Mexico and South America and Cuba in the hope of extending them. This world was as it was; we might be saved in another; even Negroes might be saved in another.

Now, it is true, Yahweh had begun as a god of this world—indeed, even of one mountain in it, Mount Sinai—but under the pressures of Jewish history and the leadership of the great prophets, he had begun to assume the headship of all nations, and of an eternal realm lying either within or beyond time. As to the kingdom He—together, later, with His son Jesus—was determined to establish, the Kingdom of Heaven, there has always been confusion in the Christian mind as to its whereabouts: on earth, in heaven, or upon an earth become heavenly. I should say that, despite Greek ascetic influence and the crudeness of life in the Middle Ages, Christian thought has generally taken this world seriously. Jesus himself set the model when He went about feeding the hungry and healing the sick. Slaveowners were happy to adopt this particular aspect of Christianity; but the teachings of the great prophets about social justice, and the teaching of Jesus, the greatest of the prophets, on the same subject—teaching that got Him into mortal trouble with the authorities—was another story. The South could not seriously consider this without destroying its economic and social order.

So the South, when it was thinking martially and defensively and in terms of a sacred soil, worshiped Yahweh, but when it was thinking about individuals suffering the hardships of life, it worshiped Jesus—the gentle Jesus, not the outspoken social prophet. Yahweh was a social god, but the society he represented was exclusive, being composed of Southern whites living in his land, the South. Jesus included all individuals, Negroes as well as whites. To anyone in need He lent a sympathetic ear and a compassionate spirit, but His kingdom was not of this world. Beyond time, beyond place, those who loved Him might enter that kingdom at last. There, by the mysterious working of His grace, even Negroes and whites, slaves and masters, might sit down together. Meanwhile, here some men stood while others sat, but there was a place for every man. Even the slave had his place, but in Yahweh's eyes, this was standing room only. Partly to clarify the social problem of who stood up when who sat down, the South developed a rich code of manners. Inevitably, because these manners were supposed to place people only in this world, and also because individualistic white Southerners had become strongly touched with a Calvinistic concern for placement in another world also, the manners and the religion tended to break apart. This was further evidence of the failure of community in the South. We must now try to trace the roots of this failure.

CHAPTER 10

THIS WORLD AND HEAVEN, TOO

All men have "manners," if only accepted ways of doing things. But when we say, as it is often said of the South, that a particular region stresses manners, we mean that it ascribes unusual importance to the way of doing and saying things, as distinct from the things done and said. In such a culture, custom has unusual strength, social feeling is strong, and life tends to be a highly public matter.

The South stressed manners for several reasons. First, because it always felt a strong tie with the past, and one way to hold on to the past is through the use of customary words and actions. Second, because it favored a hierarchical structure of society, culminating in a landed aristocracy, and any aristocracy stresses manners. This is because, first, it has time to embellish the brute facts of life, and, second, because the embellishment is one of the means employed to separate the aristocratic group from the lower orders. In connection with its maintenance and development of a landed aristocracy, the South also adopted Negro slavery. To aristocratic etiquette was added racial etiquette, the essential purpose of which was to keep apart those who had to live together. Racial etiquette binds people together on one level and separates them on another.

This divisive function of racial etiquette only presents in an extreme form one function of all etiquette. For all etiquette exists partly to enable people to live together closely without rubbing one another raw. There is in every man a longing for society and a longing for privacy. An accepted code of behavior enables him to mingle with society without being wounded too deeply by the contacts.

The South, laying little stress upon impersonal institutions—economic, political, etc.—but much stress upon personal relationships, inevitably developed a rich code of manners to govern these relationships. Herein lies the answer to the peculiar personal-impersonality of the Southerner. Ideally, he is happy to see you, he insists upon your staying, his life seems to turn around your entertainment—yet always there is a note of formality, you remain a guest; even today he doesn't drop easily into first-naming. In using, however gently, the shield of manners to hold you off and thus protect himself, he is also protecting you, and, perhaps more important than this, respecting you. In thus treating you always as a guest, he is expressing his own faint sense that we are all guests here—guests of existence, making a brief visit to this lovely world. We are at home, yes, perhaps in a place made dear by long association, but this place lies under the sun and the stars, and its outer limits are lost in the Milky Way. To be entirely at home is to be at home in the universe; to feel one's own place touched by the wonder of space.

During my boyhood I had an uncle who on Sunday served as librarian for the church library. When we took him books to be signed out, he received them gravely, wrote our names in his book, and handed them back to us with just the hint of a smile and perhaps our first names spoken. Here was whimsicality combined with seriousness, boyhood and manhood meeting face to face, a perfect fusion of the known and the strange, the personal and the impersonal, the informal and the formal. Here was home touched by the air of some far country.

This vague sense of belonging, of being at home amid strangeness, is akin to the Celtic sense of the wonder of the world. It appears among the Highland Scots and especially among the Irish. It is extremely doubtful, however, that either of these groups was numerous enough, or in the case of the Irish came early enough, to produce this effect upon the Southern mind. The Scotch-Irish were also strongly Celtic, but according to Leyburn they were too realistic, hard-bitten, and restless to have retained in any perceptible degree the Celtic sense of wonder. Whenever Southerners, therefore, felt this mood, it was probably the result of English at-homeness combined with aristocratic formality.

Now, if society is not to explode, the individuals and the groups that are separated on the surface must be made to feel united at bottom. To state this differently, the sharper and more fixed the place, the more deeply must it be structured into the whole. The corollary is, the more mobile and blurred the place, the less deeply is it structured into the whole; such a society will hardly explode; it may well fall apart.

If the social manners of the South expressed at their best the sense of existence and of man as a guest here, they expressed a religious sense. Perhaps the essential tragedy of the South lay in the fact that it lacked a religion to crown that sense. Allen Tate has stated this lack. The South, he has said, should have been Catholic. It would then have had an inclusive religion both to undergird and to crown its social order. For it had a social order that stressed community, though it was prevented from attaining this goal by the presence of slavery, especially the exploitative slavery created by individualistic Protestant moderns. It was these Protestants who gave the South its dominant religion. This religion, together with the kind of exploitative slavery it fostered, effectively prevented the South from creating that community at which its social manners aimed.

This is another way of saying that the formal religion of the South did not grow out of its complete life and therefore could not crown that life with meaning. For one of the ideals of the South, remembered from earlier centuries and influential even in spite of slavery, was social life and community. The heart of its religion, however, was an individualistic Protestantism which set man naked before God. During the nineteenth century the South became deeply religious, but this did nothing either to heal the flaw in its economic life or to bridge the gap between this world and another. When pressure from the outside became too great the South cracked. It has remained divided, even a hundred years after its collapse, because it never held within its mind a clear picture of its desire. Today the Negro is creating a new picture; whether the South can accept it remains to be seen.

I know of no better way to indicate this flaw than to compare a scene from South African Negro life with a scene (imagined) from the ante-bellum life of the South. The South African scene appears in Noni Jabavu's *Drawn in Color,* an account of the author's visit from England to her South African home upon the occasion of her brother's death. She is of the Bantu tribe, where life depends heavily upon the family. "I thought how with my people, you are not often left to be merely your private self; you represent others, or others represent you, so that you are ever conscious of relative status, classification, interdependent relationships." This family had been disrupted by violent death, and extended ritual was necessary in order to reconcile its members to the disaster, and to bind them again to life, to the community, to the remaining members of the family. So, when it was over, she says, "At last I left home, at peace with myself, ritually 'bound,' reconciled, accepting what had had to be, all savage, unseemly emotions of revenge and hate extirpated, happy again like all of us."[1]

In contrast to this, notice certain passages from Allen Tate's *The Fathers,* a tale of ante-bellum Virginia, especially the account of the funeral of Major Buchan's wife. Here are all the complex kinship groupings indicated by Jabavu among the Bantus. But the plane is mainly of this world; the sense of ritual, of religion, of the attempt to bind man to the universe from which death had severed him, is largely absent. The universe is a blank, death is the abyss into which men fall from time to time. The best that can be done on such an occasion is to draw the remaining members of the family together, and in the reassurance of their company forget that the abyss exists. Says Lacy Buchan, through whose eyes the action appears, "Excessively refined persons have a communion with the abyss; but is not civilization the agreement, slowly arrived at, to let the abyss alone?"[2]

Ideally, the rich family life of the Buchans, an expression of Southern culture, should have thrown some light into the abyss, some beam among the stars. The social life of the South should have rested upon the abyss and should have been crowned with religion. In spite of its excellence, it was not so supported. The leaders, at least, of this complex society, however Christian in their profession, were touched with stoicism. They were individualists, not fundamentally a part of the complex play of society, supporting it passionately and fiercely in crisis but confused and dazed by disaster. If they had really been Stoics, they could have borne the destruction of the social order, holding themselves proudly aloof in an impersonal universe. If they had really been Christians, they would have recognized the aristocratic order as one of the changing forms of the eternal order, and even as it failed they would have been creating another order out of the Great Mystery. The fact that the South has been confused for a hundred years, and is still confused, suggests that the region was never really one.

Even the way the South fought the Civil War suggests the flaw in its religion. For a while the Southerners fought as fiercely as men have ever fought; some of them fought fiercely to the end. But the South as a whole did not fight to the end. When that came, half its armies was absent without leave, nor did Lee withdraw to the mountains. The life of the South was extremely rich but of relatively shallow rootage. It had the materials of a great religion—a rich world to be shaped for heaven—but it lacked a competent religion. Being richly rooted in people and place—in this dear and lovely world—Southerners fought fiercely for it. But since this world was not clearly rooted in another—in spite of their devotion to states' rights and the Constitution, trying, in vain, to make politics do the work of religion—they fell away as the fight grew hopeless. They were unwilling to accept reward in another world, they wanted it in this, and as it grew increasingly improbable, they stopped fighting. They had all the religious words, they were defending Christian righteousness against modern paganism, and these words carried them fiercely to the top of Cemetery Ridge, but they couldn't stay there. Even as they went, it was a better show than a battle: the South at its most splendid, a sight to thrill forever the heart of the fighter, but not quite right. Perhaps the single-minded Puritan "Stonewall" Jackson might have made it possible, but by that time Jackson was gone.

Christopher Hollis says, "The South under defeat lost her philosophy, whereas the Poles and the Irish have kept theirs. For that of the former, unlike that of the latter, was based upon mere taste and not upon the rock of religious truth, outside herself."[3] I would modify this by suggesting that the individual Southerner did base himself upon the rock of an individualistic religion, but could not find religious support for his social order.

To return to Lacy Buchan's question: "Is not civilization an agreement, slowly arrived at, to let the abyss alone?" Whether this is civilization or not, much of the South is suggested by the question. The abyss, of course, is the mystery of life, of God, of heaven and hell. The South lived on the edge of it, but refused to think about it. It may be said for the South that at least it did not make the typical Puritan mistake of considering it too closely, too analytically, too logically, so that by the nineteenth century it had pretty well disappeared, having been dissipated by the analytical mind. The South never analyzed the abyss away. It never analyzed anything away. It experienced the moments of life, it remembered them as images, little stories, which it told and retold, often with but the vaguest sense of their meaning; it remembered life as pictures out of the past, out of several conflicting pasts, as we have seen, the Middle Ages, Rome, Greece, ancient Judea. It contemplated these images, and to a degree became like them, but because they did not agree among themselves, the South never came to agree with itself. Since it did not analyze life, it was little tempted to analyze God, the abyss behind life. It simply saw life as surrounded by mystery, ever-present danger, perhaps ineffable glory. But though it did not analyze this away, neither did it contemplate it into real existence. If it had pondered more deeply the images of its daily life, it would have seen in them the eternal mysteries of its religion; if it had brought to bear upon them a probing imagination, it would have seen within them the minute multitudinous hells and heavens it envisioned on Sunday. It praised its loyal suffering servants without seeing in them the redemptive spirit of Christ. It never forgot that it lived upon the edge of the abyss with its unknown terrors and glories, but it never learned that it lived within this abyss or that the abyss lived within itself. It had the great words, it has them still, but they remain too much memories of a largely outmoded past, not living images of the present.

In brief, as Yeats might well have said, the South never substantiated its soul. Considering the majestic fantasy of Mont-Saint-Michel and the heroic temper of social men enshrined therein, Yeats realizes that "only by the substantiation of the soul, whether in literature or in sanctity, can we come upon those agreements, those separations from all else, that fasten men together lastingly."[4] The South possessed neither the literature nor the sanctity for such substantiation of its soul.

The South tried to live, on the one hand, by a highly social culture, on the other by a highly individualistic religion. The culture did not support the religion, the religion did not support the culture. Therefore it could hardly aim at substantiating its soul; for, though much of its life was in this world, it did not really seek its soul here, and though much of its soul was in another world, it was a soul pale, anemic, alone in the vastness, and ill-nourished by the lifeblood of this. Therefore, the South could create neither poets nor saints—I mean, great, region-shaping poets and saints. For it is such persons as these that shape a region, though first the region must have, by the grace of God, sufficient energy and unconscious purpose to create the poets and saints. They, as they come into being, offer a criticism of life. They create, in art and in life itself, the image of their world, of their time and their region, seen under the aspect of eternity. They substantiate, and they make substantial, the soul of their people. Looking at them and their works, their fellows see where they are trying to go, wherein they have succeeded and wherein they have failed. The poets and the saints offer us a criticism of life; not just of life in the abstract but of our life now. The poets see our world, the saints—usually—live in it, in all its richness, complexity, and ambiguity, against a simplicity that lies at the heart both of the world and of themselves. So we see ourselves with clearer eyes, in a broader perspective; so in this broader light we learn to question our complacencies, to quarrel with ourselves, to criticize our lives and the life of our region.

Since the South was never able to create poets in prose or verse, or saints, it never really quarreled with itself. As we shall see when we come to discuss politics, it became, on the contrary, adept in quarreling with others, and for this purpose it developed the instruments of rhetoric and eloquence. Yet even with its complacency, and the great pride that before the Civil War accompanied it, the South's error was less than that of the Puritanical North. The Puritan, who fought such long and stern battles within his soul, tended to be proud of his spiritual achievements. The Southerner, partly because he made no such great attempts and therefore won fewer such victories, could remain fairly humble as he faced the great mystery. In the public world, however, the world of his person, his possessions, his land, he fell easily into pride, both because he was preoccupied with these things and because he lacked poets and saints to warn him about this preoccupation. Even so, however, pride in this world is less unhealthy than pride in another not yet attained.

CHAPTER 11

STOIC REMEDY

We referred above to the presence of Stoicism in the South. It appears that at least the more cultured South tried to use Stoicism to bridge the gap between its social culture and its individualistic religion. From the very nature of Stoicism, the attempt could have little positive effect. Stoicism never built bridges; it only helped men of a certain type to accept, and live with, the gap. It could not complete, therefore, the incomplete life of the South.

Stoicism was from its inception a practical philosophy, that is, a kind of religion, the purpose of which was to relate this world to another, to enable men to live now as though in eternity. It is, and has always been, says theologian Paul Tillich, Christianity's strongest competitor. In some of its attitudes, it is so close to Christianity that it practically merges with it, as we shall see when we consider the expression of Stoicism in the South. Like Christianity, it appeals to a world infected with failure; its appeal, however, tends to be to the spiritual aristocrat, who sees the world falling away from him, whereas Christianity's appeal is to any individual who has himself failed, regardless of the state of the world. Both grapple with defeat and human failure; but whereas Stoicism tends to be negative and impersonal, Christianity is positive and personal. Stoicism is philosophical—in a moralistic way—designed for strong men, enabling them to bear "the slings and arrows of outrageous fortune," to suffer life rather than to act upon it. Both Stoicism and Christianity show a high respect for man; but whereas Stoicism sees him as only a part, though a vital part, of an immense impersonal universe, Christianity sees him as a child of God. As a part of the universe, the Stoic may simply accept and bow to its ongoing force, or he may fight honorably against it though doomed to be defeated. As a son of God, the Christian does not fight against his Father; if he is willing to accept and cooperate with the divine laws he will find his Father most gracious, even in apparently disastrous circumstances.

Stoicism has been most important during periods of social decay and downfall. It had more influence in late Greek and Roman society than at any other time. Perhaps it was important in the ante-bellum South because the social order was trembling.

Like Christianity, Stoicism shows a sense of compassion for the human lot. But in Stoicism this compassion tends toward inaction and toward restricting itself to sympathy and respect for every man who bears nobly life's ills, regardless of the station he holds. The emperor Marcus Aurelius said that man could be happy even in a palace. The compassion of Christianity is an active compassion, aimed at righting the ills of life, at feeding the hungry, clothing the naked, saving the lost, and bringing all out of their pitiful situation into the glorious condition proper to sons of God. It is true that Christianity, at many times and in many places, has adopted toward this world a stoic attitude and has maintained that a man's wordly state meant nothing at all. It is rather hard to distinguish such Christians from Stoics; such people incline toward Stoicism because they do not really believe in the involvement of a "personal" God in this world.

The theory that Stoicism has been an important influence in the South is advanced by Walker Percy in an article in the *Commonweal*.[1] Though Percy points out several instances of the direct influence of Marcus Aurelius upon cultured Southerners, his main argument is from the stoic quality of certain dominant racial attitudes held by the whites. He is particularly effective in arguing that in the present racial crisis Stoicism is not enough; what is needed is Christianity.

Stoicism appears most clearly in the South among the aristocrats. One of the best expressions of the aristocratic *credo* appears in William Alexander Percy's *Lanterns on the Levee*. Percy quotes his aristocratic father as saying, "I guess a man's job is to make the world a better place to live in, so far as he is able—always remembering the results will be infinitesimal—and to attend to his own soul."[2] This is stoic doctrine: realize your small place in the total order; within that do your work and guard your soul. The attitude shows dignity and reserve, but it is not the outgoing attitude of the Christian, who acknowledges himself and his fellows potential sons of God.

Speaking of his father and his father's friends, Percy says: "Cap Mac and Father and General Catchings would have been at home on the west portal of Chartres with those strong ancients, severe and formidable and full of grace, who guard that holy entrance." And then he asks: "What was the pattern that gave them strength and direction, that kept them oriented, that permitted them to be at once Puritans and Cavaliers,"[3] who combined the austerities of living and the courtesy and sweetness of life?

The pattern was Stoicism, as Walker Percy suggests. The Cavalier tended to be corrupted by the superficial grace possible to his privileged station; the Puritan tended to be corrupted by the inner sternness he developed to protect himself against superficial grace. The Stoic held it was possible to combine sternness and grace, to be good even in a palace. There were at times an almost Christian lightness and relaxation in the hand he held upon the reins of self-control; it failed of being Christian only in the fact that it was he who held the reins and put himself through his paces; it was not God. A man would be saved, if at all, by the delicate works of honor and dignity demanded by the aristocratic code, not by humble acceptance of the grace of God.

In the pity that Will Percy feels for unhappy mankind, we find Stoicism touched with Christianity. For Percy tends to feel compassion for all unhappy men whether they are worthy of it or not, and this is the Christian spirit; but he fails to feel himself involved beyond this mood of pity as not only the fellow-inhabitant of the world in which unhappy men exist but as also in part its creator and sustainer. Like a Stoic, he tends to accept the world and live in it with pity and restraint. Consider his little story about his Negro chauffeur, Fode. He pities Fode in Fode's unhappy world, a Negro among the ruling whites, but he fails to recognize that he helped to make Fode's world and therefore Fode. For at this point the Stoic Percy intervenes: the world is as it is, created by the gods; Fode is as he is and must simply be respected as such. Granted that the Puritan needs a greater respect for personality than he has, the Stoic needs, from the Christian point of view, a richer sense of our tragic involvement in a world of things and people.

Finally, it is possible that in the character of Robert E. Lee there appears the faintest touch of this basic flaw at the heart of the South: the unresolved conflict between Christianity and Stoicism. If this flaw appears even in Lee, how much more so in the South generally. For Lee was, and is, almost worshiped in the South because he balanced the virtues of the South within himself, and avoided almost entirely—some think entirely—the faults. He balanced the plantation and the farm, the seaboard and the piedmont, tidewater and the mountains, grace and strength, gentleman and Christian. Among his papers found after his death is the sentence: "A true man of honor feels humbled himself when he cannot help humbling others."[4] Here is honor, normally so closely related to place and pride, attended by humility. As to any flaw at the center, any unresolved question there, Lee's biographer Freeman thinks there was none. In his eyes—and they are indeed knowledgeable—Lee was through and through the great, simple, often saintly, character he appears. Gamaliel Bradford expresses some doubt as to this perfect matching of outer and inner. Bradford writes: it was Lee "who wrote of his daughter, 'She is like her papa—always wanting something.' I wonder what she wanted." I mention Lee only because, first, I know that legends make heroes more godlike than they are, and, second, because of my awareness of this Stoic-Christian flaw at the heart of the South. I think Lee illustrates this flaw, even though in its slightest form.

We do know Lee had the highest admiration for Marcus Aurelius, an admiration he had inherited from his father, "who placed that emperor high among his venerated immortals."[5] We also know he had a sense of the smallness of human effort in the great sweep of history. Lee said: "The march of Providence is so slow and our desires so impatient; the work of progress is so immense and our means of aiding it so feeble; the life of humanity is so long, that of the individual so brief, that we often see only the ebb of the advancing wave, and are thus discouraged."[6] And all agree to his sense of personal integrity in himself and in others. There is a revealing conversation recorded between his young friend Belle Stewart and himself in 1867. She had asked him why he was sad. He replied that he was thinking of the men who were lost after he knew it was all over. But he had not told his men the cause was hopeless because "that was a fact that they had to find out for themselves."[7] This is a true Stoic refusal to interfere in the destinies of others, even though such interference might save them. In this view, a man's life is less important than the freedom to be himself.

There is also the matter of Lee's moralistic nature. This appears very clearly on various occasions. Lee's biographer Douglas Southall Freeman says that to dismissed West Point cadets who later wrote him, "he always sent friendly answers, not always devoid of the sort of preachments that crowded his letters to his sons."[8] At another place, Freeman calls him "A gentleman of noble soul. For him as for his grandfather, Charles Carter, religion blended with the code of *noblesse oblige* to which he had been reared. Together, these two forces resolved every problem of life into right and wrong. The clear light of conscience and of social obligation left no zone of gray in the heart: everything was black and white."[9] It is upon such an assured ground that moralism rests.

It may be all right for a small man to be moralistic; maybe this is the best he can do; the greatest men are not. Lee was one of the very greatest men the South produced; the greatest of its great period when it was challenging the rest of the nation. But the South tended to be moralistic, and Lee, its greatest representative, illustrates the attitude. The South tended to be moralistic because it was not intellectual and philosophical, because of the public nature of its religion, even from the beginning a matter of form and works, and because of the belated and mindless Puritanism that invaded the South with the nineteenth-century revivals. This tendency toward moralism made the South a ripe field for Stoicism, which set forth for men certain rules for life, especially in a decaying world. I should think that Lee's moralism was the product in part of a Stoicism inherited from his father and highly suited to a Southern gentleman who was a puritan as well as a cavalier.

More difficult to understand than Lee's moralism, which appears simply as an unhappy though typical weakness in a man so great, is the rather marked contrast between the sense of assurance with which he moves in the material and moral world, and the sense of humility, incapacity, and guilt with which he moves in the religious world. Freeman says that "over his acts as a man [Lee] never [hesitated]. There was but one question ever: what was his duty as a Christian and a gentleman? . . . He could not have conceived of a Christian who was not a gentleman."[10] In contrast to this assurance was Lee's often expressed sense of fault and guilt in regard to God. According to Freeman's interpretation, Lee was a Christian and a gentleman who practically always acted without fear and without reproach. But how could a man be so sure of himself in this world when he was so unsure of himself in another? It is as if there are two worlds, and excellence in one has no connection with excellence in the other. In the world of the South a man could be a gentleman and a Christian without feeling himself at home in the kingdom of God. This seems to me an example of the basic flaw in the South: the existence of a social life so rich that to be a leader in that society—a gentleman—is also to be a leader in religion, but in a social religion radically different from the spirit in which the individual faces another world. There are really two religions here: the social religion of this world and the individualistic religion of another.

This equating of God—some god—with Southern life is suggested by Freeman's comment upon Lee's countless cousins, with whom he mingled extensively while acting as the executor of his father-in-law's estate, from 1857–1859: Their "faith in Virginia's political rightness was as unquestioning as their belief in God."[11] With Virginia facing defeat, Lee wrote to his son in the spring of 1864: "If defeated, nothing will be left for us to live for. . . . My whole trust is in God, and I am ready for whatever He may ordain."[12] "If Virginia fails, life fails" does not agree with "My whole trust is in God, though he may ordain Virginia's defeat." In regard to the suffering of war and possible defeat, Lee seems to vary from the Stoic attitude that we must bear like men all decrees of fate and the puritan attitude that a personal God is punishing us for our sins and we must therefore repent.

General John M. Schofield, after four decades of army service, said of Lee, "He was the personification of dignity, justice, and kindness."[13] This praise brings together Lee's inner and his outer life: dignity and justice softened by kindness. Perhaps as a soldier, Lee succeeded in bridging the gap between Christianity and Stoicism. But maybe the fact that near the close of his life he expressed the opinion that the greatest mistake he had ever made was to enter the army suggests his realization that deep within him there was a gap between the Stoic and the Christian, a gap that army life tended to blur. For the army lays the chief emphasis upon works, as a moralistic Stoicism does; and also upon means in this world, not upon ends, certainly not upon ends in another world. Christianity points to such ends, and when Lee as a man considered these, he felt entirely inadequate. His sense of guilt may have been due to the fact that in choosing the army he had chosen a vocation alien to his most fundamental desires. Yet it must be remembered that he had chosen what was considered the ideal vocation for the Southern aristocrat and gentleman. Which raises again the question of the essential Christianity of the Southern gentleman.

Maybe there have been no essential Christians. I don't mean to criticize the South—and certainly not Lee—because even its greatest gentleman failed somewhat in being a Christian, standing with one foot on Stoic ground. My criticism is aimed at the fact that the South tried to effect the impossible combination of an inclusive social religion and an exclusive

Protestant church. And she did this because by this time the modern church had pretty well gone out of the production of saints, and since the South wasn't set up to create poets, she had nobody to tell her wherein she was wrong.

For several reasons, Stoicism found a rich soil in the antebellum South. First, because of the rising individualism of the Western World, of which the South was a part, an individualism which coincided with and was in part the cause of the decay of the inclusive community life of the Middle Ages. Second, because of the existence of slavery, increasingly under moral attack, impossible to defend in the humanitarian air of the nineteenth century and within a Christianity increasingly concerned about life in the world, but easy to defend by the Stoic doctrine that a man's worldly condition does not matter. Third, because of the growing doubt within the minds of Southern leaders, a sense of the coming eclipse of the nation, a fear of the possible breakdown of the social and economic order of the South. In such a mood a man, if he were a Stoic, could retire to the inviolable castle of his own soul and watch with stern composure the playing out of the game.

But was there any such mood as this in the South? Was not the South, on the contrary, absolutely sure of itself, eager for a future separate from the Union, happily anticipating a brief struggle to throw off the Union's yoke when it became apparent that the Union would resist? What was there Stoical about this mood?

These were the loud voices. And these are the voices that we chiefly remember, partly because their seeming assurance forms such striking contrast to the disaster that shortly befell the South. But there were others, filled with foreboding. One of the earliest was Jefferson's lament over the evil of slavery, "I tremble for my country when I think that God is just, and his justice will not sleep forever"; and the same man, now grown old, upon learning of the passage of the Missouri Compromise, the first demarcation of free and slave states, "trembled as at the sound of a fire-bell in the night." Moving forward thirty years, we come to Calhoun, certainly a fighter, no Stoical acceptant of life as it is, a few months before his death lamenting: "The poor South! God knows what will become of her!"

Some ten years before this, in the 1830's, William Gilmore Simms, probably the leading man of letters in the South and an admitted authority on the life of his times, was writing essays on Hamlet and discussing the Hamlet-like quality of the educated Southerner. He admitted that along the frontier Southerners were men of action, decisively meeting events as they arose; but along the Atlantic seaboard, the best of them, the best-trained, the leaders, had become too sensitive, too keenly aware of the difficulties and ambiguities of life, pondered too long upon the event. When, finally, and partly because of their hesitation, the situation would become impossible, they would rush desperately into action as Hamlet did, destroying both themselves and those about them. This is partly what happened in 1861.

Hamlet, of course, was not a Stoic. But the foreboding mood that made Hamlets of some Southerners could have made Stoics of others.

In our own day, W. J. Cash is of the opinion that over against the complacency of the South there always sat a "haunting fear and uneasiness." And Harriet Martineau, in her *Retrospect of Western Travels,* published in 1838, comments as follows upon the spirit of Southern entertainments: "Nothing could be gayer than the external aspects of these entertainments; but it is impossible for the stranger to avoid being struck with the anxiety which shows itself through it all. . . . I was never in Southern society without perceiving that its characteristic is a want of repose. It is restlessly gay or restlessly sorrowful. It is angry or exulting; it is hopeful or apprehensive. . . . While everything is done that can be conceived to make you happy, there is a weight pulling at your heartstrings, because you see that other hearts are heavy, and the nobler the heavier. . . . You reproach yourself because you . . . feel as if it were ingratitude to your entertainers not to think them the secure and happy people which, in alternation with their complaints . . . they assure you they are."[14]

Is it any wonder that in this uneasy world many Southerners became Stoics? It was a way of enduring the storm; it was not a way of bringing the ship into port.

CHAPTER 12

SIR WALTER SCOTT AND THE CIVIL WAR

We can follow this thread of Stoic foreboding into a consideration of Scott's Waverley Novels and their influence upon the ante-bellum South. Actually, the Stoic influence of these romances was probably slight. Their total effect, however, may have been considerable, though hardly so great as Mark Twain claimed. In *Life on the Mississippi,* he said Scott caused the Civil War by filling the mind of the Southerners with foolish, romantic notions of themselves as representing pure-hearted unconquerable "chivalry"—which is how some visualized themselves. Scott was widely read in both South and North, but the seriousness with which Southerners took his romances does suggest that they may throw some light upon the Southern mind of that period. In attempting to explain this vogue, I am relying for my understanding of the romances largely upon Alexander Welsh's recent study, *The Hero of the Waverley Novels.*[1] I shall summarize here those aspects of the novels that seem most pertinent to the ante-bellum South.

According to Welsh, the underlying purpose of the Waverley Novels was to present under the guise of historical romance the primary importance of the social order, especially as bound up with the institution of property. They represented Scott's reaction to the excesses of the French Revolution. Scott was in fiction what Burke was in politics and Blackstone in law. Scott created two types of heroes and heroines: the proper, or passive, hero who defended law and order, reason, prudence, and the accepted values, especially property; and the dark hero, who acted for the individual against these values, and in a spirit of passion and disorder. Though perhaps he lived more richly, the dark hero always came to a disastrous end, in failure, exile, or death. As a rule, the locale of his action was the wilder Scotland as opposed to the more civilized England, or the wilder Highlands as opposed to the more civilized Lowlands. The main activity of the proper, or passive, heroes and heroines was to make an excursion from the more settled land into the frontier, observe and to a degree become implicated with the darker heroes and heroines there, and at the end return safely to civilization, marry each other, and unite their separate properties in a greater estate. For instance, in *Ivanhoe,* perhaps Scott's best-known romance, the hero Ivanhoe marries the fair Rowena, not the dark and far more interesting Rebecca. To judge from the plot, Scott is always in favor of his passive, civilized heroes, though there are grounds for believing that he valued more than he admitted the passionate life of his dark heroes.

In some ways Walter Scott himself served as an ideal for Southerners. Herbert Grierson says, "To an extraordinary degree . . . Scott kept his life's experiences out of his romances," and adds that Scott kept most references to his art out of his letters and journal. "What a novel Balzac would have made out of Scott's ambitions and negotiations and reckless expenditures and labours, and the careless ease and expansion of the social life he was to all appearance chiefly interested in —and then the failure and the tragic end."[2]

Somewhat like William Gilmore Simms, Scott was more concerned with being a gentleman than a writer. Though he worked hard at his writing, it was behind the surface. He tried to cut too wide a swathe in social life and in publishing, involved himself generously but often inadvisedly in the latter, and when failure came, accepted like an honorable man all the debts involved and worked himself to death to pay them off. Southerners must have admired him for what he was. His romances, however, touched them more subtly and widely than his life.

We began with the slight thread of Stoicism; that can be followed quickly. It appears generally in the attitude of his proper heroes to accept things as they are—the status quo—though one must admit that they show a concern for the status quo and a deep anxiety about running counter to it that is hardly Stoic. It appears in the self-restraint of these heroes, and their deep respect for themselves and for others. This is illustrated best by Colonel Mannering, of *Guy Mannering,* the finest gentleman, says Welsh, in the Waverley Novels. "Mannering is a man of means whose self-respect and compassion are alike tempered with great delicacy. Though he can be moved to tears, he knows that even an offer of one's services can be misconstrued as an intrusion."[3] This reminds us of General Lee's sad comment that his men had to fight on till they knew for themselves that they were defeated.

But the chief means through which Scott touched the South lay in the similarities and differences between the stories he told and the story the South was enacting. First, in regard to property.

The French Revolution, in endangering property rights, had increased the prestige of property. However, as Welsh points out, "The affirmation of the right of property in the Waverley Novels and elsewhere must be viewed against the general uneasiness, implicit in both the natural rights theory and in Christianity, over the inequality of privilege."[4] Thus, though property was held firmly during Scott's time, it was often held anxiously. This anxiety was strong in the American South because of the nature of slave property. For "Property rests directly on a rational order of society, and is secure only by virtue of an agreement among men to respect it—that is . . . ultimately to respect . . . things as they are."[5] But how do rational men justify the holding of other men in slavery? And how can title rest safely upon the agreement of others to observe it when those in slavery haven't even been asked to agree? If Walter Scott and his English and Scottish gentlemen were concerned about the validity of titles to property, how much more so were Southern slaveowners, whose titles were being increasingly challenged by the abolitionists of the North?

But perhaps of more general interest to the South was the balance between Scott's proper or passive heroes and his dark heroes, one group representing the world of prudence and cultured society, the other the world of passion and the frontier. These were the two worlds that existed also in America. According to Frederick Jackson Turner, the frontier put its stamp upon American democracy; according to Erik Erikson the tension between the frontier and the old home put its stamp upon the American character. But there is a significant difference between the frontier of Scott's novels and the American frontier: Scott's frontier opens upon the past, the American frontier upon the future. When Scott's ladies and gentlemen made an excursion from England into Scotland, or from the Lowlands into the Highlands, they traveled from the cultured world of their present into an earlier and wilder world, a world that carried memories of a more passionate past rather than hints of an undefined future. Scott's proper heroes and heroines could make a journey to the frontier to see how poorly and briefly others lived amid their wild and passionate surroundings: seaboard Southerners went to the frontier to stay and to become frontiersmen themselves. Scott makes it clear that his passive heroes and heroines, though they are affected by their dark counterparts, must make no concesson to them in attitude or point of view. In fact, if such concession is made, the passive hero or blond heroine who makes it ends by being lost at sea, or is exiled, or departs for the American West, to be lost among the Indians.

Actually there was during the early nineteenth century a good deal of fear in America on the part of old seaboard settlers that culture and religion would be lost on the frontier, and doubtless Scott's American readers were faintly conscious of this as they read his pages. But the pull of the frontier, its sense of the future, was too great. Many of them lay aside the book to go west themselves, or closed it and took it with them hopefully to be reopened amid new scenes; and those who resisted the pull and stayed at home comforted themselves with the thought that maybe Scott was right in preferring a settled and ordered society.

We come now to Scott's dark heroine and her place in the South. We have seen that the anxiety aroused by the desire for a society stabilized in property was increased in the South by the presence of a property in human beings; we have seen that the American frontier of the future broke down patterns of culture as Scott's frontier of the past was unable to do. We now ask: Who were the dark heroines in the South to match those dangerous willful creatures of the Waverley Novels?

Practically speaking there were none. There were the Grimké sisters, who spoke out against slavery and the subordination of women and left Charleston shortly thereafter, in the late 1830's, for the North. The Southern woman was the "blond" heroine, brought up as a girl to please, as a matron to rule the home and to minister to the ills of the plantation. As with Scott, they were both prudent sustainers of order and discreet angelic presences.

But just as the geographical frontier in the South was more powerful than the remembered frontier in Scott, so was the dark heroine more seductive. No one called her a heroine or admitted publicly her seductiveness. The readers of Scott may have tried to forget her presence or to recall it only in fleeting guilt-tinged moments. But she was there, in sharp contrast to the pure "blond heroine," passionate, willful, still but half at home in the culture in which she had been forcibly set down. There is little need to repeat what I have already said about the apeal of the dark earth-woman to the passive heroes of the South. I am only suggesting that Scott's romances picked up in the American South a power they did not have in the more stable English scene, and that their essential message of the value of social order over freedom and of prudence over passion was largely unrecognized by Southern readers. It is true, the plantations were, on the surface, great orderly systems, their order made more imperative by the inequities and violence upon which they rested; it is true also that the white women of the South were pathetically eager to forget the disorder that underlay the lives of their men. Scott helped them to forget by leading them into a world where the passive heroes and heroines were both pure and successful. But it was hardly purity and settled property which won out in the South.

We may say, in general, that Scott's novels probably added confusion to the Southern mind already confused by the presence of slavery. Misreading them permitted the Southerner to romanticize his "peculiar institution" with a touch of the feudal past. And, more significantly, it helped to upset the early Southern balance between past and future. Scott's outmoded frontier of the past, Southerners interpreted as their own frontier of the future. They did have a frontier. It consisted of democracy spreading westward. With his romances of feudal life along past frontiers, Scott blurred the image of the future in the mind of the South. There would come a time when the past would not only confuse but hypnotize this mind.

Was there anything to Mark Twain's charge that Scott "caused" the Civil War? Perhaps something. The Southerner, misreading Scott, may have been led into attitudes that helped to bring on the war and to lead to defeat. Scott assured his readers that order and property would win. The South was moved toward the conflict by its defense of its property in slaves. What it did not see was that such property was essentially irrational and disorderly, related therefore to Scott's world of dark heroes and heroines, who, though they may live richly, always fail. The South was defending property rights to the disregard of human rights; in the humanitarian air of the nineteenth century this was a lost cause.

Scott also suggested to the mind of the South the possibility of lost causes. His lost causes were those of the romantic frontier, of Bonnie Prince Charlie, and of wild willful men; but the Southern plantation people who read Scott were members not only of a settled culture but also of a culture changing and breaking along geographical and racial frontiers. They had one foot in each camp. Their concern for the settled plantation order made them accept uncritically Scott's lesson about the permanence of property; their concern for rich frontiers leading toward wildness, but also, they felt, toward the future, made them follow with eagerness the adventures of Scott's dark heroes and heroines, overlooking for the most part their dismal end.

Yet not entirely. They were learning from Scott, what they

already sensed, that vital causes can be lost—they were developing a tragic sense of life.

In doing this, they were developing Scott's own suggestions. Scott wrote romances, not tragedies. But at times he came close to tragedy. The critic W. P. Ker says: "Scott gets very near to the tension of tragedy, but never quite uses it . . . there is the shadowing tragedy all through *Old Mortality* but never the tragic inference."[6] Of the same story, Welsh says: "The disconcerting thing about the end of *Old Mortality* is that the hero comes close to decisive action without knowing it and Scott comes close to producing a tragedy without knowing it."[7] And of the Waverley Novels: "The Waverley Novels would be a curious set of documents if Scott allowed his heroes to complete their several gestures toward death."[8]

And this is what his Southern readers did. They read Scott for his romance, his light and dreamlike arrangement of things, his impulsive play against the serious background of an orderly society. But when they felt the pull of the vital frontiers about them, some of them tended to become, as Simms has suggested, Hamlets, who, having remained undecided too long, finally swung about them in wild, imprudent action. The Southerner, as I have said before, was always too inclined merely to accept the lures and the pressures of the world; I shall point out later how this led him, hardly a tragic hero, into a tragic career. So he accepted the romances of Scott; he saw in himself the passive hero, the defender of law and order and property. But he also accepted the compelling lure of his geographical and racial frontiers, and almost without knowing it he became both the dark hero and the proper hero swept away on a tragic career. The high point of this career was the Civil War. Southerners entered it as though it were just another romantic adventure arranged for their amusement by Sir Walter Scott. He had cautioned them that all romantic adventures would fail but they had not understood. They were the chivalry, fighting against prudent businessmen, schemers, and calculators.

Jeb Stuart of the sash and plume fell from the saddle at Yellow Tavern, and the brilliant soldier-gentleman Lee was at last overwhelmed by a slugger who delivered through his blows the packed and calculated power of the North.

CHAPTER 13

POETIC SOUTH: ITS SENTIMENTS

We have said that the South lacked both saints and poets, either or both of which might have unified its life by revealing to it the implications which this world has for another, by crowning its culture with religion and basing its religion in its culture. But, though it never succeeded in solving this problem, it did have a rich store of materials that might have been used in the solution. Though it lacked great poets, it had the materials of poetry. Perhaps the poets failed to appear because the need for them wasn't clear enough. Perhaps the need wasn't clear enough because of the poetic nature of Southern life itself.

There's an adage, "Poets are born, not made." According to the Italian philosopher Croce, the truth underlying this statement should be expressed as follows: Men are born poets; the practical world, however, strips from most of them their poetic characteristics.

This is especially true of the modern world. The thrust into the future is so great that men are largely concerned with getting there—though nobody knows where or even what *there* is—and have little interest left for the road, the passage through the world. It is true that our leisure increases daily; and California, which boasts that it is today what the nation will be tomorrow, blooms in whole sections of houses, the occupants of which are supposed to loll in timeless sunshine on the edge of gracious pools. But the drive, the thrust is still there, as the expressways attest.

The distinction of the South is that it has moved more slowly, more hesitantly, into the modern world than has the rest of the nation. The pace is now accelerating; how fast it will become no one knows. The charm of the South has been its somewhat less than practical, indeed its poetic, quality. I know there are businessmen in the South as hardheaded as any in the nation; this has always been so. The eighteenth-century Scotch-Irish were the "Yankees of the South." But the Scotch-Irish changed even as they were changing the South; and that leisurely quality which the South has emphasized, that air of detachment from the urgencies of life, is to some degree the detachment of the poet.

It was in part this preoccupation with the creation of a poetic life that prevented the South from creating poets. By poets I mean imaginative writers, in prose or verse; and by a poetic life I mean a life touched by imagination. For the first two centuries, of course, like the rest of the country, the South was too busy gathering the materials for life itself. But with the coming of wealth in the nineteenth century, and with a growing national life, why did it not, like New England, create a notable imaginative literature? The South is flowering in literature in the twentieth century as New England did in the nineteenth. Why this century of delay?

The ante-bellum South was both too satisfied with its values and at the same time too much on the defensive to encourage and permit poets to speak freely. New England, too, had heavy streaks of complacency—e.g., the spiritual pride of the abolitionists—but it was not on the defensive, it even carried an air of victory, and its men of imagination had a chance to speak out. They also had the motivation, for the harshness of early industrialism in New England contrasted with certain at least superficial graces that were naturally a part of the old established agricultural order of the South. Among the New Englanders, there was Thoreau warning of the evils of a rising industrialism, Hawthorne and Melville revealing the dark unplumbed abysses of life. If you call Edgar Allan Poe a Southerner, he was the distorted genius of the South, speaking of the desperate emptiness that underlay the smooth surface; his images are of iron walls closing in, of graves entombing the living. William Gilmore Simms shows with less distortion what was going on. He was so impressed by the excellence of Southern life—which was related indeed to its poetry—that he was unable to draw as sharp and critical a picture as otherwise he might have. He was too provincial, too much of a Southerner, to apply to the life about him that criticism that true poetry through its imaginative insight applies. The poetry of Southern life itself prevented Simms from making such a fundamental criticism, both by seducing him by its charm and by constraining him by the unified and therefore strong culture it made possible. The South was too good—at least too pleasant and persuasive—to make Simms a great writer, but, unfortunately, not good enough—as no society is—to get along without such writers.

The poetry of the South is related especially to the South's stress upon both sentiment and images. We shall consider first the matter of sentiment. How is sentiment poetic, and why has the South developed a more than usual amount of it?

Sentiment describes that fairly steadfast emotional attitude, usually positive, that relates people to places and to other people, and that has been developed over a period of time. Says John Crowe Ransom: "A sentiment is the totality of love and knowledge which we have of an object that is private and unique."[1] I have already established that the originally spacious mind of the South, under the influence of slavery, became increasingly concerned with physical and social place, and that the originally balanced temporal mind became increasingly concerned with the mere continuation of the past. In discussing sentiment as a poetic characteristic of the South, we shall see that, though sentiment bound the South together in a complex web, it tended to bind it to a limited place and to the past and thus reinforced the effect of slavery. Even without slavery, Southerners would have stressed sentiment, but slavery made this emphasis inevitable.

Along with this sentiment, and as a part of its development, goes a certain degree of knowledge of the related persons or objects. John Crowe Ransom has pointed out how close this knowledge is to the knowledge the artist has of his subject: that is, how close sentimental knowledge, using the term without derogatory intent, is to esthetic, or poetic, knowledge. If, therefore, the South is a region favorable to the development of sentimental knowledge, it is also a region favorable to the development of poetic knowledge.

We have spoken of the South's tendency to move slowly through time, carrying much of the past with it, continually transforming the empty space of the future into places enriched, at times indeed, as now for a hundred years, burdened, by the past. Most contemporary Southerners are burdened. Either they are lost in the past of an earlier South, gone now with the smoke of war, or, in reaction against this memory of defeat and frustration, they rush into a future, the opposite of what they have known. The reason the South handles so inadequately these ties of sentiment, which bind it together in space and time, is that it has never been sufficiently conscious of what was at stake, never really understood the poetry of its life. Perhaps this ignorance, or innocence, is part of its charm. I too can say a good word for innocence; but it seems clear to me that the South failed partly because it relied too much upon the surface of life; it accepted complacently the gifts that nature lavished upon it: the world looked like a place you could live in without much thought.

Instead of thought, the South has relied upon sentiment: the binding together of space and time by emotional attitudes that bind people and places together. Sentiment can exist in considerable strength without much knowledge of its importance. A man who has lived and worked long in a given place, a farmer, for instance, may be so attached by sentiment to the place that he will refuse even an extravagant offer for it. Yet he only knows he doesn't want to sell; he has lived there a long time and likes it. So sentiment grows out of custom, and our farmer, if challenged, tends to defend custom for custom's sake.

But life is more than custom. It is a balance of custom and novelty, the old and the new, the past and the future. In the beginning, the South kept this balance rather well. But the adoption of slavery tended to unbalance it. It became increasingly difficult to think clearly about the problems slavery raised, increasingly easy to fall back upon the sentiments that had arisen in connection with it. Slavery tended to become right both because it was customary and because it had come to have a central place in the culture of the South. The slaves came to be associated with places that the whites had made their own and to which they were therefore sentimentally attached; they also had their place in the total society, in which all other men also had places, and the sense of order thus achieved created in all the participants a valuable sense of belonging, though undoubtedly the whites felt this far more than the Negroes.

We have already seen how Calhoun tried to defend a customary, static, feudal society, in which change is organic and sentiment is strong, with modern, rational political methods originated primarily by John Locke for the purpose of destroying feudalism. Calhoun made this error because in his mind he was a citizen of a modern state but in his heart the exponent of a feudal world. His mind opposed his heart.

If the South had had poets—outstanding imaginative writers—it would have done better in the long haul, though it is doubtful if even poets could have warded off defeat. They might, however, have helped the South bear it better. It did not have the poets partly because from the beginning it was too much interested in the public world and too little interested in the imaginative and critical world of the mind. It was more interested in that public quarrel with others, which appears in rhetoric, oratory, politics, and war, than in the private quarrel with itself which the poet—and the saint—keeps alive. The poet seeks the total vision; sees the events of this world as hinting at or betraying the world of spirit. It is paradoxical that the South had a total vision superior to that of the North. The proof of this is that the North has driven more rapidly than the South toward individualistic chaos and in part swept the South along with it. Yet the total vision of the South was sadly incomplete; it failed to set this world securely within another and it was along this crack the heart of the South divided. If the South had had poets it would have understood itself better, and perhaps corrected some of its faults. Particularly, it would have understood better its deep but vague sentiments, and might have been able to rear upon them a better defense than it did—which was that this was the way it had always done things, and, by God, it would keep on.

What could poets have done to help the South? Most of all, perhaps, they could have expressed its deep but vague feeling about time and space. These were the sentiments upon which Southern life rested; they were the source of its strength; they were also the source of its weakness, and contained the seeds of its defeat.

The religiously inclined person may say the South was defeated because of a religious failure. But this is really to say that it did not set this world securely within another: it did not rest its space and time securely upon the universal and the eternal.

All poets are concerned, the great poets clearly, with this world as seen in the light of some other. "The light that never was on sea or land,/The consecration and the poet's dream," Wordsworth called it. Whatever this world may be, we apprehend it in terms of space and time; but, though all men occupy space and time, they occupy it differently. We have already noticed how Southerners have differed from non-Southerners in this: Southerners are more involved in time and space, more sustained by time, more attached to place. More attached to the world. This is what strict Puritans always said about Southerners: they enjoyed the world too much. A New Englander visiting Charleston about 1800 was favorably impressed by the concentration of wealth evident in the great houses of Charleston but was shocked at the pleasure Charlestonians got out of living in them. It was right—it was indeed righteous—to use the world to build houses, or, preferably, wealth-producing factories; it was wicked to enjoy these things.

But Southerners never completely forgot another world, universal and eternal; they were aware of it, and still are: the final mystery that surrounds us, in space and time. Southerners also, in their emphasis upon community, itself occupying a place within space, would have agreed that it is impossible to pick up the world except by the handle of a community. If not this world, surely not another. And yet right at this point, the point of transition from an earthly community to a heavenly, the South became confused. Unlike the true Puritan, the Southerner valued this world so much that he was bound to consider any other in the light of this, but his earthly community, corrupted by slavery, simply could not serve as the model for the heavenly. As we said earlier, if he had had poets, he might have seen a little better where he was right and where he was wrong, and might have made such adjustments as would either have warded off the war that finally came, or failing that, at least have prepared him better for suffering such a defeat.

Take the matter of time. Poets are concerned, sometimes terribly, with the passage of time. If the South had had poets, it might have understood better the nature of what it was trying to carry into the future. It might have continued to stand, as the early Virginians did, upon a living past instead of hoisting upon its shoulders the burden of a dead past. It might have learned without disaster that all things are transient, and when their time comes, they have to go, good and bad together.

Poets might thus have purified the great piety of the South. Not destroyed it but purified it, and balanced it against ideals. Piety is devotion to the sources of our being. Leaving out the question of God as our source, we are largely what the past has made us—or not made us. For the past has also prevented our being and continues to prevent it. The problem of piety is how to respect the past without worshiping it. At every moment it is alive in us through habits of thought and action, customs, institutions, but also at every moment something is dying because of lack of present nourishment. One must be forever sifting the past to determine what is alive in the present or may live in the future. This the poets help us to do. They make clear to us what we recall with devotion, what only for material interest or for custom's sake. They keep us from worshiping the past as a whole, or indeed any part of it.

The reason it's so hard to keep piety from degenerating into an all-inclusive worship of the past is that a strong intellectual tradition is needed to act as a check upon piety, but that piety, like other sentiments, tends not to arise where a strong intellectual tradition exists. The analytical intellect tends to prevent the formation of vague emotional attachments. Thus the dilemma: no piety or too much. This is really a problem of the modern world; how to understand and harmonize the deep attachments of the heart without explaining them away.

The South never had a metaphysics, a philosophical tradition. Its manners, its religion, had deep sentimental rootage; but this was not extended by thought throughout the world and the universe. Not knowing what they were doing, Southerners did it shallowly and sloppily. They tended to accept the world, with the attachments that bound them to particular places and to the remembered images of those places. They did not recognize the universal, symbolic quality of these attachments; they did not make a point of believing in them. They were attached to them by an essentially religious piety, but they did not realize the religious quality of this attachment, and were therefore bound to the particular place and moment instead of being freed into the universal and the eternal. In brief, they tried to live in the world, to be a part of the world, without real thought. They assumed too easily the goodness of the world and of themselves. They made the opposite error the Puritans made. The Puritans thought too hard about their inner lives, or perhaps thought wrongly, with too much analysis and too little contemplation, until finally they thought them away. Southerners thought too little, and so, though they did not lose themselves in the alpine atmosphere of the analytical mind, they did lose themselves in Southern swamps of emotion and sentiment.

Take also the sense of space, and the need for poets there. Coming but recently out of Elizabethan England, the earliest Southern settlers, certainly the leaders among them, brought with them the feeling of great spaces, a feeling which the New World more than satisfied. This sense of a vast world to the west increased after the Revolution, when the Appalachians were crossed and the tree-clad Mississippi valley stretched to the horizon. Though by this time the Elizabethan flair for adventure had diminished toward prosaic search for rich land, the westward drive had been intensified by the coming of great numbers of Scotch-Irish to the piedmont of the South. With an old hunger for land, occasionally touched by the lure of distance, these people drove westward with perhaps more than Elizabethan intensity. But they were mainly seeking land on which to build a home, farm home or plantation home; they were seeking space to convert it into place. A place for themselves, first in the natural world, then in the human. Since the South was to remain chiefly agricultural, these places remained country, and were not subject to the increasingly rapid change that took place in the growing industrial areas of the North. The Southerner's tendency to move somewhat slowly through time, carrying into the future something of the richness of the past, was matched by his tendency to pause in space, to cut out a place for himself in it as proof to himself that he was surrounded by a friendly world. Inevitably he developed an attachment to such a place, and gathered much knowledge about it, some of it practical, as which soil suited which crops, some of it sentimental, as the piping of myriad frogs after the rain. He liked the place because the soil was good, but he also liked it because the piping of the frogs was familiar. He realized clearly what the richness of the soil meant: good crops, profits, a better house. He had only a vague sense of what his sentimental knowledge meant. The mystery of life and death was part of his religion; and doubtless from time to time, he connected the mystery of the wheeling stars and seasons with the unknown meaning it had for him. If he had had poets, imaginative writers, he would have come to understand these things better; at least to have been more substantially set within the world of nature. For poets see any place as symbolic of place itself, man's outer garment, the friendly yard looking out upon vastness—or, it may be, the armed frontier beyond which lie all the forces of darkness.

Yet it was not in the matter of man's relation to the land that the South has suffered most from the lack of poets. With this exception perhaps. For at least a hundred years now, the white Southerner has been too much inclined to identify himself as one who defends his land against dangerous outsiders rather than as one who loves especially this piece of earth. Poets might have kept his eyes more steadily on the things he loved rather than on the things he feared. And it was, first of all, a certain place he loved.

It is when we come to place as social place, however, that we find the Southerner becoming especially confused. For here interest entered. He was attached to the order of society under which he lived, not only by habit, not only by ties of affection for the people around him whom he had known for years in their several roles or places, but also by the material profit he gained from this arrangement. In addition to this, the whole movement from the medieval into the modern world has been marked by a changing attitude toward social place. Throughout most of the American colonial period, the generally accepted attitude, South and North, was that there is a place in society for every man, high and low, and a man is supposed to stay in his place. Actually, however, this theory was being rapidly undermined everywhere in the Western World, and especially in America, where free land continually offered to men the chance to make for themselves a better place than that into which they had been born. Because of the more definite attempt in the South to create a landed aristocracy—the ultimate of place—and because of the introduction of slavery, the old idea of inherited place continued to hold sway here long after it had virtually disappeared from the rest of the country. But even the Southerner, carrying much of the past with him, was also driving, sometimes fiercely, into the individualistic modern world. And, as we have seen, it was because he was trying to combine incompatible attitudes that he came to grief. This is seen clearly in the matter of social place. Poets might have helped him to understand and overcome his confusion; an inclusive church, itself poetic because of its inclusiveness, its universality, would also have helped. Unfortunately, he had neither.

In the medieval notion of place, the slave had a place in society, into which he was born and in which, like other men, he remained. But the medieval church, which in its doctrine, its liturgy, and even in its practice, had included all men, had now been splintered into many denominations and sects. Furthermore, the modern world, rising in the West, and especially along the American frontier, was calling men out to an individualistic struggle, in which each one would take and hold whatever place he could. Throughout the period of slavery, the South tried ineffectively to make the slaves a part of the total community, especially through the establishment of sentimental ties with house servants; but lacking an inclusive, a poetic church, it was not possible to "place" this earthly community in a heavenly setting. There was a heavenly setting, of course, to which the saved would be admitted, master and slave alike, but the Southerner made no serious attempt to prefigure this community on earth. Out of the earthly community men had to pass as lonely individuals into another world, into the order of the saved or the chaos of the damned.

The white Southerner told himself that the Negroes were "our people" and therefore at home here. He went to great efforts to convince both himself and the Negroes that this was true: "My Old Kentucky Home," "Swanee River," "Carry Me Back to Old Virginny," "Massa's in the Cold, Cold Ground." And indeed the Negro was essentially a Southerner, with an unusual capacity for making himself at home wherever he found himself. But this realistic capacity covered tragic depths. Home wasn't really here. The Negro was climbing Jacob's Ladder. Home was over Jordan, over Deep River, and he longed to cross over into Camp Ground. If the ante-bellum South had really listened to these spirituals, these true poems, it would have realized how poor were its pretensions that the Negro really belonged to the community. This was the deepest poetry of the South; it offered the truest criticism of Southern pretensions. It revealed how far from home was this society that laid so much stress upon home, how far from a heavenly place the society that laid so much stress upon place.

Indeed, if the white master had been able to see what the lowly slave was doing to him, he might have discarded, at whatever cost, the whole system; or, if not that, he might at least have learned far more humility than he did. The system itself was basically evil, though possessing the virtue of creating in the master a sense of responsibility, however limited, for the dependent slave. But more subtle than the effect of the system were the effects of the close relationship of these two particular peoples. In general the Negro was more southern than the white, more touched by the sun, less hardened by the rigors of the north. More warm and impulsive, less cool and detached. Whites living in the South became Southern as they were exposed to this sun from a deeper south. Some of them became harsh and moralistic in the attempt to protect themselves from it. Others, more fortunate, were softened without being overwhelmed.

Attempting to define racial temperament—supposing it exists—the sociologist Robert E. Park called the Negro race "the lady among the races." He was suggesting that, in comparison with the white, the Negro is more sensitive and artistic, less practical. Whatever he may have been, it's perfectly clear that this is what the white Southerner tended to make him. For he took away from the Negro any practical incentive toward material advancement, and left him only the experience of the present moment and the possibility of getting some immediate—perhaps some poetic—satisfaction from it. But then, in order to live with the Negro, the white had to become like him. The Negro let his slow gaze linger upon the fields whose products he could not possess; the more he gazed the less there was even for the white man and the more he, too, had to be satisfied with the present. The white Southerner was already poetic in his sense of a present balanced between past and future. The Negro, and the impractical system of slavery, made him even more so. More contemplative.

I overstate the case. Southerners, white and black, are not so easygoing as this. For one thing, too many Scotch-Irish came into the South. But the point is, whatever they are, they are what they have become through living together in the particular relationship they have. A visitor to the South during ante-bellum days gave it as his opinion that the most successful plantation owners were men of deep inner strength and therefore reserve combined with the ability to compromise in details. But these are almost the exact terms in which the anthropologist Melville Herskovits, who believes in racial temperament, describes the Negro: unusual reserve combined with unusual resiliency. Is it not probable, then, that the masters learned to act like this in order to handle successfully the slaves? And if such changes occurred in stolid English and hard Scotch-Irish in response to a practical demand, how many more subtle influences flowed between whites and Negroes across the centuries?

I was thinking recently about the plaintive quality of so

many Negro songs. "Sometimes I feel like a motherless child." Then I remembered the plaintive note in pioneering America: the homesickness for old streets, and settled ways, and village lights at dusk. Translated into religion, this became such a song as

I've wandered far away from God
Now I'm coming home . . .
Open wide thine arms of love,
Lord, I'm coming home.

And I wondered how the plaintive note of the pioneer crossed with the plaintive note of the Negro slave, and how perhaps white Southerners have a double sense of nostalgia. For they, too, were pioneers. They, too, left the seaboard and moved inland . . . and moved inland. And they carried with them these dark neighbors, who even more than they were pilgrims here.

But who could recognize this kinship while it was developing? And—to return to the spirituals—what white man could admit the heartbreak revealed there and his involvement in it, even though he was often uneasy himself and sometimes sick at heart. The South had no poets, nor any inclusive church, to tell it where it was wrong. How could it hear the prophetic voice of its lowest class, the slaves? So it kept on trying to make politics serve the purpose of religion, until politics ended in war, and war in defeat, and still the South did not know why it had been defeated or what course might lead it upward again.

CHAPTER 14

POETIC SOUTH: ITS IMAGES

The South was poetic, not only in the nature of its relation to space and time, but also in its heavy reliance upon images. For the poet, the artist, is concerned first of all with the appearance, the sensuous impression of things; and when he reduces the world to words, he is concerned especially with the sensuous quality of the world and the words. In brief, the poet, the artist, deals with a concrete world, a world whose sights and sounds have meaning within themselves, a world which images forth its meaning.

This is the kind of world the Southerner has tried to live in; a world composed of a place, or places, embedded in time, growing out of the past and into the future; not primarily a world of process, spinning out of a largely forgotten, or denied, past into an unimagined future. Of course, process is inherent in all life: we are always going somewhere. But some of us see more clearly where we are going because we see more clearly whence we have come. In contrast to this, the extreme modern is so immersed in process, and so hurried forward by it, that, though he sees some meaning in life, that meaning, instead of inhering in the scene about him, exists abstractly in some vaguely imagined world. The Southerner, more poetic, tends to find meaning within the scene about him and within the remembered and anticipated images that attach themselves to this scene.

This has not been the emphasis of the American mind. C. Vann Woodward thus summarizes Thornton Wilder on this subject: "It is not the concrete but the abstract that captures the imagination of the American and gives him identity, not the here and now but the future."[1] Of Southerners, Wilder says: "They were cut off, or resolutely cut themselves off from the advancing tide of the country's modes of consciousness. Place, environment, relations, repetitions are the breath of their being."[2]

It has been remarked that one of the striking characteristics of the Southern writers of the recent Southern literary renaissance is their use of concrete detail. These details are not used simply for the realistic purpose of producing the impression of actual life, but also for the imaginative purpose of suggesting the universal meaning that lies within the concrete. This use of the concrete image is in the Southern tradition, according to which men have seen the world as a place to live in, and life as inhering in the objects, persons, and scenes that surround them, and not in some vague something lying beyond and outside life, to be come at only through a process of abstraction.

One of the most outstanding of the recent Southern writers, Eudora Welty, stresses the importance of place in her writing: "I am myself touched off by place . . . place opens a door in the mind." Not only does place open a door; it holds one secure. She speaks of "the blessing of being located—contained."[3]

Very far from this is the typical modern, and American, process of abstraction, through which we arrive at a world supposedly more real and valuable. Of course, it is by a process of abstraction that anyone arrives even at the world that immediately surrounds him: the images of the objects that compose it have to be abstracted from the total situation to be recognized at all. But this is a limited abstraction, necessary for any understanding but very far from the extreme abstraction of the modern mind, which reduces all things to their molecular components and then recombines them in new forms, often useful but strange, sometimes fantastic, and recently extremely destructive. This emphasis upon a world continually rebuilt in patterns suggested by the analytical mind has not been historically the emphasis of the Southern mind.

From the beginning the Southern mind tended to see life primarily as a public, not a private affair. Sense was mainly common sense, life was mainly what it appeared to be. As we have said, the Southerner tended to accept the world, and himself as a part of it. He had his private life of course. But he was not concerned, as the New England Puritan was, passionately to analyze that life, seeking for truth somewhere within its darkest, or brightest, recesses. He had gone along with the world pretty well in England; he still carried rather clearly within himself the sense of the world community that he had inherited from the Middle Ages; sometimes a harsh, even a tragic community but a community nevertheless. He wasn't inclined to see himself snatched out of the world as a brand from the burning, bound to purify himself of a corrupt and corrupting world.

He was a man of considerable common sense. As Hannah Arendt explains, common sense is the sense that appearances make upon people.[4] Everybody agrees that an oak tree is solid, whatever solidity itself is. The Southerner was inclined to trust the appearance of the world, and the things and people in it. If a man acted in a neighborly fashion, he would be accepted as one regardless of the intricacies of his motivation. If he followed the forms of religion, he was considered religious. If on the contrary, he refused to follow the forms, he was not only irreligious, he was also a bad citizen. This was essentially the attitude of the established Church, the Episcopal, and this was the general attitude of the early Southerner.

Now all this emphasis upon the community, upon the public appearance, is an emphasis upon images, upon the look and the sound of things. It has been remarked on several occasions that the religion of the South has been mainly a matter of a few dogmas to be accepted, a few images to be recalled. Whatever theology the South has produced has been mainly concerned with hammering home a few dogmas, not with investigating and understanding the meaning of these dogmas in the over-all picture. And the religion of the Southerner, unlike that of the typical Puritan, has been little concerned with the passionate intellectual struggle to prove the mysteries of man and God and the relation between them. The Southerner has indeed sensed these mysteries; indeed, over the long run, the Southerner has continued to sense them, and to admit their reality, long after the non-Southerner, so far as consciousness goes, had largely analyzed them away.

In his regard for images and for dogmas packed with emotion, the Southerner has remained religious—however one may evaluate this religion. Undoubtedly his concern for a few religious images has given a solidity and a continuity to the life of the South, just as his concern for secular images has steadied the South and caused it to move more slowly into the modern world, in which change is all. Religion is a search for reality. Reality is not primarily thought about but seen and heard. Says Hannah Arendt: "For us, appearance—something that is being seen and heard by others as well as by ourselves—constitutes reality."[5] "Thought is endless," says the painter Edward Hopper, "but the picture exists in space and time."[6] Out of the complex flow of life, the religious mind picks an image to stand for the spirit of the whole, which may not be expressed otherwise. "The Lord is my shepherd"; "a mighty rock in a weary land"; "a living fountain." Central to the Christian faith is the cross, with its implications extending from the crossroads of decision to the cross of execution.

The religion of the South has been chiefly a matter of the contemplation of images. Whether this has ennobled the South or not depends upon the nature of the images contemplated. The blood-soaked cross, though intended to produce humility and self-reproach, may produce pride, harshness, and cruelty. I do not question the Southern emphasis upon images; they are the source of power; whether in secular or religious matters men usually act, not for reason's sake, but because of the appeal of a picture, a phase, an emotion-charged fragment of life. One of the main functions of the reason is to unravel and understand the drives that inhere in the images, in order to strengthen one drive by adding image to image or weaken another by pitting image against image. The South has not done this sufficiently. Often it has got one image in its mind as a horse gets the bit in his teeth, and has run away in defiance of other images it would have done well to recall. Consider the almost fatal devotion to "state sovereignty." Either the South has not thought enough—or, perhaps, it has not considered closely and long enough the images around which it has built its life. It may be that the South needed, and needs, a form of thinking foreign to the modern world, different from the analytical thinking that has produced this world. For the South has moved more slowly than the rest of the country into the driving modern world of process; it has carried with it more of the medieval world of pause, and place, and image. In a traditional society, such as the Middle Ages, yesterday's scene changes so slowly into today's and today's into tomorrow's, that no one realizes a change is going on and things take care of themselves. But in a culture like that of the South, in which tradition and change are perhaps equally balanced, men have continually to weigh the images out of the past to determine which are suited to the present and the future.

In our discussion of place, we noticed that the South got into trouble because it did not have the poets—or the saints—to tell it what its particular relationship to space and time meant. It ended by being enslaved by place because it could not universalize that place, and by time because it could not eternize that time. The failure to understand the images is the same failure, for it is through the images that we are bound to space and time.

I recall an incident that illustrates for me how images steady us. My grandmother, who died in 1919 at the age of ninety-four, had seen much hardship during her long life. I can hear her quavering voice still as she sang the plaintive melody:

O Land of Rest, for thee I sigh
When will the moment come
When I shall lay my armor by
And rest in peace at home?

But then the courage, the drums, the echo of the bass:

We'll work till Jesus comes
. . . .
And then be gathered home.

There is no question in my mind that the first lines expressed for her the pathos of life, the chorus the determination to live regardless of the hardship. This is the acceptance of life's mystery expressed in simple images.

The Southern stress upon manners is at the same time a stress upon public life and a stress upon images. Manners are to be seen. Indeed, Richard M. Weaver suggests that the South appears to the North like a composite of images, a kind of tableau, "interesting, even fascinating, to look upon, with its survivals of medievalism, its manners that recall vanished eras, its stark social cleavages, its lost cause, its ballads and sentimental songs. . . . It is so strange that one cannot conquer the feeling that it must be in some degree fictionized."[7] Because of this impression, says Weaver, the North never really credits the suffering of the South.

As we have said, the South tends to live in public and to hide its heart. It is concerned with entertainment, with pageantry, with the mere fact of living. Its life has taken place largely in the open, and there it has created its chief art, oratory. But all this emphasis upon public life can also be used to hide the heart, as manners serve not only to bind people together but also to keep them apart. In regard to the heart, the South has shown a stoic reserve. Unlike other Americans we have been tragic, but unlike the Spanish, as revealed in their great representative Miguel de Uanmuno, we have not spoken about it. The North is apt to hide such frustration as it has experienced through serious attention to business; the South is apt to hide its far greater frustration under a light and often playful manner. The North is distracted, the South is diverted. Being less serious about business than the North, it is felt by the North to be flippant. Perhaps whatever style it has lies just here: that it is superficially light but deeply serious.

The existence of a kind of aristocracy in the South suggests this same stress upon the surface, upon form, upon images. The Southern aristocracy never gained hereditary titles; it was continually being modified by the arrival of newcomers from the lower ranks, and by the disappearance into those ranks of former aristocrats. Yet even so, it revealed at least one mark of a true aristocracy: its members were public figures, to be seen. The aristocrat is responsible not only for government, but also, in the largest sense, for manners. This is not to say that the manners of the aristocrat were to be copied by the common man; indeed, there was an aristocratic etiquette that was in many ways different from that of the common man, and was intended to set the aristocrat apart. The aristocrat was to reveal, to make public, what life could, and should, be. He walked, he acted, he spoke as a man should. This is one of the reasons why men have upheld aristocracies in the past; they show us what life can be, what it is, ideally, to be a man. I am not saying that the image presented by the aristocrat has ever been perfect; indeed, it may be very far from the Christian image; I am only saying that men live, not mainly by exhortations, but by what they can see. One function of the aristocrat was to give men an image of humanity touched with splendor. This is a form of poetry and it brings us to a consideration of that elusive appeal that for many has clung to the South.

CHAPTER 15

ALL THAT GLISTERS. . . .

The realistic, earthy attitude of our century of total war, an attitude as common to Southern writers as to any, has blown the myth of the magnolias sky-high. They used to stand for a rare supernal innocence. Now even the streetcars are named "Desire," and the only reason we haven't had "Adultery Under the Magnolias" is that the dead fallen leaves are too harsh and noisy.

If any haunting appeal survives this naturalistic barrage and penetrates our minds at all, it receives a doubtful welcome. For, touched as we are by liberalism, believing in freedom and the rights of the underdog, we wonder if we should entertain this antique attitude. Supposing the South does possess some vague charm, was it not based, does it not rest upon racial exploitation, and should it not therefore be condemned?

We must admit that the South paid too much for its glamour. Not all that glistered was gold. But we need to remember, modern man especially, that the shine of life is important. Men do not live simply to live, to work another day, to eat another meal. They live because life seems to hold more than this. They live greatly, and create great societies, when they feel a quality of glory, of splendor, beneath, behind the surface of life and occasionally breaking forth in light.

Our mixed reaction to this quality of the South is illustrated by the response of a New England friend of mine to an article I wrote several years ago. I had leaned heavily upon the natural charm of an old South Carolina tidewater plantation: the live oaks draped in Spanish moss, the sleepy reaches of the river. In the conclusion I had pointed out how blind to the total situation were the people who had once lived here. My friend was angry on two counts. First, because he had been entranced by a picture that was later revealed to be largely illusory; second, because he had permitted himself to be entranced by a picture built, he felt sure, upon an immorality. Behind his reaction lay hidden the question: what is the relation of charm to goodness, of glory to truth, of manners to morals?

My friend's reaction was in part fascination, the attitude of being drawn to an object and at the same time repelled by it. This is part of the appeal the South has for the rest of the nation. Though the Bible doesn't say so, this is probably how the elder Brother felt about the Prodigal Son: he scorned him because he had wasted his inheritance, and envied him, secretly, because he had been to Paris! In the phrase of Robert Penn Warren, it is out of "the Great Treasury of Virtue" that the North both looks down upon and, very secretly, envies the South.

Even to speak of the charm of the South may seem to moralists like glossing over the evil of the South, clearly evidenced historically by slavery and open segregation. Life is far more complex than moralists imagine. There is indeed a moral imperative, but there is also an esthetic lure. Of course charm may be assumed and therefore be false and misleading, but so may morality, as the term *hypocrisy* indicates. Nevertheless, there is a true charm and there is a true morality.

What makes it more difficult is, they do not always go together. There have been charming scoundrels and boring saints. In spite of this difficulty—which is simply an instance of the imperfection of life—men still value both charm and goodness.

The first poem in the *Collected Poems* of Edwin Arlington Robinson is entitled "Flammonde," and is about a man who was short on goodness, certainly on respectable goodness, but who possessed an indefinable charm. After he had gone

From time to time
In Tilbury town, we look beyond
Horizons for the man Flammonde

"The flame of the world," I should guess, forever fading like the sunset but forever luring us on.

To move from esthetics to morality and from the individual to the region and to condemn the nineteenth-century South as a whole because it supported the institution of slavery is, first, to make the mistake warned against by Edmund Burke, of condemning an entire people, and, second, to read back into the past the moral attitudes of the present.

Admitting, then, that men value both charm and goodness, and that, unhappily, these qualities often exist separately, let us ask to what degree a quality of charm belonged, perhaps still belongs, to the South. The myth assumes charm, and myths are based upon reality, even though the reality is often little more than the abiding wish that certain things may be true. It isn't difficult to find within the South of the last hundred years sufficient motive for the creation of this myth. Through war and Reconstruction, the Old South fell swiftly from high estate to low, from honor to degradation. Furthermore, as we have seen, the South, even in its greatest days, was never entirely sure of itself. It was, therefore, almost inevitable that in the disappointment and confusion of the post-

Civil War period, the white South should remember only the charm of ante-bellum days, and should dream, without knowing it was dreaming, of "fair women and brave men."

But, strangely—or perhaps not so strangely—the South was aided in its creation of this dream by the North. For now that the industrial North had broken the agrarian South and destroyed the slaveowning South, and had thus removed the economic and moral threat of that region, Northerners could afford to praise the charm of the South, certainly of the ante-bellum South. Not only could they afford to praise it; in a sense they could not afford not to praise it. For they had pretty effectively destroyed it—in a not very charming fashion!—and the easiest way to forget their actions was to praise that now harmless remembered charm that contemporary Southerners were insisting upon.

But this is only to say that the postwar South, with considerable help from the North, created a myth of the Southern past such as would soothe the Southern heart and quiet the Northern conscience. The question to be considered then, is this: Was the myth built upon anything more than postwar need? Had there ever been in the South a quality of life that might properly be called charming, enchanting, or splendid? The question is difficult. The ante-bellum South is touched by such a golden haze that it is almost impossible to determine what splendor was really there and what was only attributed to that earlier time by the unhappy post-Civil War generations. We, today, reacting against the myth-making propensities of our grandfathers, are inclined to deny the whole thing. This is as erroneous as to accept it all. I believe there was in the South, I believe there still is in the South, something of that quality that the myth enshrines. It is my purpose here to try to describe it, to indicate its causes and its serious defects. It is possible that the South failed because it misunderstood the problem; it is possible that it failed because there is no solution.

What is this quality which the myth enshrines? I think it may be variously defined as *charm, enchantment, splendor, glory.* Of these words, the mildest is *charm,* the strongest *glory.* I think more people would recognize the charm than the glory, partly because charm is more pervasive and abiding, glory more limited and transient. A person may be consistently charming, he is glorious only in "glorious moments."

But if one recognizes the charm of the South more readily than the splendor, it is not simply because charm is more persistent and pervasive, it is also because of the feminine connotation of charm and enchantment, and the masculine connotation of splendor and glory. As I have already suggested, the culture of the South was predominantly feminine. This explains the feminine character of its pervasive, and evasive, appeal. Indeed, the more masculine traits of splendor and glory are traits that appeal especially to women; esthetic rather than moral traits.

It is undoubtedly this feminine quality of the South that has attracted the interest of the more masculine, the more solid, sober, realistic North. Woman is, or at least was, at both the base and the pinnacle of Southern life. For the feudal slogan, "Dieu et le droit," the South tended to substitute "Ma dame et le droit." This made of woman both the beginning and the end of man's endeavors. In other words, God. Of course, this subordinating and uplifting of women was the work of men, since this is still predominantly a man's world. It may be, then, that our talk about the solid, realistic, masculine North in contrast with the shadowy, romantic, feminine South is merely what men choose to think about the nature of men and women. Maybe the men are the romancers, the women the realists. This doesn't matter, so long as we agree that the basic temper of the North inclined to the realistic while the basic temper of the South inclined to the romantic, and that these contrasting temperaments to some degree attracted each other.

But not to the same degree. The South has never been attracted to the North as the North has been to the South. The North has had something the South has lacked, primarily driving energy and business acumen; and the South is now increasingly eager to posses these traits. But it wants them, not for themselves; but because of the higher standard of living they will bring; whereas the Southern traits we are talking about have never brought anything in any market, and could hardly have been admired by the North because of their monetary value.

That is, not until recently. For it now appears to the wizards of Madison Avenue that charm has monetary value. I call them wizards on purpose; they charm us into buying their products. But this is a most recent occurrence.

Nor does it help us define the charm that has been historically credited to the South. Until recently (*i.e.,* Madison Avenue) this charm never brought anything in any market and had no monetary value. Perhaps this suggests a clue as to its nature. As money is a highly specialized form of exchange, so money is usually exchanged for special values, for special skills and products. This is exactly what the Southern quality we are talking about is not. It is not special but general. Not exclusive but inclusive. Said Barrie: "Charm is that which if a woman has she needs nothing else." A more haunting definition is that by Camus: "Charm is the ability to get the desired answer without asking the question." Charm is then the expression of the entire person, hinting at the total situation, suggesting life itself, always implying completeness and wholeness. This becomes clear when we compare the words *charm* and *enchantment.* Both have the quality of magic, both arise from a situation or a person. Charm is simply a lesser enchantment, enchantment a greater charm. They are alike in that they are expressions, complex, unanalyzable, of the entire person or the entire situation. They suggest wholeness and exist only where wholeness is.

It may be a diabolical wholeness, as the terms *witch* and *wizard,* dealers in charms and enchantment, suggest. It is far less apt to be a godlike wholeness. There was Saint Francis, but he was only one. Apparently the union of charm and goodness is hard to come at in this world. It may have been inevitable that the South should fail.

As for splendor and glory, it's a little harder to realize the wholeness they suggest. Take the adjective *splendid.* It comes from the Latin *splendidus,* and means shining, and the shine of most things is superficial, the effect of reflected light. But the shine can only exist where there is a sun to cause it and eyes to see it; that is, where there is a world, where there is at least some kind of wholeness. Or take *glory.* The word immediately connotes war and, at one time, the shine of armor. But the real glory of the soldier lay in his courage, his loyalty to something larger than himself, his willingness to sacrifice his life for the larger whole. The glory of his paraphernalia was only the outward look of this inner wholeness.

The phrase "the charm of the South" seems a more natural and true expression than the "splendor" or "glory" of the South. Partly because it is more vague, evasive, more modest; partly because, being all these, it is—shall I say—more feminine. It may be that women make better Southerners than men. It may be that the men were more imbued with that lust for the future—the abstract, formless, unembodied future—that became the earmark of the North. It may be that because of this they could less successfully show the quality of completeness that all our key words suggest. It may be, of course, that men never can show this quality of completeness as successfully as women can.

A talented and traveled friend of mine once remarked, "The appeal of the South is simple enough; it's the appeal of the fairy tale. Everybody wants to believe in fairy tales. The simple evil, the simple goodness, the quick reverses of fortune. The South is a strange, a magic land, where anything may happen." As I shall indicate, I think the appeal of the South is more than the appeal of the fairy tale. But I might point out that the fairy tale, like poetry, clarifies our desires, pinpoints our wishes. The world of the fairy tale is not the world we live in; our world is much more resistant, obstructive; but how we wish, sometimes, we could manipulate it more easily! It may be that the South did, foolishly, envisage the world too much in fairy-tale terms; but it did something in creating at least a superficial image of human desire.

I should say that the charm of the South is more closely allied to the charm of light opera. The lovers meet, and laugh, and weep, and sing against the sunny background. We know, of course, that life isn't like this; but, oh, we say, if only it were! We are touched with nostalgia for our lost past.

This is part of the appeal of the South to the contemporary world. Caught in our rushing, urban, industrial, and international world, we recall with nostalgia what seems an idyllic past. Especially do we think of the South in this connection, both because the South is that part of the nation that has the richest past, much of it still alive, and because there is already in existence the myth of the golden South.

Commenting upon the importance of the past in the South, T. Harry Williams recalls "a phrase Woodward borrowed from Toynbee, that Southerners know history has happened. They know this because Southern history has been compounded of tragedy and many of the elements of that tragedy are still apparent today. More poignantly than other Americans, they realize that the past impinges on the present, and more often than their fellows in other sections they relate the present to something in the past."[1]

Indeed, there is a sense in which Americans outside the South have no past; at least no past that can be clearly seen and known. The old line says, "We do not miss the springtime until the flowers are gone." It is worse than this. We do not know the springtime until the flowers are gone. In this sense, non-Southern Americans cannot yet know the American past. They are still living it; still entangled in it; still doing, but now more successfully than ever, what they started to do at Plymouth Rock in 1620. But what Southerners began, in 1619, with the arrival of slaves in Virginia, they had to stop in 1865. At that moment the preceding two-and-a-half centuries dropped into a kind of past that other Americans know nothing about. That time was done with and gone—a true past—and since then, one of the South's main questions has been, what to do with it. That the South has not yet capitalized this rich past, that it still finds it more of a liability than a resource, doesn't change the fact that it is there, and because of its difference from the present can be recognized and can give to the region a variety of remembered experience unavailable to the rest of the nation.

There will come a time when Americans will understand the tragic nature of their Civil War. When that time comes, the defeat of the South will be recognized as the defeat of one America and the birth of another, and all Americans then will have such a past as the South already possesses—possesses but as yet hardly uses.

But beyond the appeal of the South to the nation since the Civil War, was there in the Old South an actual way of life that created this quality of charm, at moments perhaps, of splendor? I think there was and to a degree still is.

The most evident fact, and the one that has remained unchanged from the beginning, is the perennial appeal of sunny lands to people of colder climates. At its extreme, this is the appeal of the tropics, with their strange glamorous fruits, and bright colors. The South, of course, is not tropical; only the southern fringe is even subtropical. Yet it abounds in vast and mysterious swamps, where the gray moss hangs like a dream; and everywhere the woods, fed by heavy rainfall and hot sunshine, are forever reaching out to repossess the fields. To northern people, used to a spare and orderly nature, and influenced by the presence of such a natural world to be spare and orderly themselves, such a luxurious world has tremendous appeal. Not that these people from a sterner climate would be happy remaining in the relaxed air of, say, the Deep South. Most of them, unless they had retired, would soon long for the stripped, productive nature of their own towns and fields. But all northern people, certainly those from cold, fog-bound shores, dream of sunny lands, some "island-valley of Avilion,"

Where falls not hail, or rain, or any snow,
Nor ever wind blows loudly; but it lies
Deep-meadowed, happy, fair with orchard-lawns
And bowery hollows crown'd with summer sea. . . .[2]

Something of this is the natural charm of the South even today; the sunny, December pines of Pinehurst and Camden and Aiken, the shining black water of low-country rivers, the shadowy live oaks hung with Spanish moss.

It is the open, sunny quality of the Southern scene that makes it so easy for the people who live there to feel themselves a part of the whole. The world belongs to them and they to it. It is this sense of man's life as being rounded by and included in nature that supports, deep down, the flash of glory that, at rare intervals, accompanies Southern life. A more stern, a more separative nature, would not permit men to identify themselves so easily with the whole.

The natural scene has remained largely unchanged. But there was more to the charm of the South than this. If this had been all, there might never have been a war. The South would simply have flowed along until Northerners had made enough money to use it as their winter playground. Then they would have come, paid for the sunshine and the equivalent of the motels, and gone North again in the spring with everybody satisfied. But the South had more than climate. It had an openness, a frankness, a charm of manner—to relate it to the climate, a sunny quality—which created in the North, along with simple approval, some envy, and some anger that people should seem to be happy in such a patently evil society.

The natural charm of the Southern scene was very soon accentuated by the presence of great landed planters, in Virginia first, then in South Carolina. I do not say these planters always bought fairly this appeal, nor that it was always founded on character; many of them were slick politicians, ruthless adventurers. To some degree, however, even these, under the weight of landed possessions, grew in strength of character and became worthy of the public responsibility that had become theirs. Whether they became morally responsible leaders or not, there was a spaciousness, a splendor however superficial, in the long avenues, the fields running to the far woods, the snowy cotton fields of the later South, the broad hospitable piazzas or galleries, and occasionally the glint of white columns in the morning sunlight. And there were often handsome men and gracious women on these piazzas, walking on these lawns, handling fine saddle horses. Undoubtedly this had at times the quality of light opera. Especially as the outlook for the South grew darker, these social manifestations grew lighter, until one is finally amazed at the gay parties in Richmond, when the city was almost surrounded and many of the participants were wounded soldiers; and one begins to wonder whether this gaiety was as superficial as it had appeared on the piazzas and lawns, whether these people were not of a breed that had learned to smile even in the face of death. However that may be, in earlier, peaceful years, they had smiled and chatted and sung together, as though life were light opera; and undoubtedly many of the less fortunate felt about them as one feels about light opera, that this is the way we should like to live if only we could; that though we know we cannot, we should like to play life and have time for gracious words and actions. We have noticed already the emphasis of the South upon play. This was a part of it. Admittedly, too few people were playing at the expense of too many; but at least the leaders of the South knew—and maybe the generality—that there was more to life than Carlyle's "Work, for God's sake, work!"

It is, however, unfair to the aristocracy of the ante-bellum South, certainly of the eighteenth-century South, to suggest that they thought only of play. Like any aristocracy, they thought of themselves to a degree as being in a play—though perhaps few of them phrased it in just these words. In part, they were fulfilling the immemorial role of the aristocrat. It is the nature of an aristocracy to be observed, to be in the public eye. It is true that an aristocracy, usually being wealthy, can buy broad living space, both outdoors and in, and might be expected thereby to gain privacy; and in a certain limited physical sense this is true; but with the space and the wealth go servants, who will observe and note. Consequently, the aristocrat learns to live ever in the public eye. The truer aristocrat he is, the more seriously he assumes the responsibility to act like one; with the assurance, ease, and grace, with the dignity and command, that every man would adopt if he only could.

The aristocracy of the South was in part fulfilling its immemorial role. But only in part. It was never a true, Old

World aristocracy, with title and position descending from father to son, but a brief aristocracy of a few generations, rising out of the commonalty by both luck and ability, descending to the commonalty again when luck or ability failed, surrounded always by commoners who here and there as the years passed were breeching the aristocratic ranks. Much of the concern of the Southern aristocrat, therefore, was with staying on friendly terms with the commoner, who held continually increasing political power, and who in time might well belong to the aristocracy himself. The Southern aristocrat could not, therefore, play the aristocratic role with characteristic assurance. The newer the frontier on which he found himself, the less assurance he could muster.

But though the South never created an aristocracy of the first order, it did create an aristocracy, that is, a group of men who felt a high responsibility to the state and who assumed with some dignity the roles of leaders. The poet Yeats, himself an aristocrat in temper, remarks that in all vital cultures men have the sense of filling roles. They play their parts, they have their places in society. The criticism of the Southern aristocracy is not that they played parts, but that they played with divided minds and confused hearts. The parts they assumed were not great enough, or not assumed with sufficient devotion. They were too eclectic, too unintellectual. They tended to think of themselves as the new Romans. It was not enough, primarily because it could not be deeply believed in. For they were trying to return to that ancient twilight of Stoicism through the mist and broken light of a millennium and a half of Christianity. The role as they played it was too limited, too social and political. As we shall see, the South overplayed its political hand at the expense of its religion.

They didn't really know what they were doing. To the Southern aristocrat, life was a game which he played according to the aristocratic code, and he played it out to the bitter end: the well-bred young men of the South showed up well both as officers and as privates in the trenches of Petersburg and in the ballrooms of Richmond. Playing this large and manly game, they created at times the effect of splendor. But with the downfall of the South, something went wrong. There appeared now a fissure between this world and another that cracked the heart of the South after this world had failed. They had played the game for this world. They had not realized it might be for another too. Their actions under the Southern sky had not been projected against an eternal sky. They had not known how to relate worldly fame to unworldly goodness. They had had no Dante to project against the eternal sky a divine comedy which would have included their worldly games.

Unlike Puritan New England, the South was not inclined to deny the world and scorn earthly glory. It was inclined to accept it, but with too little understanding. The Southerner's society was set up for this world. When he faced another, he tended to face it like the Stoic, alone, all the rich ties of the world swallowed up in mystery or annihilated in nothingness. The splendor that had touched his days, especially if he were an aristocrat, faded swiftly now; it could not break into that ineffable splendor that the Puritan sought and occasionally found in God. For not only the Southern aristocrat, but also the Southerner generally, had assumed, too easily, that God was in the world, and it was this assumption that lay behind his search for fame and glory here. He had assumed that life was good. But he failed to consider sufficiently—to contemplate—the images of the world he loved, failed to harmonize them and thus to universalize them. The possibility of splendor was always present, but it was a local, or an earthly, splendor. It was the splendor created by an aristocracy that did not really understand and accept its function in the world. This aristocracy failed because it was incomplete, hanging between the Middle Ages and the modern world, continually deteriorating under the individualistic thrust of its members, and without a universal church to clarify and crown its aspirations.

Part of the legend of Southern splendor, and perhaps also part of the reality, is connected with that aristocratic type, the cavalier. I have tried to avoid giving the impression that New England was Roundhead, the South, Cavalier. That is nonsense. A small number of defeated Cavaliers did flee to friendly Virginia during Cromwell's Protectorate; a few were important. If they tempered Southern society, it was because that society had leanings in that direction already. Certainly their tendency to the broad and lavish life, their gambler's propensity to win or lose all, lent color to the South. They held both their possessions and themselves loosely, they threw themselves into the game. Splendor by its very nature cannot accompany lives that are held too closely and prudently. There must be daring, the risk of all for all in material things, at its height in spiritual. This was the spirit of the Cavalier, and it was the presence of this spirit, carried first perhaps by but a few, that helped to touch the South with splendor. Speaking of this touch of chivalry in the South and its effect upon dramatic action, John Temple Graves says: "Insofar as it is sacrifice in terms of drama, large or small, and offers a man a gallant picture of himself, Southerners do, perhaps, respond more than others to the chivalric impulse. . . . It may be that there were few cavaliers in America but there has been a legend of cavaliers. There has been a tradition of light-hearted, dramatic, notwithstanding disinterestedness."[3]

This sense of the brave show, the spacious and splendid life, symbolized by an aristocracy, was accentuated in the nineteenth century by the romantic impulse, which came to America some fifty years after it had come to Europe. For Romanticism emphasized the importance of the individual, and the whole Southern sense of life as a public affair was already stressing the individual as he stood among his fellows. The ideal of the Southern community was a group of distinct individuals. Romanticism also came to the North, but there, as we have seen, it expressed itself largely in the individual flights of transcendentalism. In the South it was a much more social affair: the Southern romanticist, keenly aware of the importance of public life, became romantic even in public and as a member of society at large. This suggests that the society at large may have been romantic. If so, it carried within itself, by definition, a touch of strangeness, something of the uncommon, the rare. It may be that the appeal of the South we are examining was, and is, simply the appeal of the romantic to a realistic civilization. However, this distinctly romantic quality seems not to have appeared in the South until the Romantic Movement reached these shores. The eighteenth-century Southern provincial and American was rational, a planner not a dreamer, having small regard for what we call romantic strangeness. When this appeared, it expressed itself in two main ways. Its serious expression was the drive toward Southern nationalism, which paralleled the contemporary European emphasis upon cultural nationalism. Its less important drive was its return to the Middle Ages in some of its leisure-time activities. There must have been, therefore, at least throughout the seaboard South, a considerable feeling for the imagined charm and splendor of the Middle Ages. The European romanticist returned to the Middle Ages out of the surrounding ugliness of early industrialism and across what he felt to be the barren rational eighteenth century. The Southern romanticist also passed over the eighteenth century, though it was far less rational, far more human, along the American frontier than in the salons of France; but as to his own contemporary world, though he may have been fleeing from it, he was also celebrating it. His interest in the Middle Ages was probably motivated in part by his growing unhappiness over an economic and social system that was being increasingly condemned by the world and was increasingly imprisoning even the whites within its harsh walls. Perhaps he turned to the Middle Ages partly in order to forget the darkening world about him. But he also thought he saw there, not the opposite of his life, as did the English romanticist, but its ideal and crown.

This brings us back to the question: To what degree did there really exist in the South the quality of charm, perhaps of momentary splendor, which these Southern romanticists claimed? We have seen evidences of this quality in the Southern scene itself, and in the Southern aristocracy. Let us consider more generally the life of the people.

We have already suggested that the essential appeal of the South is the appeal of wholeness. The basic weakness of this appeal, as we shall see more clearly, is that the "wholeness" it aimed at was limited and incomplete. It was wholeness at a certain level, and that not the highest. It is this failure in height—or depth—that dimmed the splendor of the South and falsified its charm. But whatever charm and splendor it possessed was due to its accent upon the whole. For it is the realization of wholeness that causes experience to emit charm and splendor. The moment, the word, the gesture, the action shine because they mean, suggest, symbolize far more than themselves. The prime illustration here is the mystic vision.

When I indicate the mystic vision as the ultimate in glory, I seem to let the South out entirely, for the South has been almost entirely lacking in mystics; to find a hint of them, you must go to Puritan New England, and to the greatest of the Puritans, Jonathan Edwards. There were moments in the life of Edwards when the glory and splendor of God suffused the world; every bush burned. I am not quite sure what place Edwards found for man in these visions. But I'm not concerned about Edwards. I am concerned to point out that glory and splendor are related to a sense of wholeness. It is significant that, desiring to speak of this quality in the life of the South, we have to go beyond the South, to Puritan New England, to find an illustration of what we mean. Since this prime illustration occurred in New England, it would seem that, instead of suggesting glory as a quality of life in the South, we should mark it as especially a quality of life in New England and in the northern tier of states influenced directly by New England.

This should have happened, and this was the hope of Jonathan Edwards. Perhaps it was the hope of all true, early Puritans, who were sent into the wilderness to find God, to meet him face to face, to behold his glory undimmed by earthly veils, however lovely. Why did the hope not materialize? Indeed, why did the South, where men were less concerned to find God in the wilderness, find more glory in life?

I can only suggest the answer. I make it from where I stand, both within and without the Puritan fold. It seems to me that the Puritans asked too much of men; aimed too high; were proud in doing so and became more proud because they had done so. Martin Luther, with the intensity of Jonathan Edwards, could behold the glory of God sustaining, without evident supports, the earth and sky, and lamented the fact that men had to see the pillars. The early Puritans of New England emphasized inwardness too much. Go too far inward, and even though you search for God there, you will find a wilderness.

One cannot say in a few words what really happened to the early Puritan vision of New England. In general, being too intense to be sustained, it broke in two. One part became the beautiful but ethereal idealism of Emerson; the other the materialism of the Yankee trader. Emerson remembered the other-worldly light; the Yankee trader the worldly commitment. The light still lingered, palely, about Emerson's study at Concord; it had faded completely from industrial Lowell.

The South, essentially non-Puritan, never aimed so high. The Southern settler was as religious as the New England Puritan but in a different way. For the most part, he was not seeking God in the wilderness, either of America or of his heart. He assumed—too easily, as history was to prove—that God was with him, a part of the world he had left, a part of the world he had come to, His presence suggested and acknowledged by the public worship held in the Episcopal Church. The Southern settler was inclined to accept the world with its combined good and evil, to accept himself, only quarreling with himself, and with God, in his most private moments and about his most private affairs. For he had, as we have seen, a strong interest in public life, which took the form in this new country of a strong interest in politics. Not cherishing, and therefore not realizing, the inner vision, he had but little of the Jonathan Edwards sense of the ineffable glory of God. Concerned, on the contrary, with public life, first of the local community and later of the province and state, he developed a strong sense of that earthly glory that is the crown of public effort. Though he was not unaware of tiny flecks of glory that shone throughout the world—for he was religious—he never really succeeded in relating these to public glory, and all of it to the glory of God. Perhaps public glory cannot be related to the glory of God. Perhaps when man seeks glory he turns away from God.

As Hannah Arendt points out,[4] modern man hardly seeks glory of any kind any more; he seeks material advantage. Not seeking glory, he naturally misses it, and pays for its lack by the vacancy and boredom of his days. For, as Robert Oppenheimer says, "We hunger for nobility; the rare words and acts that harmonize simplicity and truth." And in *Brother to Dragons,* Robert Penn Warren tells us that

the only
Thing in life is glory . . .
For drink's a kind of glory too, and man
Can't live without some glory after all,
Even a poor kind.

The modern world has forgotten this. The contemporary South has not quite forgotten it; the Old South knew it very well.

Concerned as we are with politics largely for material advantage, it is difficult for us to realize that men have been concerned with politics, with public position and responsibility, largely for the satisfaction of being in the public eye, of receiving such limited or large glory as the position bestowed upon them. It is here that one charm of the historic South lies. Practically every man was concerned, beyond the limits of his private advantage, with the public world, with a part in it, if the chance seemed right with a splendid part in it.

Such action, in Hannah Arendt's definition, is action itself; it is done not so much for what may come of it, but because it is valuable in itself: the stance, the gesture, the stride, the eloquent word. The proper reward for such action is glory; the esteem, the admiration, the wonder of other men. We have already said that the South carried this esteem and this wonder too far; it asked of politics what politics could not give; it paid too much for the splendid forensic battle; trying by political action to force the nation to remain agrarian, it had its own agrarianism destroyed.

If the Puritan failed because he sought God too privately and intensely, hoping to find heaven's glory unadulterated by the things of earth, the more relaxed Southerner failed because he was too much concerned with men, with the appearance of things. Being thus concerned, he found a public glory in the gestures and words of his leaders, but he did not think enough, he did not probe his life, or life itself, earnestly and passionately enough to discover how this glory hinted of, or at times detracted from, the glory of God.

For one thing, the Southerner imitated the chivalry of the Middle Ages; but did not, to use a phrase from Yeats, substantiate it in a great poetry or an inclusive religion. The soaring cathedrals of the Middle Ages are rooted, most vividly through their flying buttresses, in earth. Rising out of the dirt, the pain, the frustration of mankind, they point toward God. It is this recognition of the contrast between the actuality of life and the hopes and dreams of men that give them their splendor. Medieval knighthood was far from being an ideal profession. It was often a dirty business in a dirty age. But at least men tried to hold all things together under the eye of the church; and knighthood was one of the means toward this end. How could the showy knighthood—the chivalry, they called themselves in the late ante-bellum South—how could it represent such an inclusive vision? In no true sense did the slaves belong to the life the chivalry defended. Furthermore, most of the chivalry had by that time adopted, at least in spirit, an individualistic Protestantism that, instead of bringing the slaves into the community, was effectively excluding them from it.

Glory accompanies the sense of the whole. The South attained to a greater sense of the whole than did the North because both temperament and conditions kept the Southerner more aware of the whole than was possible in the business-oriented, and therefore private, life of the North. But the South, failing to find a religion suitable to its life, partly because it had in slavery a life unsuitable to any religion it could come up with, failed to gain consistently that sense of a universal and eternal whole which is the source of essential glory.

As the nineteenth century passed, the South found the earlier sense of glory increasingly blurred. This happened for three reasons. First, the frontier accented individualism: the community grew weaker, community standards more lax, the sense of the public eye less important. Men still sought "glory," but they sought it now in less reputable ways: gambling orgies, fights, drinking bouts. Second, with the increasing chance of wealth on the moving frontier, men became increasingly materialistic, absorbed in getting rich, concerned about the main chance. This is essentially private life; there's no real glory in it. Third, revivalistic religion, natural along the lonely, individualistic frontier, made approval and condemnation more private and inward, turned men from outward honor and shame toward inward justification and guilt.

It is noteworthy, however, that in the revivals themselves, the coming of inward goodness was expressed most publicly, sometimes most dramatically. Men turned from the limited splendor of drunkenness, gambling, and violence to the inverted splendor of a striking public repentance. They sinned splendidly, they repented abjectly. But as the splendor itself had become a limited thing, implying not the wholeness of a community but only the wholeness of an individual's will at the moment, so the repentance itself tended to be limited, expressing mainly the determination not to be that kind of fool again.

If we turn for a moment to the heroic annals of the Civil War, we find an image where the completeness of individual and group shines with splendor. Such an image is hardly Southern, except as Southerners are fighters. It is an image natural to war, and explains war's tragic glory. For in war men are wedded indissolubly to one another and to a cause, the individual is lost and found in the group, the part in the whole. This happened at the Battle of Shiloh, in the spring of 1862. The Confederates were advancing doggedly through the peach orchard where the bullet-clipped petals were floating down. They advanced, says one commentator, with bowed heads as against a snowstorm. The words suggest the pure intensity of the fighters, their wholeness of will, their subordination to the job in hand. These farm boys had faced storms before. Now, again, with bent heads, they advanced together through the falling, deadly flowers. The image comes straight from Homer.

The charm, the splendor, perhaps the glory of the South went pretty much to seed along the swiftly expanding frontier, and under the influence of revivalistic religion. But this still leaves the question open as to the relation between this quality in the South and moral or religious goodness. Did the South buy this at the expense of true goodness? If men must have glory in some form, even in drunkenness as Warren argues, is this evidence of man's weakness or of his strength?

The key to glory is wholeness. When Jonathan Edwards saw the world suffused with glory, he saw it suffused with God, the universal inner fire. Few men attain to this sense of wholeness. Certainly the American South has not been the place to create such men. The basic question is, Did the glory that the Southerner strove for, and at times attained, lead him toward this universal glory or away from it? Was it for the total man strength or weakness?

What he attained, he attained because of the sense he and his fellows had of a man's part in the social whole. He had it because he was playing his part in the show, acting his role. The glory was the spirit of the whole reflected from him. Alexander Pope, writing in the eighteenth century and, significantly, an *Essay on Man,* said,

> *Honor and shame from no condition rise;*
> *Act well your part, there all the honor lies;*

This is the century that created the great early South.

I have already referred to the thesis of W. B. Yeats that in all great cultures men have had the sense of playing roles, of acting parts. And, though Yeats does not say so, it is probably this sense of every man's being a part of the whole that gives to great cultures their sense of greatness, their touch of glory.

But now, does any man play a role before God? Is not a man's realization of God either his realization of his own nakedness and barrenness, or entire forgetfulness of himself in the mystic vision? In neither case does he act a part. It is true, the priest acts. It is his function to act out before God the role of man, so that men may see what the human role is. But the human role before God is one of abnegation and self-forgetfulness; and it is probable that the priest, acting out this role, does not generally experience the presence of God. He is not "practicing the presence of God," he is revealing the proper attitude of man before God.

In the great society, men are supposed to live in the public eye, seeking honor and avoiding shame. In the Christian life, men are supposed to call no one good but God, to pray in secret, to avoid letting the left hand know what the right hand does. How is one a Christian in the great society? How do we adjust—is it possible to adjust—goodness and glory?

I suppose the answer is, glory must always be held subject to the criticism of goodness. As true peace is the fruit of justice, so glory is the fruit of goodness, of wholeness. The weakness of the South was not that men sought glory, but that they did not remember that glory is held under God, that all human acts are subject to divine judgment. This is to say, as we have said already, that the social order of the South was not crowned by, nor did it live under, the continual judgment of its religion. The Southerner did not use the glamour and splendor of this world to remind him of another; rather he let it blind him to the existence of another. He found this world so satisfying in its public display and political action that he made of it most of his life. It is true, he did possess an inner private life, where, alone, he faced life's mystery. But this, among the best of the Southerners, tended to be a rather passive acceptance of his own smallness in the universe, and a Stoic willingness to accept the mystery in itself and in its working out in life; hardly the Christian's concern for a positive relationship with the mystery, and the expression in the world of this positive relationship.

It was the gap between the quiet, retiring, inner life of men and their large and free expression in the public arena that helped to cause the misunderstanding between North and South. There was no such sharp division in the North. Public life there was less the forum, where one strove for glory, than an extension of the market, where one strove for profit. Laws tended to be passed rather to profit the lawmakers and their friends than to strengthen and make more splendid the community itself. This happened in the North both because of the relative weakness of an aristocracy with its code of *noblesse oblige,* and because of the greater emphasis upon business and private profit—itself partly an expression of the Calvinistic theology. In the North, then, public life was more largely an extension of private life.

This being the case, men were more apt to use public life, not only to increase private profits, but also to extend private beliefs and judgments. It was much easier there to project goodness into politics, and to use laws as a means for the extension of goodness. The Southerner, making a much sharper distinction between private goodness and public glory, continually felt that the Northern politician was a demagogue, muddying the waters of public debate with private opinion. The Northerner, on the contrary, looking at the realistic nature of Southern politics, the insistence upon political balance and harmony, the refusal to discuss ideals in the public forum, concluded that the Southerner had no sense of goodness at all; that he was personally as bad as his realistic politics made him appear. Our conclusion is that this judgment was unfair. At the same time, we have to admit that the Southerner left a dangerously wide gap between his private goodness and the power world of his politics.

Stoicism permitted this gap. In this Stoic philosophy—or religion—the individual stood in direct relation to the universe, a tiny though free element in that universe. Valuing so highly the individual, the stoic played down society and all forces beyond the individual. A man was free to resist them all. As for himself, the Stoic would not use the forces of society even in the attempt to help other men; this would show a lack of respect for their personalities. It is this extreme emphasis upon the individual that has made Stoicism popular among self-reliant people especially at a time when the social order is going to pieces. We have already suggested that the rather widespread appearance of the Stoic attitude in the Old South indicated a premonition of the impending breakdown of society.

Let us summarize here our conclusions about the pervasive appeal of the South. It was and is in part legendary, in part real. Its reality rests upon the importance of the community and the public conduct of this community; upon the relative importance of the whole as distinct from individual detail. It is this concern for some harmonious whole, whether of landscape, of a social group, or of a political state that gives to life in the South that evasive charm or that sudden touch of splendor. The corroding acid was the presence of the Negro slave. He was here because of the modern individualistic concern for private profit and advancement; and this motive, operating both within and without the South, led the nation into the fierce divisiveness of a civil war and prevented the South from ever attaining that universal, that religious wholeness, of which her social order dreamed.

Milton calls the desire for fame "that last infirmity of noble mind." Perhaps this can be said of the South: she desired fame too much, goodness too little; but her infirmity was that of a noble mind. This infirmity led her into the political world.

CHAPTER 16

POLITICS AS RELIGION

The South has always been a great land for politicians. This isn't mere happen-so. It results from the character of the people and the nature of their life.

Certainly the character of the early settlers was modified by their life here. It is highly probable, however, as I have already pointed out, that these settlers brought an attitude that inclined them toward politics. From the beginning they tended to be interested in public rather than private affairs.

This sense of the public, this regard for public judgment, was connected with the sense of community. When we say that the Southern settlers brought more of the past, of Old England and the Middle Ages with them than did the more separatist group that settled New England, we are saying that they brought also a stronger sense of community. For the movement from the Middle Ages into the modern world was, perhaps most of all, a movement from common life to individual life. The rise of modern man is the rise of individualistic man.

It may seem at first glance that the villages of New England, themselves copied from the Old World, indicated a closer relation to the medieval community than did the isolated farms of Virginia. But the villages of New England were mainly structures of prudence: protection against both the weather and the wiles of unbelief. They were primarily religious settlements, autocratic religious settlements. The rulers knew that it was much easier to control the lives of people living close together than of those scattered far apart. As for the danger from Indians, it is possible that the northern tribes were more warlike, and probable that the Puritans were more suspicious, since they were certainly more suspicious in general than were the more relaxed and accepting southern settlers. We know that the early Virginia settlers were inclined to treat the Indians moderately, and even set about organizing a college at Henrico for their Christianization. This trusting spirit, however, was pretty well destroyed by the great massacre of 1622.

The London Company had tried to make the early Virginians live in villages. They had not succeeded; either because the general trust in the world about them, or the lure of profit from tobacco, or both, were too great. But these settlers, moving up along the rivers and clearing land for tobacco, were not misanthropes. Indeed, it can be argued that in the long run their fairly isolated lives made them even more desirous of company, and more sociable, than were the town dwellers of New England. Perhaps the main thing is that the more balmy climate of the South lured them into the open and thus in the long run made of them individualists who, somewhat strangely, were fond of company and sensitive to the will of the loosely organized community.

Now, as Hannah Arendt points out, the economic life was considered by the Greeks, and indeed by most men until we enter the modern world, a private affair. Public life was, preeminently, the life of politics. This became the ideal of the South during the eighteenth century. It was assumed that working men, business people, had little time, interest, or ability for politics. It was also assumed that the men who attained prominence through the ownership of property—in the South mainly landed property—should assume public responsibilities and should become political leaders. This was their obligation, and their honor. All men valued politics, discussed politics, and took such part in politics as their economic situations and the customs and laws permitted. The southern settlers were disposed, by their basic attitudes and ideas, to value politics and the public life.

Politics—local politics first—was also emphasized in the South because there was need for strong local government on the loosely strung-out farms and plantations. This was centered in the plantation government itself, an autocracy controlled by the planter. But neither planter nor farmer was primarily concerned with a strong centralized government. Such a government is of value primarily to trading and manufacturing interests, which depend upon distant communication, transportation, and finance. The interest in politics in the South began at home, and when it did spread to the national arena, it was still primarily concerned with the local situation, and with national power only so far as was necessary to protect the local situation.

In the province of South Carolina, almost from the beginning, local and state politics were very important. South Carolina was, for over fifty years, the "Southern Frontier": England's frontier against the great empires of France and Spain. And, so far as the colonists could see, it was nip and tuck as to who finally would control North America. It was only after 1732, with the settlement of Georgia—at first a narrow strip in eastern Georgia—that South Carolina ceased to bear alone the burden of the Southern frontier and could relax somewhat her concern about Spain and France. But having stood in this exposed position for fifty dangerous years, South Carolina learned from the beginning—indeed, learned too well—that government is important, that political power is important. It was this insistence upon political power that made South Carolina the leader in establishing the Confederacy.

The South also emphasized politics because of its aristocratic leanings. All aristocracies have to emphasize political power, since the aristocrats are a small minority with special powers and privileges and since they are concerned to maintain the *status quo.* Especially was it necessary to emphasize politics in the kind of aristocracy that existed in the South. For this was no titled, no permanent aristocracy. It was composed for the most part of men who had risen to power, and who also, as time passed, realized that through carelessness or dissipation they could lose this power. These men were surrounded by the many who did not belong to the aristocracy but who remained on the outside only because they had as yet shown insufficient energy or had lacked sufficient time to join the ranks of the leaders. But there they were, all the way from the ne'er-do-well to the successful yeoman farmer who was rapidly on the way to prominence. One man in the community might belong to the aristocracy, but there might be several others whose children might rise to that position. Because of this instability, this ever-changing personnel, the Southern aristocracy was always conscious of the needs and responsibilities of its position.

The question arises here as to the degree of control exerted by the aristocracy of the South upon the life of the region. To what degree did the aristocrats control the political destiny of the South? They probably controlled it pretty completely in colonial days. The landed aristocracy of the South copied their lives after those of the English gentry. Most of the common people of the South, coming from the same background, accepted and approved of this organization of society. It is true that the more the frontier expanded and the farther the settlements lay from the seaboard, the more the frontiersmen were removed from the influence and power of the coastal aristocracy, and the more they thought and acted for themselves. This became especially true with the great influx of Scotch-Irish during the second and third quarters of the eighteenth century. But the great sweep toward democracy did not really begin until the Revolution. During the colonial period generally, the South had an aristocratic government.

Indeed, as Edmund Wilson has pointed out in *Patriotic Gore,* the great sweeping pictures of the Southern aristocracy that long ago became a part of the Southern myth are not based upon the final days of the ante-bellum South but upon its colonial period. This was the time of the great plantations, of eighteenth-century courtesy and gallantry, of charm and of intellectual culture. With the coming of the nineteenth century, this world became increasingly insecure, and increasingly lost the influence of its simple dignity. William H. Prescott, speaking in 1859 of his own state, South Carolina, indicated his realization of this. "Forced, perhaps by circumstances, to think of ourselves more than was profitable, we have learned to talk about ourselves much more than was needful. We seem, somehow, to have become uncertain of our old position. I cannot help thinking of those days not so far removed, when South Carolina stood among her sister states with no defiance on her brow, no hatred in her heart—admired, honored, loved."[1]

The South lost its simple dignity because the Revolution not only freed the colonies from England but also gave voice and volume to the will of the common man in America. Following the Revolution, the frontier exploded across the Appalachians into the great central valley, and this movement swept democracy upward and lessened correspondingly the power of aristocracy. It is significant that during the first half of the nineteenth century voting and officeholding rights were steadily extended until by the time of the Civil War through most of the South these rights were held equally by all.

As to the manner of aristocratic control, even in colonial days it was rather a matter of personal influence than of actual power. The yeoman farmer, the renter, the laborer, followed these leaders because they believed in them. When an individual did not command respect, he was apt not to receive it. But the farther west the tide of settlement flowed, and the briefer, therefore, the period during which a man had held leadership in a given community, the less influence he had.

One other thing should be said about the interest of the aristocracy in politics. The aristocrat emphasized politics both because he had to maintain position and because his culture told him that this was the responsibility of the man who had economic power and resultant leisure. Seeing him concerned about politics, the average man also became concerned, both because he made no absolute distinction between himself and the aristocrat, and because the movement of the frontier threw the common man more and more upon himself. In fact, in both politics and manners, the aristocracy of the South served the usual function of aristocracies: to give to society in general an image of the way to live. Not that the poor struggling farmer thought he had to live like an aristocrat—that would have been a foolish putting on of airs. But he was made aware that there was more to possessions than the possessions themselves, that they demanded a certain style of living, and that when he reached that point he, too, would adopt that style. Meanwhile—and this is important—he would live even his poor and hard life with what style, however simple, he could command. In an expanding America, this style demanded an increasing concern with politics.

Up until, say, the Missouri Compromise in 1820, we have

in the South simply a healthy interest in politics. A highly social people, a people who love to take part in public action, a people moving rapidly out from under aristocratic control into the wide reaches of the frontier. But now begins that quarrel with the North which in the end will make the South desperate in its use of politics, will indeed make it assume that politics can defend any situation regardless of the moral nature of the situation itself. Roger Burlingame points out that the agitation over the Missiouri Compromise "was not to keep the land from ruin, but to maintain a balance of power in Congress between the slave and free regions. For the first time, then, we see a definite political division based on the institution. . . . So the aspect of slavery as a political weapon further diverted consciences from its moral color."[2]

In brief, politics in its all-inclusiveness began to take on the character of religion. This was the result primarily of tremendous pressure from the outside, but it was also the result of the tendency of the Southerner to consider religion a matter of certain public forms and of certain private attitudes and beliefs—attitudes and beliefs that related one to God and that were of no real concern to other men. As for dealing with other men, he would act politically.

This may not be too bad if there is a basic agreement with the men we deal with as to the nature of life and its fundamental values. Given such agreement, we can safely throw all our problems into the political arena. But it was the unhappy position of the South that, in the first place, it never came to any sure agreement even with itself and, in the second place, it found itself in increasingly bitter disagreement with the North. It has been said of the South that, unfortunately, the political questions it had to face were often matters of life and death. Through the middle of the nineteenth century, it was defending a slave-based society, a society resting upon a certain kind of exploitation of labor. This was opposed by the at least nominally free society of the Northern states—though this "free" society was frequently conscienceless in its exploitation of labor. Furthermore, the South, because of the nature of its slave labor—a race in appearance very different from the whites—had superimposed upon its economic scheme a social scheme. This, by the way, is the nature of any plantation system: it is not only a system of economic relationships but also a system of social relationships. This means that the plantation system in the South became a way of life; and the relationship between whites and Negroes, as determined by this plantation system, also became a way of life. The white South became increasingly unable to imagine a life wherein a different set of racial relationships might obtain. To challenge the economic system of the South, therefore, was to challenge its way of life; that is, to raise a life-and-death issue.

It is also true, as Allen Tate has suggested, that the religion of a people is directly related to the way it makes its living. This is not the Marxist doctrine that religion is the mere shadow of economic life. It simply maintains that men relate themselves to the material world and the spiritual world in the same way; their view of the material world is, with the proper changes, their view of the spiritual world.

Now, when, as in the South, the relation to the physical world through the plantation system and chattel slavery has become a way of life, to attack this basic productive system was to attack even the religion of the South. To make this worse, the religion of the South, as we have seen, was never really codified; always there was a conflict between an inclusive social order of status and an exclusive social order of individualistic democratic progress. Therefore, to raise questions about the religious order of the South was to raise questions about the most fundamental and the most uncertain point. This consequently aroused the South to the most desperate defense.

So political action grew more intense in the South. For we had here an aristocracy, dependent upon a graduated society that ideally rested upon religion and was crowned by religion, engaged in an increasingly stern struggle, both with a rising democracy within its borders actuated by an individualistic religion, and with an even more extreme democracy without its borders. As this struggle grew more intense, political action increased in importance and public life became more and more constricted. Men sacrificed personal freedom in order to maintain slavery and the entire social system based upon slavery.

A part of this freedom was the freedom the artist, the poet, must have if he is to express his vision of society. There have always of course been men in the South who realized that the region was paying too much attention to politics. Most of the following references are to South Carolina, but since that state has certainly been as politically minded as any other Southern state, they need not be discounted. Early in the nineteenth century, Governor D. R. Williams tried to persuade the state to balance agriculture with manufacturing, in the attempt establishing a clothing and hat factory at Society Hill, but the state refused to follow him, continued to plant cotton, tried nullification because of the high tariff, and, as the historian Wallace says, "futilely sought a political remedy for an economic ill."

Of course, the prime illustration of South Carolina's emphasis upon politics is John C. Calhoun. In a senatorial debate of 1837, Calhoun formulated a brief for the South. "Defying those who would industrialize the nation, Southerners thereafter took refuge in a doctrine of localism and depended upon the Constitution to protect their institutions from outside assault."[3] In brief, Calhoun would control by politics, not by economics, national economic forces.

In 1853 we find the South Carolina leader, Benjamin F. Perry, lamenting that the South's—or at least South Carolina's—obsession with national politics had taken the leaders' attention away from the economic needs of the state. Perry said, "What might not South Carolina now be if her Calhouns, Haynes, McDuffies, Hamiltons and Prestons had devoted their great talents and energies to the commercial and internal improvement of the state instead of frittering them away in political squabbles that ended in nothing."[4]

One of the serious writers of South Carolina in ante-bellum days was Henry William Ravenel, who has left us his *Journal*. Speaking about the question of slavery in the territories, Ravenel said, "Our people do not reflect enough upon these things for themselves, but are led on by politicians and made to think that our safety, honor, self-respect and our very existence depend upon these issues."[5]

Continuing these illustrations into the twentieth century, we find a list of certain alumni of the University of South Carolina published in 1901 and called "Jewels of Carolina." The list includes only "generals, governors, congressmen and senators."[6]

About the same time, in 1907, one of the leading sociological thinkers of the South, Edgar Gardner Murphy, speaking about the ante-bellum beliefs of the South—states' rights, constitutional liberty, and others—said this: "These faiths, however sacred to us, are today irrelevant. Slavery, secession, were ended at Appomattox, and whatever may have been their former justifications, they are to be justified no longer."[7] Murphy called these political beliefs faiths, and this is what they largely were. South Carolina not only emphasized politics, South Carolina—and the South—tended to replace religion with politics, and to make politics, religion, and the moral life one.

Even more recently, we have the Southern historian Ulrich Phillips saying in effect that we are again in the situation of a Southern writer of 1860, who declared that our problems were more than politics, not to be settled by the political wisdom of Webster, Calhoun, and Clay, but were social and industrial. The writer of 1860 asked, "Is it unjust to hold the Negro in bondage? Is Negro slavery inimical to the rights of white men? Is it best for both, the white and the black man?"[8] These are moral and religious questions. These are not political questions. But the South insisted on discussing only political questions.

Still thinking of the past decade, we may ask, what white Southerner has talked about human rights? We insist upon talking about states rights. The emphasis upon civil rights is an emphasis upon human rights; note how bitterly the white South fights against any talk about civil rights. This is the same Southern tendency to keep questions in the political realm and to prevent them from becoming moral and religious.

The Southerner's early and continued interest in politics and public life, the result both of his basic outlook and of his situation vis-a-vis the North, worked against the development of an interest in the arts. It must be recognized, of course, that for a long time pioneering conditions in the New World made interest in the arts impossible. But when wealth and leisure came, an interest in the arts did not follow in the South. Southerners were inclined to take their literature, their poetry, from the North or from Europe. It is probable that from the beginning the set of mind of the dominantly Puritan New Englander, his emphasis on the inner life, turned him more toward art than did the mind of the Southerner. It is true that the Puritan also tried to set up, as the basic structure of his outer life, a theocratic state, but the test for citizenship in this state was, in the beginning, experiential and religious. From this inner life, it was easy for the Puritan to move, on the one hand, into the literary life, whose operation is private, or, on the other, as the "Yankee," into the "private life of profit." Living more in the public world, the Southerner felt his obligations to the public world. As soon as he could relax the material struggle, he felt called to public life and to politics.

The effect of this sense of public obligation is illustrated in the life of the ante-bellum Charlestonian Hugh Swinton Legare. Legare's deepest interests were literary: he developed these interests through a stay in Europe; he should have been a writer. But public opinion forced him into law and politics. There his literary studies were a handicap rather than a help; he had to achieve against them rather than with their aid.

An instance of this public opinion is shown in a criticism of the minor Georgia poet of the same period, Richard Henry Wilde. Wilde spent six years studying in Europe. Of his use of this period, a friend of his said: "The mission to which Mr. Wilde addressed his faculties and gave years of toil in Europe was not in harmony with his relative duties to mankind and with that position which his eminent talents and finished education had secured from the world. There was [in Europe] delight for the senses, but mildew to the heart. The voluptuary, the man of fashion, the idler, were gratified; but the moral hero, the public benefactor, the man of enterprise and the scholar of a just ambition, desirous to leave a record of popular utility, would turn with generous self-denial from such enchantments." It is interesting that in this view the function of the scholar is not to conserve truth, or to discover it, but to leave a public "record of popular utility."[9]

Also apropos this Southern concern with politics, there is the comment made by a Northern tutor in Virginia in 1837: "A knowledge of the politics of the day turns to a very good account as almost every gentleman here is more or less a politician."[10] And one of the characters in A. B. Longstreet's novel *Jack Hopeton* says: "Everywhere else there are numerous roads to distinction; here, there is only one—politics."[11]

In New England the Romantic Movement expressed itself in the transcendentalism of Emerson and the humanitarianism of Thoreau—and, indeed, of William Lloyd Garrison. There was no such expression in the South. There was Edgar Allan Poe, one of the greatest of the American romantics; but he was practically driven from the South. And there was William Gilmore Simms, a romancer who in some things rivaled Cooper, but whose strength often fades off into sentimentality and whose hope was perhaps as much to be accepted by the gentlemen of Charleston as by the literary critics of America.

This suggests the kind of handicap the South has always put before its would-be artists. It is not simply that it has condemned them for pursuing their more private lives, it has lured them into public life. Simms wanted to write, but he also wanted to be a country gentleman. The South, seduced by the charm of the world, was now seducing its own artists.

In contrast to this, there was little in the early industrial society of New England to seduce Emerson and Thoreau. They were angry, they were disgusted with their society. Therefore they were strongly moved to create, through art, a world of their own. The Southern writers found their society too attractive to offer any strong criticism of it. They tended to go along with it, to reproduce it, with its show, its sentimentality, its occasional splendor.

As we shall see a little later, the South lacked individual literary creators, poets, partly because Southerners in general were engaged in the public enterprise of creating the South.

Of course, they were in the first instance making a living, like men everywhere. But this living tended to be more than the private world of profit; it was also the public world of human relationships. The charm, the appeal, the poetry of the South lies partly here, that men were engaged, sometimes to their own economic hurt, in creating a public world. They did not feel they needed poets to express for them the dissatisfactions of life; life had too many satisfactions in itself. The fact is, such a people need poets, and religious thinkers, and philosophers, perhaps more than any other. Loving the world, finding satisfaction in the world, but without poets, philosophers, and religious thinkers, they become complacent and sentimental. As the South did.

There's one other thing to be said about Southern politics and the romantic impulse of the South. This impulse did not express itself in transcendentalism and humanitarianism; it did express itself in regional politics, in the cultural nationalism of the nineteenth century. Here, instead of the single person's being glorified, the entire region was. Following this impulse, the South thought increasingly of itself as a distinct "nation," radically different from the North. It was this impulse that brought freedom to the European dependencies in South America and freed Greece from the Turks. Byron, who wrote appealingly of Greece and who, indeed, gave his life in the Greek fight for independence, was very popular in the South. When the South left the Union, then, it was seeking not only economic self-control but also that political self-control that it felt, romantically, belonged to it as a "nation."

So much for the most important circumstances that not only rendered the South politically self-conscious but that led it to emphasize politics beyond reason. Let us consider now the essential weaknesses of Southern politics.

The basic weakness appears in the thinking even of the nineteenth-century South's greatest statesman, John C. Calhoun. In his politics, Calhoun was a faithful follower of John Locke. Locke had laid the foundations for modern politics, the politics proper to individualistic, democratic man, determined to break away from the authoritarian institutions of the past and to set up, in the light of his own reason, rational institutions suited to his individualistic purposes. The first aim of Lockean politics was to break the hold of the traditional, feudal, sacred past. John C. Calhoun not only adopted this rational politics, and learned how to manipulate it so that he was able to lead the South for more than two decades; he even attempted to add to its armory the device he called the "concurrent majority." On one level, it was entirely reasonable that he do this, since he represented a minority and was therefore forced to encumber and delay majority action as long as possible.

But what was he using this complicated, checks-and-balances Lockean politics for? As we said earlier, to maintain in power a region that at least in the thoughts of its leaders was highly conservative, even feudalistic. He was using the politics of a rational, individualistic society to maintain a prerational, organic society, in which custom and tradition, and not reason, had been the moving force. In such an attempt, even in the absence of outside interference, the political means would change or destroy the social end. The outside interference came, finally in the form of the Civil War, and made academic the question as to what would have happened if the South had been able to continue for some time this self-defeating course.

As to the question, why did Calhoun and the South attempt to follow such a contradictory course, the answer is that this was merely the public indication of that contradiction that lay at the heart of the South. For the Southerner was trying both to hold on to the past and to grab the future. And the farther west he went, and the longer he lived there, the more impelling the lure of the future became. But the more compelling also the drag of the past, as embodied in chattel slavery. Calhoun with his clear, logical mind, simply made apparent the division that lay at the heart of the South.

His personal life also illustrates this division. He was the son and grandson of Scotch-Irish frontiersmen, hard-driving, logical, looking to the future. But he married into the low country, plantation aristocracy of South Carolina—though the woman he married was a cousin, also a Calhoun. In the long run he brought to the defense of this aristocracy the logic and drive of a Scotch-Irish frontiersman; in other words, he brought to the defense of the past the instruments of the future.

He had to fail; the South had to fail.

Another way of saying the same thing about the South is to say that its effective political images were too far from the images about which its most distinctive hopes clustered. This is the case even today; perhaps more today than ever. The political images were the product of the modern world, rooted in Locke. The Constitution, States Rights, State Sovereignty, Checks-and-Balances, Individual Liberty. As would be expected of modern creations, these are high abstractions. I don't mean they are not real, that they do not carry terrific emotional weight. I only mean they are considerably removed from that concrete reality of the everyday world, of the definite place, of the present time in which, as we have seen, the Southerner tends to live. This reality is represented by the more human terms: home, kinsman, hospitality, kindliness, courtesy, courage, and honor.

The Southerner tended to accept these basic, concrete facts of his life as he accepted life in general. He did not build a great poetry upon them, or a philosophy, or a church. Therefore, he never really understood them; never knew them in their universal and eternal meanings; never lifted them out of the moving pattern of his life and contemplated and criticized them. Both lured and forced into the wider, more public arena of politics, he gave his attention, his thought, and his emotions to political slogans. He supposed that by defending the political position represented by these slogans, he was defending his life. He was trying to defend by political means human and religious values that he really didn't understand. Consequently, as we have seen, the means themselves, politics, became imbued with a religious quality, and political defeat, finally military defeat, seemed to be the defeat of God himself.

Perhaps the Southerner who carried furthest this belief in the importance of public life and politics was Thomas Jefferson. Because of his greatness, and his importance in the founding of the nation, he strongly influenced the South in that direction. Jefferson was an eighteenth-century rationalist, who apparently felt that a man's religion, so far as it was not a reasonable matter, was a purely private matter, without public effect and of no public interest. He felt, as Allen Tate puts it, that man's destiny could be encompassed by politics. This was the expression of the eighteenth-century belief in man's control of himself by reason. All that was needed was a group of rational institutions, and this Jefferson, and others, attempted to provide in the American government. Calhoun, who also believed in reason and tried to get men to follow it, came increasingly to the belief that men acted only from self-interest; that despite the political safeguards Jefferson and the others had set up, the majority, which increasingly meant the North, would treat the South in whatever way it thought most profitable. There was little place in Jefferson's mind for this kind of irrational selfishness. Of course, Jefferson, too, distrusted power, distrusted it extremely, but he felt that it could be controlled by political checks and balances. But the question still remains, if the people are watchdogs over their rulers, who is the watchdog over the people? Under the theory of the divine right of kings, God supervised the rulers. In Jefferson's democracy, the people took the place of the kings, but nothing took the place of God. Therefore the tyranny of the majority, which Jefferson was beginning to fear before his death and which Calhoun fought futilely against.

Though Jefferson with his theory of religion as private and politics as the one public business increased greatly the original tendency of Southerners to live and move in the public arena, he also helped to set in motion an opposing tendency. The deepening religious interest of the South during the nineteenth century was to some degree a reaction to Jefferson and deists like him. He of course, with Tom Paine, was the best known of the deists—or "atheists" as their opponents usually called them; and it was partly in fear of such men that nineteenth-century revivalism went to the extremes it did in the South. But this religion was still a private affair between the individual and God, however public its revivalistic expression may have been.

Now, as we said, the Southerner in his absorption in politics brought into clear consciousness certain effective but highly abstract phrases, or images, such as the Constitution, States Rights, etc., and thereby pushed into the background the simple homely images by which he really lived. But in this regard Jefferson was too abstract even for the South. As early as 1800, according to William Sumner Jenkins in his *Pro-Slavery Thought in the Old South,*[12] Jefferson was being attacked because of his abstract political theory. Everyone admitted that he was a great speculative thinker. But this frightened the slaveholding South, which was aware of the extremes that had followed the rights-of-man theory in France. Such an abstract theory, acted upon in America, would destroy the entire slave system.

It appears, then, that Jefferson was suspected by religious

people because his rationalism left little room for religion and by slaveowners because his rationalism might leave little room for slavery. He was properly feared by both, since his rationalism was a tool that would not only help free the enslaved but also help to break the life-giving bonds that tie men to the corporate community and to God.

Here again, in Jefferson *versus* Calhoun (and Calhoun *versus* himself), we see the mortal conflict that lay deep in the heart of the South. In the decades preceding the Civil War, Jefferson's influence waned and the rights-of-man theory was driven underground. Yet even as this was occurring, the aristocracy was losing ground and the South was becoming more democratic. And, to jump to the present, what do we have? Southerners swear by Jefferson, he is the patron saint of the Democratic party, and yet the caste system advocated by Calhoun is still the fact in most of the South and the ideal in much of the white South. We are still in the woods.

We may consider this attempt to substitute politics for religion from another point of view. As regards forms of language, the South has been noted for its rhetoric and its eloquence. The purpose of such speech is to persuade others. If you describe this type of speech as carrying on an argument or a quarrel with others, you may describe religious speech, at least in part, as carrying on an argument or a quarrel with God. The great Judeo-Christian example of the quarrel with God is the Book of Job. By and large the South—the white South, that is—has never really quarreled with God. In accord with its highly public temper, it has been inclined to be complacent about its inner or private life, to accept the world and itself as given, and to go on from there. It could do this, first, because the world as given was, at least for the white South, an unusually pleasant world, and second, because as soon as this world came into conflict with the North, there was always a sufficient quarrel with non-Southerners, a quarrel which for a long time the South had some chance of winning, to keep the South occupied. Men are hardly going to quarrel with the nature of things so long as there is a considerable chance that they may change the arrangement of things. The South, therefore, the ruling South, that is, both from temperament and from the nature of its political situation, spent most of its energies quarreling with men and had little left for any quarrel with God.

The quarrel with God is in a way the quarrel with oneself. We have spoken of the lack of poets in the South. "The poet," says W. B. Yeats, "quarrels with himself, the rhetorician with others." For a long time the white South was too busy quarreling with others to quarrel with itself. Therefore the lack of poets; therefore the lack of a social-minded church. Within recent years both of these lacks are being filled, and primarily because of the long failure of the South to succeed in its quarrel with others.

But the Southerner was not the only American who laid too much emphasis upon politics. All Americans have been politically minded and have tended to try to make politics do the work of religion. The failure of the South, at least vis-a-vis the North, was that the religion the South had did not strongly reinforce its politics. Let us contrast for a moment the interplay of politics and religion in the North and in the South.

At the very beginning, in New England, the state was the arm of the church, politics one of the means to religion. Though this relationship soon broke down, the tone accompanying it still exists. Politics can still be made to wear the aura of religion.

According to W. L. Miller, this was clearly apparent in the American Revolution. At that time politics demanded that we speak to the world in political terms, such as "inalienable rights." "But those terms, in and by themselves, would never have supplied the drive to victory, however mightily they weighed with the literate minority. What carried the ranks of militia and citizens was the universal persuasion that they, by administering to themselves a spiritual purge, acquired the energy God had always, in the manner of the Old Testament, been ready to impart to his repentant children. Their first responsibility was not to shoot redcoats but to cleanse themselves; only thereafter to take aim."[13]

Perry Miller suggests that one enduring result of the Revolution was the belief that it had not been revolutionary, but simply a protest of native piety against foreign impiety. In this connection, it is significant that though the French Revolution was against the church and religion, the American Revolution had no such object.[14] As a consequence of this closeness of religion and politics during the Revolution, the foreign visitor Grund was able to note in the 1830's that Americans looked to religion to promote civil liberties, and so religion took color from patriotism.

Southerners were, therefore, only Americans in their inclination to make political liberty a faith, and to crown politics with the aura of religion. What distinguished the Southerner in ante-bellum days was the gap between his politics and at least an important part of his religion. As the Civil War crisis approached, both the North and the South tried to find religious support for their respective political positions. Religion was, however, a much greater aid to the North than to the South. This was because the individualistic social order of the North was closer to its individualistic Protestant religion than the social order of the South to essentially the same religion. The South was trying to fight a conservative war, though its citizenry was strongly touched with democratic Americanism and expressed this in their individualistic Protestantism. After the South had been attacked, its soldiers could fight for "hearths" and "native land," but they became confused as they tried to incorporate in their aims "God" and their "altars." For this was the same individualistic Protestant God the Union soldiers were fighting for. And the social order out of which the Union soldiers came stood for democracy and the individual and progress and the future. The god of the North was more strongly and variously attached to the life of the North than was the god of the South to the life of the South. The life of the South did not support completely its politics as the life of the North supported its politics. It was perhaps because of this wide gap between its life and its politics that the South laid more weight upon its politics than they could bear; indeed, tried to make politics bear the weight of religion.

As a result, the political role became a matter of life and death. The players, who originally had entered the forum mainly because they liked the action and the applause, now began to see themselves as acting "in the great Taskmaster's eye." When, with political (and military) defeat, He let them down, they were let down indeed; the game of life was lost. For a hundred years now the South has been trying to discover new rules under which the game can be played.

CHAPTER 17

"THE TRAGIC SENSE OF LIFE"

During this period the South has developed a tragic sense of life that is peculiarly its own. The seeds of this were present even among the whites before the Civil War. Defeat and frustration merely underlined the attitude that already existed. Today, the Southerner as an American believes in success, takes individual defeat as a temporary setback, and has never known national defeat. As a Southerner, however, he has known both national defeat and long frustration. Both white and Negro Southerners have known this, but because the experience has been different, and because they have taken it differently, we shall discuss them separately, taking the whites first. Though we begin with the Civil War, we shall be mainly concerned in this chapter to explain the development of the tragic attitude during ante-bellum days.

The defeat of the South in the Civil War may be called not incorrectly, a tragic defeat. For, though it is not difficult to understand why the South was defeated, it is not possible to view that defeat with complete satisfaction. Too much goodness was involved in the downfall, some of which America could use today. It was the South's possession of these strains of goodness that gives to its defeat a tragic cast. Like the typical tragic character, the region, for all its excellence, had its fatal, its "tragic" flaw.

Yet, though the history of the region may be called a tragic history, the Southerner himself does not strike one as a tragic character. I know there are exceptions. In the summary eye of history and certainly of myth, South Carolinians generally acted like tragic characters in the late 1850's. "Hotspurs" they were called, and they rode fast, proudly, even insolently into the darkening future. This was true tragic *hybris,* and if these figures are typical Southerners, then the Southerners are tragic figures. In the parade and bluster of the last decade, the South has underscored a part of this image; any nobility that may have been connected with 1861, however, is largely absent. Indeed, the South has rebelled and blustered so much that many non-Southerners think the Southerner is like this. This opinion is due to the poor press the South gets. This isn't quite true. The press being what it is, the South gets the kind of press you would expect. If our politicians put on circuses—and they do—why should a circus-hungry press—and people—disregard them?

Yet, whatever outsiders may think, I doubt if knowledgeable Southerners will agree that this insolence, bluster, and parade is an expression of the essential Southerner. Nor would they be inclined to say that the Southerner is a tragic character; indeed, I think this is about the last thing they would say. Such a characterization would run counter to their whole sense of the Southerner as relaxed and humorous. If this estimate is correct, then we have the situation of a people of a generally nontragic character suffering, as a people, tragic frustration and defeat. This suggests that Southern history should not have happened to Southerners; and it may be that it is this not-quite-suitable combination of people and events that underscores the quality of pathos that haunts Southern life. I was suggesting this quality when, in an early chapter, I spoke of Southerners as children entering unawares the dark woods of the modern world. Pathos—and childhood—suggests innocence, which in the South is curiously mixed with guilt; it suggests also the feminine culture of the South.

The nature of the tragic character has been sketched for us by two great ages, the late Greek and the Elizabethan. These were ages in which men thought highly of man, ages of great attempts, great achievements, and great failures. In the tragic vision, the individual hurls himself against the walls of ignorance, or custom, or church, or state, or even the vague but still massive walls of life itself, and is in the end stopped by these walls or impaled upon them, but is remembered because of the great attempt he made. The literary tragedy is man's tribute to the stripped will of man; a recognition of its worth and of its doom within this limited world. With everything lost but the will to continue the tragic hero continues.

Dealing with great attempts and great failures, tragedy always raises more or less clearly the question of justice. What is justice? Is it attainable in this world? Though only the drama *Prometheus* shows a god fighting and suffering for man against the gods, all tragedies raise more or less clearly the question of the justice of life. This is one of the great questions, and historically men have imagined tragedies as being enacted by men of at least earthly greatness, aristocrats, nobles, kings. With the coming of the modern world, the importance of admittedly great men, aristocrats, nobles, and kings, has faded, and the average man has become of increasing importance. It is difficult for us now to raise the great questions because we do not think greatly enough of man. Only admittedly great actions can raise great questions.

But though we live in a world short on heroes—short on tragic heroes—we also live in a world infused with a sense of tragedy. One of the great books written by an early precursor of that world was entitled *The Tragic Sense of Life,* published in 1913. Its author, Don Miguel de Unamuno, was one of the early existentialists. Though it may be impossible to define existentialism, one of the main attitudes of its adherents is of life as a desperate affair, the individual forced moment by moment to create his own life, to use a phrase from Unamuno, "in the depths of the abyss."

Though the typical Southerner is not, in my opinion, a tragic character, he has a deeper sense of life as tragic than do other Americans. Whether this makes him more of an existentialist or not does not yet appear. Since existentialism is in part the intellectual expression of extreme and isolated modern individualism, it would be somewhat surprising if the Southerner with his strong social sense should be an existentialist; and yet in his emphasis upon the concrete, upon the present moment, upon the fact and not the theory, he shows an existentialist attitude.

We now go back to the beginning to determine how the Southerner developed whatever tragic sense of life he has. He began, as we said, with a fairly relaxed, acceptive air. There was in the attitude of his immediate predecessors, the great Elizabethans, the makings of tragedy; Raleigh spoke of the "star-stretched greatness" of man, reached too high himself and was cut off. But no great degree of this carried over into the commercial Southern settlements; and, as the seventeenth century yielded place to the eighteenth, men became more practical and more limited in their interests.

It is true that the frontier, which from the beginning exerted some influence, and which from the Revolution on was a magnet, accented individualism and the tendency of the individual to rebel against outer control. But the looseness of social organization in the South and the general tolerance of individualism was usually so great that men did not need to rebel in order to express their individuality. The nature of the life itself gave them sufficient latitude.

Then came the Scotch-Irish, a darker, more willful, more

passionate breed of men. Life had treated them more harshly in the Old World, and they were prepared, both by their experience and by their Calvinistic interpretation of that experience, to live more harshly in the New. They seem to have been aware, as we have said, of their tendency to individualism and lawlessness, and were generally disposed to set up quickly a strict church that might restrain their rebellious natures. Nevertheless, the very existence of such a strict institution within a region otherwise unrestrained must have inflamed rather than restrained the spirits of at least some men, and developed in them that proud individual will that could brook no interference and that in its complete working out might become truly tragic.

Where the restraint worked, however, and doubtless in most cases it did, it was a puritanical restraint; and puritanism is hardly the soil for the tragic character. It is true, there are differences of opinion on this question. Joseph Haroutunian, in his book *Piety versus Moralism: The Passing of the New England Theology,*[1] sees a sense of the tragedy of life as essential to Calvinism. On the contrary the late Perry Miller,[2] who was an authority on New England, argues that Puritanism lacks a sense of tragedy. I am inclined to agree with Miller. The Puritan relied too much upon the Covenant with God, of which, as time passed, he made a legal matter. Though this did not remove entirely the mystery of God, it pushed it into the background. It is true, the Puritan learned how to face a hard world, but this tended to make him hard and narrow and to prevent the great sweep of the truly tragic character. Also, in a sense, he refused to find the world really hard, since he was assured that God meant it all for man's good. He tended, therefore, to play down that tragic sense of the great mystery and impossibility of life. In the Puritan view, life is hard but never unjust.

If the coming of the Scotch-Irish, then, pushed the Southerner toward the tragic sense of life, it was rather because of their bold thrust and passionate intensity than because of their strong puritanical leanings.

But though the continuing moving frontier tended to bring out those individualistic and indeed insolent characteristics that mark the tragic character, this tendency was counteracted in the South by the order and restraint needed for the conduct of a complex organization like the plantation, and, more importantly, by the increasingly necessary unity demanded of the white community because of slavery. Before the end, this unity was demanding that men keep silent on the essential question of tragedy—the subject of justice. There was no time to raise the question of universal justice when Southern whites, theoretically democrats and equalitarians, were holding Negroes in bondage. There was no room for rebels against either God or man.

Yet, even while Southern whites were becoming individually more social-minded, less individualistic, less rebellious and potentially less tragic, the South itself was taking up a course that would bring disaster, and was developing and permitting to be developed in its citizens a singleness of purpose that might eventuate in tragic action. The question of justice was being increasingly raised, but instead of being that universal justice with which tragedy is concerned it was political justice within the union of American states. Here we see again the South's tendency to reduce all questions to politics, and then to take sides as though one were standing with God against the Devil—as Dr. James Thornwell, at the beginning of the Civil War, said Southerners were.

But it should be pointed out that this singleness of purpose, this wholeness of heart on at least the political level was not merely the result of the increasing tension over slavery, it was also due to the original social nature of the Southerner, his tendency to merge private and public life, his concern for the entire community. This concern gave him a certain wholeheartedness, especially in moments of crisis. I say a certain wholeheartedness, for, as we have seen, his heart was never whole at the deepest level. Standing with considerable wisdom between the past and the future, he was yet never clear as to just how he stood: now he sought too desperately the future, now held too hard to the past. Being thus not clearly placed in time—though, even at that, he was more clearly placed than his Northern compatriot—he occupied an uncertain position in eternity. He couldn't really decide how God stood in regard to it all.

Caught in this deep uncertainty, and having as neighbors citizens who were certain what time was for in the business either of saving souls or making money, the Southerner drew together with his region and headed into a struggle that he did not completely want and therefore a defeat which he was not prepared to suffer.

Whatever degree of wholeheartedness the Southerner attained, at whatever level he found it, he attained at the same time some degree of innocence. We approach here that delicate problem of the relation of innocence and guilt in the Southerner. It has seemed to many outsiders that the white South, nominally Christian, yet supported by a patently unjust labor system, ought to be overwhelmed with guilt. The fact is, it is not. It is possible, indeed probable, that the South's burden of guilt is far more stifling than we realize. It is probable also that the failure to admit, perhaps even to recognize guilt, is due in part to complacency, moral obtuseness, hardness of heart. But I think there has also been a strange quality of innocence in the South, the result of the interaction of the people and the situation. It was in part this innocence that made the less innocent, more sophisticated North suspicious and angry; it seemed to the North like sheer deceit. It was also this innocence that helped to take the

South down the disastrous road it followed. It is this combination of innocence and guilt which makes the South hard to understand. What were the grounds of innocence in the Southern character?

What are its grounds anywhere? The main ground is wholeness: the fact of wholeness creates the quality of innocence. William Blake cuts to the heart of the matter in that quatrain which he calls, significantly, "Auguries of Innocence":

To see the world in a grain of sand
And a heaven in a wild flower;
Hold infinity in the palm of your hand,
And eternity in an hour.

He is innocent who can see wholeness. On the contrary, he is guilty who is separated, and feels guilty as he is aware of it.

We do not usually think in these terms. We are too simply moralistic. We say he is legally guilty who has broken a law and morally guilty who has broken a moral law. But to break a law is to be shut out from wholeness, from society, or from the moral universe. Punishment is the price we pay for reinstatement.

In the Garden of Eden story, Adam and Eve became separated from God. The proof of this was their disobedience; the punishment, their realization of their guilty separation and their attempt to separate themselves still further by hiding from Him "amongst the trees of the Garden" and from each other behind fig-leafed aprons. Their further punishment was their expulsion from the Garden and from God's immediate presence.

It has been said that just to be born is to be separated from God and therefore guilty, and there's something in this, man being the creature of infinite desires he is. Yet some men have lived more completely than others; some societies have encouraged more completeness than others; and such men and such societies, because of their relative completeness, have a quality of innocence unknown to more separated individuals and more separative groups. We highly modern individualists have been so materially successful that we have even tended to equate guilt with the lack of material success, whereas its main cause is the very individualism, the separatism, we have cherished. No wonder we cannot understand why we are bored, unhappy, and despairing. But let's go back to the general problem of innocence.

Usually when we think of it we think of the child and of the saint. They are very much alike but very different. The Christian admonition is to become *like* little children. The child is innocent because his world is still whole, undifferentiated, unbroken, the counterpart of his own simple, impulsive inner life. It includes even the moon in the sky as a toy to be played with. The saint is innocent because his world, having been broken, is whole again, the counterpart of his own continuing inner life. It is sometimes said that innocence means newness, detachment from the past, life just in the present. This does describe the innocence of the child: he has no past either to incorporate into the present or to keep out of the present. It does not describe the mature innocence of the saint, an innocence filled with sophistication. As the Bible puts it, be wise as serpents and harmless as doves. Whatever innocence the average man may reveal, it lies somewhere between these two poles, the innocence of the child and the innocence of the saint. The saint, too, lives in the present; but it is a present into which has been incorporated, as into one whole, all the richness of the past; and to the saint's view all the past is rich, all an evidence, somehow, of God's love.

So, in attempting to understand the innocence of an individual, or a group, it is not enough to say that, like the child, he faces the world with no memory of the past, detached, uninvolved, with clear eyes. The question is, not how limited and restricted is the view, but how well organized it is, how well everything in it hangs together. According to our analysis, the early Southerner brought much more of the past into his present than did the early New Englander but it was the Puritan New Englander who was oppressed with the sense of guilt, that is with the absence of innocence, and not the Southerner.

The truth of the matter is, the Puritan was more burdened with the past than was the nonpuritanical Southerner. The Southerner only became burdened when he tried to speed his progress into the future by means of an anachronistic and dying institution. The Puritan deliberately cut himself off from the past, and from much of the world, because he could not incorporate it into his bright but limited vision. But, because it was really a part of his larger self, he had to hold himself separate from it and it was this separation of himself from a part of himself that gave him the sense of guilt. To the Southerner, the past and much of the present were woven together in one world. Since he had had to cut himself off from less than the Puritan, he felt a stronger sense of wholeness and exhibited therefore some innocence.

In fact, much more than we are accustomed to think, innocence is the product, not of the novel, never-before-apprehended moment, but of the slow accretions of custom, undisturbed, undivided by the acid, analytical mind. W. B. Yeats, wishing for his daughter the gifts of innocence and beauty, asks:

How but in custom and in ceremony
Are innocence and beauty born?

The wholeness that belongs to both innocence and beauty tends to belong to a society in which present and past are woven together through custom and ceremony. The South may have depended too much upon mere custom, too little upon a rich and significant liturgy—indeed, the lack of this may have been its chief weakness—but whatever innocence it had was in part the product of "custom and ceremony": the casual and yet effective binding together of men and of groups of men, of the past and the future, in one society. Insofar as this was effective, men lived in it without thought; they were innocent of thought; they were innocent.

In an isolated, tradition-bound society it may be possible to be fairly innocent of thought without falling into disaster. But the South was never such a society. Increasingly, during the early nineteenth century, the western frontier pulled away from the seaboard, increasingly the strain along the Mason-Dixon fault grew greater. Twisted and compressed by these inner and outer forces of change, the South dreamed ever more deeply of the now-vanished custom and ceremony of the eighteenth-century plantation. In most of the stories of this time, written either in or about the South, the plantation is the Southern ideal. But the actuality about which this plantation myth was built was the long-vanished seaboard plantation of the eighteenth century. The contemporary nineteenth-century plantation had fallen into decay along the seaboard, and along the frontier was bursting at the seams as it responded to the expanding individualism of the time and the place. The old accompanying innocence was disappearing. With this growing separation from its early self and from the rest of the Union, the South began to develop a sense of guilt.

The individualistic, separatist spirit of the Scotch-Irish, accentuated by a century on the frontier, increased this sense. For the Scotch-Irish were the most puritanical group in the South, and as such were furthest from innocence, most conscious of guilt. The Puritan felt guilty first because he felt his separation from God. Attempting to close this gap, he cut himself off from the world—oh, in the North he developed the Yankee, to manipulate it, but neither he nor the Yankee could afford to love it. Disentangling himself from the world, therefore, and from love, he increased his sense of guilt; and the more he made of the world a wilderness of stone, the guiltier he felt. The only way out of the wilderness is the lightning flash of God's grace, as on the road to Damascus. Without some such intervention, he is headed for wilder wildernesses, and the further he goes to find God, the less God is there.

The Scotch-Irish, the "Puritans of the South," were prevented by their own modified Puritanism and by the inertia of the South from wandering so far. But they did help to develop the sense of guilt that for so long lay obscured, like a hidden strain or stain, beneath the fairly placid surface of Southern life.

It is well at this point to contrast a sense of innocence that appeared mainly in the North during the mid-nineteenth century. The paradox is that it appeared there, in a rapidly disintegrating individualistic culture about the same time as a quality of innocence was being canceled in the South by a growing sense of guilt. As Henry Nash Smith has pointed out in *Virgin Land: The American West as Symbol and Myth,*[3] the innocence of the North was produced by the presence of the vast, untouched reaches of the West, the innocence of which, it was believed, would make innocent the men who settled there. In these untouched spaces, they would be washed of the evil and guilt of the past. The wholeness of nature would make man whole.

I should add to this that the burden of guilt, heavily imposed upon New England by the strict Puritanism of the seventeenth century, and by the progressive loss of wholeness in the increasingly intense individualistic struggle of the early nineteenth century, had become too much for man to bear. At last the Northerner reacted against it, and, like the Romantics, he concluded that in the innocent world of nature he would become whole again.

It was an impossible dream. For the Northerner carried with him into these spacious new lands the same constrictive, rational, guilt-laden mind he had developed. The West may have been, as it was called, "The Garden of the World," a new Eden for a new Adam. Only, Adam was not new. He brought with him his individualistic and increasingly materialistic drives. The Garden was so rich that Adam, beginning as a subsistence farmer, soon found himself involved with the rise and fall of world markets, and, even more desperately, with the financial power, expressed especially through railroads and banks, of the East and of the wicked Europe he thought he had left behind. By the end of the nineteenth century, the dream of innocence was gone. Its disappearance is recorded, for instance, in E. W. Howe's *The Story of a Country Town,* and in Hamlin Garland's *Main-Traveled Roads.* When the western fringes of the Garden became the Dust Bowl of the 1930's, it was clear that nature, if ever innocent, had been sadly tarnished by man.

The Southerner, less an individualist and separatist, had less guilt to be relieved of. We have to be careful here. It's easy to say, he should have been overwhelmed with guilt. This is moralism. This is abstracting from a system an aspect we dislike and judging the abstraction alone. From our point of view, slavery is wrong; we would feel guilty if we maintained or even defended it. Our dearest ideal seems to be equality, with liberty running a close second. But there have been times when men, basically as good as we, considered equality diabolical. Liberty and equality are both values; but so are dependence and hierarchy. More basic than all of these is the need to belong: to something bigger than ourselves; to a society; to the universe.

Even at its greatest, the South never met this need. Yet, especially during the eighteenth century and along the Atlantic seaboard, the Southerner handled slavery with such a sense of the complete social order and with so little sheer, disruptive individualism, that he developed little conscious guilt in regard to it. He had therefore less need to pin his hopes on the untouched, virgin, and innocent world lying to the west. In fact, from the very beginning he was more inclined than his Northern counterpart to accept the whole world, himself included, with its mixed good and evil. His innocence, indeed, lay partly in the fact that he accepted the world, though, undoubtedly, much of this apparent innocence was complacency. But as he came to depend increasingly upon one aspect of his world, slavery, to take him swiftly into the future, he found himself losing progressively the wholeness of his early view, turning increasingly to the past to justify himself, and therefore becoming increasingly entangled in the past, and increasingly burdened by the guilt caused by this entanglement. For, now, he was not as at first wearing the past easily as a garment, but deliberately seeking in the past some fragment that might aid him in justifying, that is, in making whole his increasingly fragmented society. The more rapidly he drove westward, in the spirit of the modern individual on the make, the heavier the moral burden of slavery became. And this simply because the slaves became increasingly means for the advancement of the slaveowner, decreasingly people in their own right, who had for years or generations held a fairly assured though highly unequal place in a relatively stable community. Even today the effect of this original individualistic drive continues to show in the greater intensity of the racial struggle in Mississippi than in South Carolina.

In the general indices of sociology, Mississippi and South Carolina are considerably alike. But the racial tone is different. With the invention of the cotton gin in 1793, South Carolina slipped from the spacious eighteenth century into the driving nineteenth. But Mississippi was not settled till the nineteenth. As a friend remarked, "South Carolina fell into sin, Mississippi was conceived in sin."

It should be clear by now why the Southerner could not move west in the spirit of the free Northern yeoman. The Southerner either took slavery with him or he looked forward to the benefit, and the burden, of slavery on the frontier; or he looked forward to the difficulty of living as a simple yeoman in a region in which at least some others would own slaves. And the more, and more rapidly, he moved, the less he found about him the old, established, customary, and therefore, in some degree innocent, community; and the more, therefore, he was aware of the guilt that accompanies all separation caused by the desire for individual advancement. After the bitter defeat of the Civil War, and forced now into subjection to a nation of which he felt himself but insecurely a part, there is no question that he would enter with little innocence any West left to conquer.

But this takes us ahead of our story. If the Southerner's growing sense of guilt had been properly related to the social order that was its chief cause, he might have corrected the flaws of that order without a disastrous war. But under the influence of the puritanical Scotch-Irish and the growing individualism of the nineteenth century, he came to connect his guilt simply with his separation from an abstract God, and not from God as He might appear in other people, including those held in slavery. Indeed, the more guilt he felt for his private sins, the less he felt for his public, though all the time it was the existence of slavery, increasingly condemned by the growing humanitarian spirit of the nineteenth century, that furnished the reservoir of unconscious guilt that spilled over into conscious guilt for personal sins.

We have, then, in the South, at the close of the antebellum period, a badly confused society. A society being disrupted by the individualistic pull of the West, by its own deepening sense of guilt, the result largely of the slave system but attributed to personal sins, and by the moral and political pressures of the North. As a protection against these disruptive influences, the South developed a superficial assurance in regard to slavery and a loud Southern nationalism.

This struggle within the South was a tragic struggle because it resulted from a flaw within a society that revealed many excellencies. Among these, I need mention only the courage advocated and exhibited by any aristocracy, the strong sense of social duty within a society of admirable looseness—the individual balanced against the group—and a will to freedom at almost any cost. We have to admit that the social unity of the whites and their will to freedom was in part a reaction to the presence of Negro slaves. Nevertheless, these characteristics were within limits excellent ones. Furthermore, the slaves were also in a limited way a part of the community, the older the plantation as a rule the more truly a part. Unfortunately, as we have seen, they were supposed to be a static element in a dynamic social order, and therefore could never find any true place.

The Southern intellectuals and artists—unfortunately, there were too few of them—sensed the tightening struggle, the darkening air, but without really understanding it. William Gilmore Simms, as we have already pointed out, one of the best-informed men in the South, was fascinated during the 1830's with the problem of Hamlet. He saw sensitive seaboard Southerners as Hamlets, faced with social problems too complex for solution, and in danger, therefore, of adopting desperate remedies. Says William R. Taylor, in *Cavalier and*

Yankee, Simms "came to look upon his own personal lot and that of the South as essentially tragic. The South in its newly awakened consciousness was seen as necessarily at war both with itself and with the larger American society of which Simms continued to feel himself a part."[4]

During the same decade, the thirties, the South Carolina intellectual, Hugh Legare, wondered why "a society so charming and so accomplished [as our lowland aristocracy] be doomed to end so soon, and, perhaps, so terribly." "We are (I am quite sure) the *last* of the *race* of South-Carolina. I see nothing before us but decay and downfall."[5]

Taylor goes on to say that, for Southern visitors abroad during the second quarter of the nineteenth century, Europe was "a mirror which threw back a distorted image of what was happening to the South, an image which threatened revolution, class warfare and the extinction of polite culture. . . . The South saw itself as experiencing in a few years a historic decline which in Europe had spread over centuries. . . . The idea of the gentleman underwent an equally abrupt change, and Jefferson's conception of a natural aristocracy made up of men of superior virtue and superior talent tended to be replaced by an image drawn from revolutionary Europe of the gentleman as a doomed aristocrat. Among Southern intellectuals, tragic exaggeration was all the rage."[6]

Discussing this sense of Southern doom, Herbert M. McLuhan writes: "The passionate and tragic sense of life as opposed to the life of multiple and divergent purposes is already discernible as a basic life-style long before the Civil War, as the work of Poe strongly testifies. The ominous sense of fatality that was already haunting that life comes out in all his work."[7]

Perhaps this is the place to discuss an idea we suggested much earlier, when we pointed it out in contrast to the

Southerner's dominant circular and indirect movement of thought and action. This is the capacity for swift and sometimes terrible direct action. I am thinking here primarily of the white Southerner. There are several reasons for this. The most important is the Southerner's close relation to the rest of the community. The society has been so homogeneous, its basic problem so similar, that in a crisis the individual springs immediately into action knowing that those around him will support him. In a sense this is impulsive action, and reveals the Southerner in his general impulsiveness, his usual disregard of delaying thought. But it is an impulsiveness that rests upon long social agreement and especially upon one situation.

This situation was the centuries-long presence of the Negro slave, with the continuing danger of slave insurrection and continuing white agreement to control it in a split second. As we have seen, slavery carried with it some sense of and belief in leisure, but it also brought to the whites the need for swift and perhaps violent action.

This kind of action probably also existed as a balance to the thoughtful, circling attitude of the Southerner. After too much circling, after too much coiling of the spring, there is apt to occur the sudden release, like the rattlesnake's unwinding in his deadly stroke. Among the most sensitive Southerners of the mid-nineteenth century, this seems to have been the tragic mood that Simms feared: of pondering too deeply upon the event, until finally, like Hamlet, one strikes in hopeless desperation. For most Southerners, however, the mood and its release were not tragic but merely the natural, general, and probably accepted result of the situation in which the Southerner found himself.

It is possible to relate this kind of action also to the climate: the sultry, quiet, too quiet, summer afternoon breaking in tornadic thunderstorms. The Southerner is the product of both the social and the physical climate. But of course he made the social climate that then in turn helped to make him.

To return to the sense of doom which, as the nineteenth century advanced, increasingly overshadowed the South. In the social world this was balanced, and wherever possible drowned out, by lightness and gaiety. Harriet Martineau was just one of the many who observed that the generally assumed lightness and ease overlay a deeply disturbed mind and heart. The Southerners had early stressed the graces of life; a people concerned with public life, they had developed and enjoyed it. As the scene darkened, therefore, they became increasingly gay, trying to overcome the darkness with a little light, trying like the dancers in Brussels on the eve of Waterloo to drown with music the sound of approaching guns. But this gaiety was more than a pose; it was an expression of the life-style of the South; it danced in Richmond drawing rooms throughout the long assault.

Here, in these drawing rooms, was exhibited both the strength and the weakness of the South. Here was a people, on the surface and in public gay and happy, in private and in the depths of their hearts torn with fear and anguish. They danced like ladies and gentlemen, smiling, never admitting "how ill all's here about the heart." It's a fascinating attitude; within certain limits admirable. But there are limits, and the end is confusion. No man need wear his heart on his sleeve, but sooner or later the outer must echo the inner, the world the heart. This is the composite vision that the great religions, however precariously, achieve. Perhaps the South has charmed men because it has danced so well above the abyss, but sooner or later the piper must be paid. The South has been paying now for at least a hundred years. There are some recent indications that it may be on the verge of bringing together the inner and the outer worlds, of finding a more solid floor for the public dance than the aching hearts of separate individuals. We shall consider these when we come to the growing influence of the Negro in the South today.

But that the loneliness still remains is suggested by the mid-twentieth century writings of Miss Eudora Welty, of Mississippi. This is what Louis Rubin says, in his recent book *The Faraway Country:* "Miss Welty depicts these little social communities, these family and town groups, as protective devices that serve to ward off knowledge of certain vast, ungovernable facts of human existence in the world. Participation in the family and the community makes it possible to shut out the consciousness of time and mortality, to screen from one's vision what the unhappy Virgie Rainey, who cannot belong to the community, faces in *The Golden Apples:* 'a horror in life . . . the separateness, . . . Death is denied, ignored; the family life goes on, organized, tranquil, ordered. . . . Violence is denied; one pretends that it never existed. . . . They are concentrating on the daily ritual, the bemusement of life."[8]

They are diverting themselves; diverting themselves from facing the terror and the glory of life. Or, as Lacy Buchan, one of the characters in Allen Tate's *The Fathers,* says, they are leaving the abyss alone. The South has always diverted itself, has always been a land of many diversions, entertainments, parties. Certain ante-bellum visitors suggested this was due to the boredom of life on the great plantations. Somewhat perhaps. But there was something more. There was the inner loneliness that Shelley Fairfield records in her diary in Eudora Welty's *Delta Wedding:* "Does the world suspect that we are very private people? I think one by one we're all more lonely than private and more lonely than self-sufficient."

And yet, though the South could not face the abyss, and created a complex social life to avoid having to do so, the situation did not permit entire forgetfulness. James Baldwin has remarked that the essential function of the Negro in American life is to hide the abyss from the eyes of the white. He is the floor above Nothingness. If he rose to equality, there would be no screen between the white and outer darkness. This perceptive comment may be transcribed for the South. There are here two basically opposed myths about the Negro: one that he is a savage, and terrible, the other, a child, and lovable. The Southern white set up the screen of social life against the abyss primarily because he could not face frankly the moral problem posed by the presence of the enslaved Negro. But then the Negro himself took on some of the terror of the abyss: he was the savage. Yet events proved that he could be lived with: he was also the child. Thus, the Southern white, though he could not face directly the abyss, was always reminded of the mystery, the terror, and sometimes the tenderness of life.

But in all this play of social life against the abyss, there is evident the flaw that cracked the South: the social world does not lead into the private; it is, on the contrary, a wall against privacy. Culture does not lead into religion. We have a highly social culture *versus* a highly individualistic religion. Yet it is possible that the very style of the South lies in this balance between the sensed terror of life and the determination to gloss it over. Perhaps this is that combination of seriousness and lightness which, according to Robert Frost, is necessary for style. "The style is the way the man takes himself," he says; "and to be at all charming or even bearable, the way is almost rigidly prescribed. If it is with outer seriousness, it must be with inner humor. If it is with outer humor, it must be with inner seriousness. Neither one alone without the other under it will do."[9] Perhaps the South diverted itself, not simply from boredom and not simply to avoid the issue, but also because this is the only way to face the ultimate issue with any style, and the South did value style.

As for the Negro in the South prior to Emancipation, it can be said of him even more certainly than of the white that he was not at heart a tragic character. He had no part in creating his harsh American fate; and it is possible that he possessed a native temperament that enabled him to bear that fate remarkably well. It should be admitted that the existence of racial temperaments is doubtful. However, as we have noted, Herskovits thinks that the Negro does show at least two important racial characteristics: an unusual degree of both reserve and resiliency. The Negro may be more varied in the African scene than Herskovits suggests. We know that slave traders and plantation masters made clear distinctions between certain tribes. Leaving aside this question, we can admit that the Negro in America has tended to reveal the character which Herskovits describes. This is not the typical tragic character. For traits like these enable men to bend before the storms of life and stand upright again, not to crash in pride and magnificent ruin like the tragic hero.

In this regard the American Indian is often contrasted with the Negro. In early colonial times the Indian, too, was enslaved, but tended to break under the strain. The white man has a sentimental regard for the Indian on this score. Remembering his own love of freedom, he says in admiration, "The Indian was too proud to be a slave." He forgets that he himself came by this pride fairly recently. He also admires the Indian because he had to push him fiercely foot by foot back across the American continent, and then, to salve his own conscience, he felt sorry for him because he had thus disposed of him. It has also been suggested, by Herskovits I believe, that the American plantation was more bearable to the Negro than to the Indian because the Negro's agricultural life in Africa had been far more like the plantation than the Indian's hunting life in America.

The important thing is that the Negro does not seem to have brought to his American experience the tragic temperament nor to have developed it here before the Civil War. This is not to say that there were no tragic individuals among the Negroes: bold, imprudent, singlehearted men who would be free or die. Generally, however, such men seem to have been lonely, scattered individuals. The mass of Negroes were more realistic, prudent, and pliable; they estimated correctly the overpowering weight that could be quickly massed against them, and accommodated themselves, with whatever grief and pain, to this weight. Even as they moved slowly toward the work goals their masters set them, so they moved slowly toward the goal of freedom that doubtless all of them desired.

But here again we need to recall that sense of community, admittedly imperfect, which existed in the South. The Negroes were never a true part of this community; they were even less a part than were their fellows on the plantations of Catholic South America. Yet the community was there, in some ways they belonged to it, household servants rather intimately. In our liberal air, with its accent upon freedom and justice, we find it hard to believe that anything can compensate for the absence of these two characteristics. Yet we should not. Within the century we have seen a flight from freedom toward totalitarianism. This occurs partly because Western man has forgotten that man wishes to be free only that he may belong, that he may become a part of something larger than himself. Men do hate forcible bondage, but only because it prevents them from accepting willing bondage—or, if you prefer, from binding themselves to others as they wish. That the Negroes of the South developed certain ties to the community beyond the mechanical bonds of slavery, that they felt themselves enclosed to some degree within the community, is indicated by the fact that today, fighting for freedom and justice, they still show a strong sense of community, and a strong desire, not to be free of it, but to belong more truly to it.

The Negro, then, has moved circumspectly toward freedom; his has not generally been the bold and suicidal stride of the tragic character. Yet at one level he has advanced more directly and rapidly than the white. This is the religious level. Here he was not confused, slowed down, and turned aside by the contradictory wishes that filled the white man's mind: both to maintain the total community remembered from the medieval past and to move more rapidly into an individualistic, exploitative future; both to accept the world, with its pleasures and pains, its mixed good and evil, and, in revulsion, to deny the world and run frenziedly after God. The Negro was caught in a changeless plantation-and-slave system, he had small chance to exploit anybody, and there was little place for puritanism in his rich, warm love of life. Perhaps he loved the immediacy of life more because, being kept so close to it, there was little else he could see. He has, in these latter days, and among a growing middle class, developed at times a strict puritanism; but this can be explained mainly as a reaction against the mythical love of life that in part his condition stimulated in him and in part the whites attributed to him.

The Negro was deeply religious when he came here. Life was not the simple measurable thing he could see; behind all actions, objects, moments, there were presences with which a man had to deal. When, therefore, the white offered him some aspects of Christianity, partly to salve his conscience, partly to encourage obedience and order, the Negro was quick to take what was offered him as the religion of this new land, which was now his, or at least in which his lot was cast.

What he received, he interpreted in the light of his own experience. Doubtless in those areas where the paternalistic system worked best, especially in the old seaboard states, he came finally, through the limited and sometimes prudent affection he received, to a sense of God's love as expressed in the simple figure of Jesus: child—and he loved children—and finally lord and master. But—what the white had not intended—he came by way of the Old Testament to the sense of God's justice that finally would save "his people." He saw himself as one with the Israelites in bondage in Egypt, acted out their suffering and anticipated their escape. This story meant nothing to the white Southerner; it had been too long since he had been enslaved; it never even occurred to him that this Biblical story could have meaning for the Negro; and though the Negro in his spirituals sang this story openly before the white, the white thought the verses merely odd and interesting.

The Negro remained for a long time in the house of bondage, and it was while he was there that he discovered the strength that lies beyond tragedy. He pleaded with God, he argued with Him, he enacted through the years Job's great drama. And he came out finally where Job came out; he accepted the hardship, suffering, and mystery of life, and he experienced occasionally the light that lightens the path of those who do not deny the darkness.

A people not deserving the hard lot that befell them, maybe they had to do this to survive. But they did it. Maybe the Southern white has not done it because he has not had to. I suppose the question is, how much defeat does a man have to suffer before he begins to capitalize defeat? I daresay this depends upon the man. The significant point is that even before the Civil War the Negro had learned the lesson of adversity. The white hardly sees it yet. At the opening of the

Civil War, though there were a few who sensed the falling darkness, the majority were bright, too bright and insolent, riding high toward a defeat they were not prepared to suffer, and would, even a hundred years later, find it hard to understand.

CHAPTER 18

PAUSE FOR REFLECTION

Let us summarize what the Southerner was on the eve of the Civil War, poised precariously at what seemed the zenith of his achievement. Only as we understand what he was then can we begin to understand what he has become in the last hundred years.

As we have seen, the South's most perceptive observers were aware that he had already passed the zenith. "The poor South!" said Calhoun in 1850. "God knows what will become of her!" But such perceptive observers were few. Most Southerners felt that the South was still riding high; and an increasing number of Northerners felt it was riding too high for the safety either of Northern, that is, Christian, ethics or of industrial profits.

Looking back now, we can see that the critical moment in the life of the South probably came about 1820, the year of the Missouri Compromise. By that time the institution of slavery had so woven itself into the regional life that the South was bound to present an unavoidable moral and economic challenge to the North, and, in defense of itself, would inevitably be drawn into moral and political conflicts that would undermine it.

During the early part of the nineteenth century, the

Southerner expressed a group of interests that so balanced one another as to set up within him a series of healthy tensions—tensions strong enough to drive him forward but not so strong as to bring on disastrous inner or outer conflict. The most important of these were as follows: first, the tension within time itself, between past and future, expressed mainly in the tension between aristocracy and democracy, between the plantation and the frontier; second, and related to this, a tension between the dream and the reality, between romance and realism; third, a tension in space between the regional and the national; and, finally, a tension between the outer political world and the inner religious world.

The tension between past and future, expressed as the tension between aristocracy and democracy, was, in part, the tension between the plantation and the farm. The most important step toward the democratic future and away from the aristocratic past was the American Revolution and the consequent opening of the transmontane frontier. The days of the great planations, upon which aristocracy rested, had gone with the abolition of primogeniture and entail. The seaboard plantations had also been severely damaged by the loss, in Virginia, of the prime money crop, tobacco, to the richer lands of Kentucky about the close of the eighteenth century, and, further South, by the overproduction of cotton through the opening of the fabulous lands of Alabama and Mississippi during the first quarter of the nineteenth century. Yet the plantation was still the dominant ideal whether on the seaboard or along the frontier, and the possession of a plantation gave certain aristocratic privileges to the possessor. Though family became less important every decade, there was still the general conviction that some men were intended to lead, and the possession of numerous acres was one title to leadership.

During the second quarter of the nineteenth century, and as a partial result of the disappearance of the great stable plantations of the eighteenth, there began to appear in the minds of many white Southerners a growing tension between the dream and the reality. This expressed itself especially as a tension between the past and the present, for the dream was not a utopia, to be attained in the future, but a Golden Age remembered from the past. It was during this quarter-century that, with the aid of writers both Southern and Northern, the legend of the plantation arose. The stories generally claimed to be describing nineteenth-century plantations, but they were really re-creating imaginatively the great plantations of the eighteenth century. This imaginative effort was evidently due to a growing uncertainty about the present and a consequent nostalgia for the past. For the present, certainly in the seaboard states, looked bad. The soils could not compare with the new soils of the frontier, the population was fleeing West to richer lands, and serious men were deeply concerned over the economic future of their states. It is significant that the plantation legend of the South, though it received its final form in the days of the Redeemers, from 1880 to 1900, was already flourishing before the Civil War. Even then, while some Southerners rushed westward, others looked longingly backward; perhaps some looked longingly backward even as they rushed westward.

Now, of course, there is always this tension within men, this desire to hold on to the past even while taking hold of the future. Indeed, this is what life, developing, is: the continued incorporation of the new into the old. The situation in the South was as yet hardly dangerous; but as we look back upon it now, we see the South becoming sentimental about its past. This is a part of the unrealistic, romantic quality of the South, but there are several significant things about this romanticism. First, it was a looking backward, toward a Golden Age, not a looking forward toward Utopia, as in New England Transcendentalism. The South would have said—

and probably still would say—that it had few illusions about the nature of man; men would not become suddenly good; it was not, as the romanticists thought, simply a matter of changing a few institutions. The South could hardly think of changing any institutions, what with slavery weaving itself ever more closely into its total life. So it did not become romantic in its conception of man.

Even its romantic nostalgia for the past was unlike a comparable nostalgia that had recently appeared in Europe. There it was a reaction against both a dehumanizing industrialism and a dehumanizing eighteenth-century rationalism. The industrialism—except in its variant, the plantation economy—had not appeared in the South; and the eighteenth-century rationalism had been muted by New World conditions. The Southern romantics, therefore, had no cause to jump over the eighteenth century as they looked toward the past. The eighteenth-century plantation was still their ideal, though, it is true, they went back to the Middle Ages for the feudalistic aura they conferred upon it. In brief, there was a real and continuing economic base for the romantic life they imagined. Here, then, more than a hundred years ago, we find in the South that intricate mixture of the romantic and the realistic that W. J. Cash describes.

As to the tension between the region and the nation, this was, in 1820, beautifully balanced. The region did not exist yet as a solid political entity; this was to result from the loss of the Civil War. However, it had already begun to realize itself, as John Alden points out in *The First South.* "The First South frequently behaved as a section before 1789," says Alden. "It was increasingly taken for granted by men of the Revolutionary generation that the South was a distinct area with special and common interests that could not be ignored in the affairs of the nation."[1] In comparison with the national feeling that exists in the United States today, that existing in the first half-century of the nation's life was relatively weak. The paradox is that the South, which today has the least clear, unmixed devotion to the nation, had, about 1820, the most. It was New England that had the least. New England had threatened secession before and during the War of 1812. The South had strongly supported the war, and for some years afterward it held this as a reproach against New England. From this point of view, the true patriots then resided in the South. It was only when the rising political strength of the New England manufacturers made that region a threat to the agrarian South that the South began to focus its patriotism upon its region. From then on until the Civil War it tried, unsuccessfully, to draw the West to its aid against what it thought were the un-American policies of New England. When it withdrew from the Union, it did so in the belief that the Union had been false to the original compact, the Constitution.

In 1820, however, such a desperate measure was hidden in the future. Although the aged Jefferson reacted to the Missouri Compromise as to "a fire-bell in the night," it is doubtful that many were aware of the far-off danger. The Southerner, as we have said, having emphasized place and places and a man's place in the world, and being concrete-minded, was honestly attached to his local community and, if he belonged to one of the original states, to that state and the political government he had known longest. He was also deeply attached to that more abstract unity, the young nation, partly because he had fought hard for it and had been most important in organizing it, and partly, if he came from one of the newer states, because he was conscious of his need for a strong central government to aid him in conquering the wilderness.

There was also at this time a reasonable tension between politics and religion in the South. Though men's interests rested heavily, and increasingly, upon the slave system, these interests had not yet become so entangled with ideals that men could not consider them in political debate. The question of slavery was still being argued on both economic and moral or religious grounds. There were as yet more abolition societies in the South than in the North. The final full-length debate on slavery came in the Virginia House of Burgesses in 1831–32. By a very small vote, the proponents of slavery won. Then came the abolitionist attack from the North; and from that time on slavery became increasingly the way of life of the South and a sacred institution; and Southerners, defending it politically, began to pour into that defense a religious drive that should have been directed, not to political defense, but to moral and religious understanding and reform.

As we have seen, the Southerner was inclined from the beginning to consider religion a private matter, important, fundamental, but still private; the rest of his life was public and political. When, under the pervasive influence of slavery, public life became critical, he poured into that life a passion heavier than it could bear. Against this passion stood the opposing passion of the abolitionists. The political forum could not contain the contestants; they adjourned to the battlefield.

The point of this summary is this: the Southerner as we know him today, though he is the clear and as yet unhappy product of the last century and a half, existed so strongly as a definite American type before this time that we can still see the original visage, however marred or sublimated it has been by the fires of history. Our task now is to define these changes and relate them to the original.

PART II

Its Bitter Testing

CHAPTER 19

GHOSTLY PAST

It has sometimes been said that the Old South was the one region in the United States that produced a distinctive culture. Disapproving as we do of slavery, the economic base of the region's life, we are apt to question the assertion. But in the sense that there was a concerted and to some degree successful effort in the Old South to create a unified life, the region did exhibit a true culture. This effort was probably the outgrowth of two causes: the nature of the people themselves and the challenge of the enslaved Negro. The people had at the beginning, and further developed, a rather marked concern for life in the present, for living in this place now. Cash calls this hedonism, and perhaps in a general sense it was, though the term suggests a too great focus upon sensual pleasure. As for the presence of the enslaved Negro, this was a disruptive element at the base of a theoretically free society, and its control demanded an extraordinary unity throughout the rest of the society.

Interestingly, though perhaps not strangely, this unity took part of its tone from the Negroes themselves. Thus, the presence of the enslaved Negro forced the South to strive for unity, and the character of the Negro, as we have already sketched it, caused the South to give to its life a certain tone.

In a dual sense, therefore, the Negro helped create Southern culture.

But, though for these reasons the South went further in the creation of a distinct culture than any other American region, it did not really succeed. Perhaps no culture ever really succeeds; perhaps every one contains in itself the seeds of its own destruction. If this be the case, we shall say that the seeds of destruction were more powerful and swift in the South. This of course is to repeat what we have been saying: that despite all its striving for unity, the South never attained it; that even without outside pressure, it would have changed radically of itself.

The outside pressure came, the South was defeated, occupied, colonialized. It was defeated partly because it was already divided against itself in the many ways we have indicated. Defeat deepened and widened these divisions.

Really deepened and widened them, though it has been one of the main functions of Southern politics for the last century to obscure all these divisions except that between the races. This, politics has widened, as we shall see later.

Military defeat, occupation, and colonialization not only permitted the South of the last century to fall apart along the lines of cleavage already apparent before the Civil War, they also prevented the South from grappling with its basic inner problem. In any attempt to understand the present South one must not forget the terrific human and material losses inflicted by the Civil War. This was in a way the first modern war, and Sherman was its prophet. Though the South was not as totally involved as is a contemporary nation under attack, it was highly involved; and when it was defeated and overrun, it had to make its way up, not only with many of its greatest leaders gone, but also with the largest part of a generation of potential leaders gone; it had to make its way up, not only across "the frontier the Yankees made," to quote

Cash, but across the economic wasteland the Republicans, now in power, continued to make. Though there is no doubt that the South has lagged behind for a century partly because of its own spirit, which has been mainly the retrospective spirit of the whites, one should never forget the grinding poverty of postwar Negroes and whites, and the heavy loss of leadership and potential leadership in the war itself. It has been said rather often that the South has sadly lacked leadership during the last ten critical years. This is true, and this is a delayed result of the Civil War.

There were at least four lines of cleavage within the spirit of the South that were widened disastrously by military defeat, occupation, and radical social change. These were the division of the future from the past, of the South from the rest of the world, of Negroes from whites, and of formal religion from life. We shall discuss these in order.

We saw how realistically the early South was settled in time, with its "foothold mortized in granite." How it brought a rich heritage, mainly from England, rooted this in the New World, and proceeded to build an order that established the patterns of the Old World in the free air of the New. We have seen also how, adopting slavery in order to move more rapidly into the future, it began to look to the past in an attempt to justify it, and to seek Old World and even ancient social images by which to live. Even while doing this, however, its mind was filled increasingly with the dynamic image of the western frontier and it was stumbling into the future, dragging with it the new industrial form of the ancient evil, slavery.

It was the presence of this contradictory self-image within the mind of the defeated South, shown here in the matter of the relation of past and future but present also in the other cleavages we have mentioned, that made it so difficult, indeed that still makes it so difficult, for the South to comprehend, accept, and use its ante-bellum past. The South was cut off as a political entity before it attained maturity. There was no assured, successful past that the Southerner could recall; he could not say, "There is the image of a success that we can try to repeat amid the conditions of the modern world." There had been no such success. The situation might have been vastly different if the South had had more time in which to attain its dream. If, after such attainment, it had been defeated and overrun as it actually was, it is entirely possible that it might have accepted its defeat, and, with a clear memory of its earlier success, might have built fairly soon a successful society upon the ashes of its failure. It had no such image, it has no such image now, and it finds it very hard to abstract from its confused history those desires that may have both survived defeat and are also available for use in the contemporary world.

We spoke earlier of Sidney Mead's idea that Americans have never had enough time, and commented that in this the Southern American was different: he brought more time with him, more history, and he found more time here. But now we see that even the Southerner didn't have enough time to work out his original ideas: his typically American plunge into space rang the curtain down too soon.

The Civil War was a traumatic experience in the life of the South, cutting across its memories, and therefore falsifying both what came before and what came after. Says Walter Hines Page, "The Civil War stopped the thought of most [of its participants] as an earthquake stops a clock. The fierce blow of battle paralyzed the mind. Their speech was a vocabulary of war; their loyalties were loyalties, not to living ideas or duties, but to old commanders and to distorted traditions. They were dead men, most of them, moving among the living as ghosts; and yet, as ghosts in a play, they held the stage."[1]

The past was not seen in the light of the future, nor the future in the light of the past. The past, therefore, in spite of all the glory that some saw in it, was dead; the future was brutal and mechanical, either rolling down upon the present of its own weight or brought on by manipulative men, whose wills were but slightly humanized by the remembered virtues of the past.

In its defeat and humiliation, the South remembered the glamour of the past. The plantation had long been on the decline (though there was a spurt of renewal in the 1850's); yet the South remembered an idyllic plantation life. And the myth of the gracious plantation (which had taken form with the plantation's decline in the 1830's) became, now that the South had undergone almost absolute failure, perhaps the region's most powerful myth. For it brought together the myth of leisure and the myth of happy interracial relations.

It is significant that one of the strongest forces creating this myth of the past was the same group of men who, during the 1880's and '90's, was busily creating the myth of the New Industrial South—Henry Grady, popularizer of the phrase "the New South" and his peers. To some degree, they may have been acting as statesmen, trying to fill the mind of the South with delightfully narcotic memories even as they changed radically and necessarily the structure of the South. In part, however, they were probably acting as they had to act. Since by the adoption and promotion of industrialism they were denying and negating the agrarian cause of the South, they had, for their own self-esteem, to praise in loving though false pictures the past they were denying.

They were praising the Old South primarily because there the Negro had his rock-bound place. But we shall consider this in detail a little later.

We should point out here that this extreme emphasis upon the past was an extension of the earlier romantic mood of the

South. As we have already noted, this romanticism had expressed itself in several ways, these being, mainly, the individualism of the frontier, nineteenth-century cultural nationalism, which drove the South in upon itself, and certain medieval, feudalistic tendencies which expressed themselves in plantation life. But this was the lighter side, the leisure side. The basic life of the plantation expressed the order of the eighteenth century combined with the materialistic urge of the nineteenth.

But now, beneath the driven wedge of disastrous defeat, the relatively shallow romantic mood of the ante-bellum South was split off from the underlying economic and social order upon which it had rested like blue haze upon a hill, and, thus separated, became a fact in its own right. The past, which formerly had served but to color and in certain confused ways to justify the South, now became, at least in memory, the South itself. The romantic past, instead of being only one of the ways of looking at the world, became one with the world. We must remember that by this time, the South's past contained not only the, to some degree, splendid structure that had existed before the War, but also the epic heroism of the War itself. It is possible that the South, in spite of the underlying misgivings of many years, entered the Civil War with at least a surface sense of epic splendor. We shall see later that with the approach of disaster, it became increasingly aware of the tragic fate which had befallen it: good men, caught in the trap of interest and custom and regional pride, not wise enough to find a peaceful way out, and therefore involved in a death struggle of brother against brother. This is the tragic, as distinguished from the epic view; and the epic view is, from the point of view of the modern world, a romantic view, taking us back to the simpler life of the movement of peoples during the late Dark Ages and the early Medieval. It is possible that the postwar leaders of the South remembered for a little while this more mature, this tragic view of their past life, with all its superficial unity cracking under the stress of war. But, if they did, they forgot it in the fires of Reconstruction, and came out of that experience with the Civil War remembered as a foreign doom thrust across the happy pathway of the South. Now broken and divided, they sought unity in the remembered dream of a perfect past. No longer did the romantic past merely play over the surface of the present: it served as an anodyne to help men forget the present.

Unable to understand and bear the tawdry details of contemporary life, the South in defeat filled its mind with heroic, and therefore romantic images of Civil War exploits and idyllic images of ante-bellum plantation life. The main point to note is that Southerners in doing this were not being the usual individualistic romantics, they were being social romantics. They were romantic en masse.

Not all Southerners swallowed the plantation myth of the ante-bellum South. Many did not, especially among the smaller farmers, and in states like North Carolina and Tennessee, where the plantation was not so widespread nor politically powerful. Ralph McGill, born and brought up in eastern Tennessee, probably speaks for these, but also admits at the same time the strength of the plantation myth. Speaking of life in these valleys, he says, "But the old clan virtues endure. And so do the independent spirit and the feeling that the people of the plantation areas are somewhat alien and soft and that they somehow took advantage in putting their stamp upon the South."[2]

Arnold Toynbee also suggests differences within the South in this matter of attitude toward the past. He uses North Carolina on the one hand and Virginia and South Carolina on the other to illustrate his thesis that in history nothing fails like success. The latter two states had been successful and famous during ante-bellum days; the former had not. When war wiped the pages clean, the North Carolinian, having nothing to forget, turned to the building of the future. The South Carolinians and the Virginians could not forget their glorious and now vanished past, and spent much of their time recalling it. They even have a different look in their eyes, says Toynbee—they are dreamers.

Which may well be true. It is difficult to observe oneself. But this Southerner can testify that the inhabitants of Belfast, Ireland, look to him like hard-headed Presbyterians, while the inhabitants of Dublin have the vague look of dreamers, remembering a heroic past, or plotting, in Sinn Fein (this was 1919), a heroic future.

Perhaps what we're saying is that the plantation gave to the South, willy-nilly, its most impressive image of itself; so impressive that even Southerners who never liked it have been affected by it.

All this suggests the idea that it is dangerous to have a past, though childish or imbecilic not to have one. With his New England idealism, Emerson said, "Life only avails, not the having lived." True. But there is no life without having lived. We are historical creatures. We carry the past into the future, and it carries us. The Southerner has always known this, though the last century has sadly confused him. He has tried to carry a past abstracted from the future into a future abstracted from the past. Insofar as he has succeeded in this, the past has been to him a burden, the future a threat.

He hardly knows it's a burden, he's been carrying it so long. But, in being thus abstracted from the present, the past is ghostly; and we do not live with ghosts, we die with them, for they are dead; or, perhaps, we live an unsubstantial life like theirs, floating vaguely across the landscape. William Faulkner, in *Absalom, Absalom!,* says of Quentin Compson that he lived amid the fellowship of defeat. "His very body was an empty hall echoing with sonorous defeated names . . . he was a barracks filled with stubborn back-looking ghosts."[3]

I know a South Carolinian who grew up during the same period the storied Quentin was growing up in in Faulkner's Mississippi. "What did I learn in school?" he repeats. "I learned that the greatest days of the South were the years from 1861 to 1865—during which she was committing suicide." In this view, the essential picture in the history of the South is Pickett's splendid but futile charge at Gettysburg. The troops still advance in order through the wheat and are mowed down and advance and nothing comes of it—and still in our memories they advance. The mind of the South, always poetic, always seeking images, found, unfortunately at sundown, an image it cannot forget. But what has this ghostly image to do with the present? No one knows.

It is worth noting that in thus dividing the future from the past, and thus splitting living time into at least two not-living parts, the Southerner has permitted history to force him away from the concrete into the abstract, into a world beyond his primary interests and abilities. He can walk right sensibly around a fact, but give him a theory and he may go mad.

But perhaps for all of us, not simply for Southerners, the past is like the Gorgon's head. Looked at directly it turns the beholder to stone. Perseus, pressing the attack against the Gorgon, got around this difficulty by viewing the reflection of the head in the polished mirror of his shield. One can safely observe the Gorgon's head of the past only by viewing it in the mirror of the future. Only the man who has a future, who is going somewhere, can afford to look at the past. He looks at it to estimate his direction, and to understand whenever possible the pitfalls and aids that life may bring. Any man who is not actually dead is going somewhere; but it may be safely said of the South during the last hundred years that it has been very hesitant about its movements. During the last few years, in reaction against the Supreme Court decision, we have the militant segregationist, who, upon questioning, generally admits that he isn't going anywhere at all. He is simply clutching onto the past. Such a past is always dead and corrupts the man who drags it along.

The Southerner has always been inclined to regard the past with piety. This is to say, the Southerner is historically minded and has a certain respect for the sources of his being. But with the loss of the Civil War and the succeeding racial humiliations, this healthy respect for the past was enormously intensified and became a religious force in the South. The postwar South deified its past, and compensated for the weakness it saw by the power and splendor of its god. Whatever was inherited from the past, whatever customs or traditions, became sacred. In this recessive mood, the forward-looking power of ideals failed. My uncle, who was by the best Southern standards a good man, and who died in 1914, once remarked to an aunt, "Ideals are a sin, Alice. We should love God." God could be seen in all the facts of the world around us. If He was going anywhere, that was his business. Apparently we weren't going anywhere, except perhaps little by little and only half-consciously, along with the drift of things. We shall have to consider this attitude further when we examine the widening gap between formal religion and life.

But one is reminded that this unfortunate fascination with the past seems to stand in sharp contrast to Bertrand Russell's praise of the past in his essay "A Free Man's Worship." To be sure, Russell attributes to the past "magical power," with "its motionless and silent pictures . . . like the enchanted purity of late autumn. . . . The Past does not change or strive; like Duncan, after life's fitful fever it sleeps well; what was eager and grasping, what was petty and transitory, has faded away. The things that were beautiful and eternal shine out of it like stars in the night. Its beauty, to a soul not worthy of it, is unendurable; but to a soul which has conquered Fate it is the key of religion."[4]

There is truth in what Russell says. The reason the South's past lacks the power he attributes to the past is that the Southerner, at least the white Southerner, has not generally conquered fate. This can only be done by love. Nietzsche says, "It is not enough to accept fate; you must love it." The Southerner, following his early weakness, his complacency, has accepted his history only in the sense that he has let it roll over him. He has not understood it, affirmed it, made it a part of himself. Therefore, instead of being to him an inspiration, it is a burden; or, more exactly, it is an inspiration to aimless acts and dying gestures, and not to a true self-affirmation in the terrible world he lives in.

CHAPTER 20

SACRED SOIL

As the Southern past became sacred, so did the Southern region in which that past had transpired. We have noted the Southern emphasis upon physical place; have seen how this was transferred to Virginia and the Carolinas as a modification of the landed estates of the English gentry, how it was encouraged by the Southern land and climate, and by the fact that the South, in contrast to the North, remained agricultural. It is true, these agricultural operations ran all the way from the immense slave plantations to the family farm, and the sense of physical place developed by these several groups varied widely. Yet all of them lived amid the scene of their toil and looked out from their cabins or their mansions upon the fields of their labor. It was therefore inevitable that they should develop certain attachments of sentiment, or, to speak without derogation, sentimental attachments, for these places. Those who found life hardest, among both the Negroes and whites, may well have hated the land even while they loved it. One of Faulkner's characters, Mink Snopes, took great pleasure in burning off his fields in the spring; he had fought futilely the sterile land, and now he would joyfully put fire to it. But it was alive, it was a part of something bigger than itself, it lay at a certain angle under certain stars, and the vistas of its rows ran to the woods and the broken sky among the trees.

Such attachments, of course, have existed all over the United States wherever men have farmed. I am only saying that the continued agricultural, and therefore relatively slow-moving, habitual life of the South made these attachments to place stronger here than elsewhere.

These attachments were a part of the Southerner's emphasis upon the concrete. He tended to live in the world of his immediate environment, and that world lived in him. If he dreamed of the future, the distant, the frontier—and he did—it was with the general intent, not so much to parlay this open, abstract space into the self-enclosed and more profitable space of the factory and the town, but to make of it his place. To reduce space to place; to cut it down to human size, down to his size. Granted, he sometimes had pretty expansive notions of his size: he aimed at big plantations. But usually the concrete and the personal element entered; he cared about things and people, himself of course included.

Being rather strongly settled and deeply centered in the actual world, as a farmer in the natural world, the Southerner developed the strength of the provincial: he tended to be sure of himself and at home. But how wide was the home in which he lived? How far did it extend? To the local community? The state? The nation? The world? The universe? Being the social man he was, home for the Southerner always included the local community; with the appeal of state politics in the South, this tended to include the state; with the great involvement of the South in the nation during its early days, it tended to include also the nation; it was in part the failure of this national concern that confused and embittered the Southerner.

As for the world and whatever lies beyond, there is always in the conditioning of provincials an attitude that may include the totality of life but does not necessarily do so. It is only by the handle of the community that we are able to pick up the world. But those who live in a community may fail to use it as a handle. They may value it for itself alone, and not also as a symbol of the great community of man. If I am deeply attached to my place, as under the sun and the stars, as under God, if I am sufficiently provincial, if I love the concrete object and the individual person enough, then I shall become at the same time universal, and shall behold other men as also living under the sun and the stars, under God.

We have seen that the Southerner could never root himself quite deeply enough in one place for his spirit thus to flower in imagination over the world. He tended to be at home in his immediate environment; the Negro showed a remarkable tendency to make himself at home; in fact he did far better than the white. But, as we have said, it may have been the presence of the enslaved Negro that prevented the white from extending imaginatively, beyond the horizons of space and time, the local communities to which, as a lover of physical place and the concrete object, he became so attached. He tried, half-heartedly, to build a universal community. He told himself the Negro was a part of this community, and in certain ways he was. But at the deepest level the Southern white was an individualistic Protestant modern, who did not really believe in community, who did not bring the community before God or hold his membership in it under God, but who faced God in an awful, breathtaking aloneness.

In brief, though the communities of the South rested as farming communities in the bosom of nature, they did not rest in the bosom of God; only the individual might hope for this. The community tended to be only of this world; its image could not be projected against the sky. The dynamic religion of the South was the religion of the frontier individualist, the modern Protestant, and its God was an individualistic God who saved or damned men individually as he saw fit. It is true, a man could strive for salvation by good deeds; but the South has never had very much faith in work. Only by grace could men really be saved, and the ways of grace were past finding out. The South has always maintained a healthy respect for the dark mystery of life.

But as the political world grew darker, and the war clouds of the fifties began to gather, the South began to see this individualistic God as also a tribal God. The Southern cause was His, the South His holy land. Thus, under the stress of the times, the South brought together, however unsubstantially, its social order and its religion. It had never been able to do this before; it only did it now by modifying its religion —by substituting for the universal God it had needed for its inclusive social order a tribal God, whose tribe was the white race, to which the Negroes were attached as hewers of wood and drawers of water. In this view, the South was God's special province, in which things were done generally according to His will.

Thus, to the normal Southern love of place was added the religious love of a sacred place, and when this sacred place, now the entire South, was invaded and overrun, that became the object of the Southerner's devotion. It must not be forgotten that the South fought for its life, at least its political life and the base of its economic life, foot by foot across its mountains, down its valleys, and up its rivers. Even if it had won, its fields and forests would have been enriched by this sacrifice; when it lost, these fields and forests became sacred soil. This is the opinion, expressed in 1891, of the Southern scholar, Basil L. Gildersleeve: the Confederate War was fought "for the holiest of causes," "in defense of 'the sacred soil' of our native land."[1]

The North engaged in war to save the Union, but by winning the war and forcing the South to remain in the Union, it succeeded in creating in the minds of white Southerners an enduring image of the South as a special place, set apart, different from, and better than the rest of the world. It has been said that the day the political South died, the South itself came into being. This is true, although, as we have been pointing out, the region was a long time preparing unconsciously for what under defeat it would become. We are trying to analyze now what it did become. Especially are we trying to describe how those earlier flaws, or faults, or perhaps healthy tensions, became through defeat the deep divisions and conflicts of the post-bellum South.

The South, which had in it the makings of a healthy provincialism, became unhealthily provincial. It become enamored of the ideal of the "loyal Southerner," and skeptical of all outsiders, especially outsiders from the North. Having defended itself so long—indeed, since the Missouri Compromise—and finally so futilely, and now having become so poverty-striken both economically and politically as to be unable for a time to defend itself at all, it became highly defensive. This defensiveness easily became aggressiveness. The South carried a chip on its shoulder. It would fight, or at least brawl, at the drop of a hat. It became chauvinistic.

In this manner the South became separated from the world, especially from the rest of the nation. Its very soil became sacred. The North was at best secular, at worst pagan. Loyalty to the South became the highest virtue, disloyalty the deepest shame. In brief, the South became god.

Yet not completely, nor to all Southerners. The group which was most fanatically devoted to its image of the South was the group which, perhaps, had been most ruthlessly treated by the South: the poorer whites, or, if you wish, the so-called poor whites. Perhaps this is natural; perhaps there are always masochistic tendencies in fanatical devotion. It is not accurate to say that these people loved the South; but they swore by, and tried to live by, what seemed to them its most important institution: racial segregation, with its clear implication of white superiority. This made them superior on at least one ground. But this leads us to our next chapter, the interracial gap.

Here we need only remind ourselves that, though the South in defeat became in a sense an object of worship, this was never absolute. (There have been, in recent years, half-humorous recognitions of the possibility of the dead goddess' resurrection: for instance: "Save your Confederate money; the South will rise again.") But the white Southerner has never been wholehearted about this. He has been for a hundred years now a man with two countries. He says, and on the surface of his mind thinks, that he is a citizen of the United States; in a national emergency he acts simply and wholeheartedly like one. But outside of crises, and deep down, he suffers from a faint indecision as to his nationality.

This is not due simply to the fact that he set up another country and had it wrested from him, and was forced on hard terms back into the nation he had attempted to leave. His doubt is deeper than that. For it was he who, in the persons of the South Carolina guerrillas—most notably Francis Marion, "the Swamp Fox," and Thomas Sumter, "the Gamecock"—had in 1780–81, broken the will of the British in southern swamps and forests. It was he who, primarily in the persons of the great Virginians, had had the most important part in the creation and early direction of the nation. He had seen the nation run away from him, and he believed it had run away from its great charter, the Constitution, following the strange gods of egalitarianism and abolitionism, spawned out of his own Jefferson's Declaration of Independence. (Confusion within confusion!) He had felt himself forced to withdraw from a nation growing daily more strange, was then defeated by that nation, and compelled—and also permitted—

to become again part of a nation which, by the addition of the Fourteenth and Fifteenth Amendments to that Constitution by which he had always sworn, had now become immeasurably stranger than ever.

Yet, somehow, it was still his nation; his forefathers had helped to create it; he had never wholeheartedly wished to leave it; and there were times when he was pathetically glad to be again within it. This becomes especially clear in the years following Reconstruction. The year 1876 witnessed, interestingly, the end of Reconstruction (the withdrawal of Federal troops came in the spring of '77) and the centennial celebration of American independence. In both of these events the South felt itself again becoming a true part of the American nation. It supported the Spanish-American War with enthusiasm; here was a chance to forget regional humiliation and frustration. In the heat of battle, the ex-Confederate general Joe Wheeler forgot momentarily the sad years of the locust and shouted: "Come on, boys. Let's get the damn Yankees—I mean the Spaniards!" I fought—or, more accurately, formed one of Pershing's million-man reserve—in World War I, not for South Carolina but for the United States. The same may be said for Southerners in World War II. One listens now, in these days of the cold war and the Cuban crisis, to Senator Strom Thurmond, of South Carolina, and wonders whether he's talking like a fighting Southern American or like a Southern politician. Probably like both.

The point of all this is that, even today, the white Southerner does not know clearly who he is. He is somehow a Southerner *and* an American. At a time when the world needs desperately men who can pass beyond the nation, he hasn't yet quite arrived at it. This may be a good thing. Historically, the South has not been isolationist. Neither its economy nor its history suggested it. If it has moved in recent years toward isolationism, this is because of the present racial crisis. As that crisis is resolved, we may hope that it will again observe the international scene with reasonably clear eyes.

Meanwhile, we have had in the white Southerner the paradox of a man who practically worshiped his native region and yet also felt himself a citizen of the nation. It is undoubtedly true that the mere passage of time has weakened the sense of regional worship and strengthened the sense of national citizenship. But this paradox should be noted as an illustration of the general character of the Southerner. I said just now that he had never been wholehearted about "this sacred soil." The truth of the matter is that the Southerner created an order that encouraged in him the natural wish to be wholehearted but that at the same time, because of both inner and outer conflicts, put such wholeheartedness entirely beyond his reach. He has responded to this difficult situation in two opposing ways: he has either accepted the fact of contradiction and has learned to live with it, or, finding this impossible, he has relapsed into the shallow but bitter certainty of fanatical devotion to one aspect of life or another.

He either reads life's lesson admirably or miserably misreads it. Perhaps better: at moments he reads it admirably, at moments miserably misreads it.

CHAPTER 21

IN HIS PLACE

The basic rift in the South, from which the others followed, was caused by the adoption of chattel slavery, not by the development of a landed aristocracy. The aristocracy of the South was never permitted to crystallize; continuously, it received infusions of new blood from the general citizenry, and from time to time saw its own members fall out of the running. But to rest the aristocratic core of an expanding democratic society upon slave labor fixed forever in its place was an impossibility. The contradiction was to have economic, political, and finally religious overtones. The rift was to widen and endanger the whole society.

It led finally to war. Defeat in that war led to a widening of the rift. Just as defeat led the South to an unhappy focus upon a past abstracted from the living present and the future, and upon a region unrealistically abstracted from the surrounding world, so it led to a focus upon the abstraction "race"; whites became whiter than ever, Negroes darker. Actually they became lighter, but the lighter they appeared, the darker and more dangerous they seemed. Now more than ever in the mind of the white the Negro had to have a fixed place.

We have seen how the emphasis upon social place was related in the South to the emphasis upon physical place. They were both remnants of the more cicumscribed, slow-moving Middle Ages where men lived among solid things and people, only etherealized as symbols of another life, not as mere abstract means to a better life here. This later, abstract vision was the dangerous gift of the modern world. The South was more slow to accept it than the North. It held on longer to places and to people in place. But when it put the Negro alone into a fixed place, and that a most disadvantaged one, it set up a strain too great in the long run to be absorbed.

During the period of slavery, however, the place of the Negro was so solidly fixed that the white South did not have to give it primary and continued attention. It is true, there was always some undercurrent of uneasiness, strongest where the slave population was largest and when the abolitionist attack was hottest. A part of this uneasiness arose from the consciences of the whites, who were also to a degree nineteenth-century humanitarians and, however vehemently they denied it in public, sensitive to the attacks of the abolitionists. Indeed, defenders of slavery acknowledged at times that it was not the insurrection of the slaves that the South had to fear but the possible failure of their owners to maintain the institution. Garrison himself said that he had to convert the North, not the South. (He may have meant that he had no hope for the South.) Yet, in spite of whatever uneasiness about slavery existed in the South, the place of the Negro under slavery was more solidly fixed than it was to be after emancipation.

Indeed, the free Negro concerned the ante-bellum South more than the slave did. The relations that existed between whites and free Negroes paralleled the relations that would exist between whites and all Negroes after emancipation: they were primarily race relations. The relations between whites and enslaved Negroes were primarily labor relations.

The relationship between whites and most Negroes—who were slaves—in ante-bellum days showed in certain circumstances an intimacy that has largely faded during the century of freedom. The chief circumstances that made for intimacy were the nature of the work performed by certain slaves; household duties and responsible jobs brought whites and Negroes close together. No one will deny that prudence was a part of this concern for the Negro; but to suppose that there was nothing but prudence here is to underestimate both the complexity of human nature—for instance, we tend to grow fond of the people we're raised with—and the influence of Christianity. As un-Christian as slavery appears to us now, it is well for us to remember that early Christianity co-existed with slavery. No one would seek to justify slavery now, but if we are going to understand and properly evaluate basic interracial forces still operative in the South, it is necessary to understand slavery, not as an abstraction, but as it existed in the nineteenth-century South.

In spite, then, of the gap that slavery opened in the life of the South, ameliorating circumstances prevented this gap from being as dehumanizing as it could have been. But just as military defeat and occupation widened tremendously the other gaps in Southern life, so they widened the gap between whites and Negroes and made it now both an economic and, perhaps even more importantly, a racial gap. It is interesting that the rift between the South and the rest of the nation—an outer gap—was matched by this division between groups within the South—an inner gap. But this always happens. "The world we live in is the world that lives in us"; and when inner unity fails outer unity fails also.

When war and Reconstruction were over, and the white South had assumed at least political control again—it is only now assuming economic control—perhaps its chief concern was to get the Negro back into "his place." There was no desire to get him back into slavery; in fact, there was rather widespread gratitude even among former slaveowners that they were now relieved of an economic and moral burden; but there was a desire to place him in some kind of peonage. In the long run, this is what took place; and the effect of this still operates in the mind of many a white Southerner. His feeling toward the Negro, though in part a caste and racial feeling, is also, more than he knows, a class feeling, and is similar to the feeling of the aristocrat for the peasant. This should make the future a little easier than it might otherwise be; as the "peasant" reaches, say, a middle-class income and style, the white will be more disposed to treat him as a member of that class. But we will come to a discussion of this later.

After Reconstruction, then, the mind of the white South began to be almost obsessed with the idea of keeping the Negro in "his place." That the Negro, who had always occupied the lowest place, would have, at least for a long time, a low economic place was, of course, almost inevitable in a land stripped bare by war. But the passion to put him there and keep him there was the result of his temporary escape from that place during Reconstruction, together with the economically disastrous events which accompanied that escape and which the white was naturally eager to believe the newly free Negro had caused. This last statement is not quite true. Actually, the whites were more inclined to view the Negro, not as the primary cause of the "troubles" of Reconstruction, but rather as the instrument of these troubles, in the hands of unscrupulous whites, Northern "carpetbaggers" and Southern "scalawags." According to the myth, all such men were "unscrupulous." We now begin to see through the myth and recognize honorable men among them. The most important thing is that the myth admits that even Southerners could be unscrupulous, both by being disloyal to that mythical entity the "Old South" and by filling their own pockets at society's expense.

The Negro, so the belief ran, was a pliant instrument in the hands of the unscrupulous white. Therefore, neither he nor society could be safe unless he were kept in a subservient place. Though this determination might have been motivated by political prudence, there was doubtless more passion than prudence in the South of those days. The passion had been stirred by the presence of the freed Negro, who, for a brief time, with the aid of federal troops was able, at least in ways, to lord it over his former lord and master. White pride, humiliated by defeat and occupation, easily saw evidences of such insolence.

What made matters worse for the Negro was that he had lost the immediate and close protection of his former master and had won increased enmity on the part of the mass of whites who had never had any responsibility or concern for him in the past. He had been freed from an individual owner, who had protected him out of self-interest, if for no other reason, and had become the ward of any white who for any reason chose to notice him. If the white South has been corrupted in the last hundred years—and it has—here is the basic cause of its corruption: almost absolute power with but the slightest responsibility. That astute observer of Southern life, Edgar Gardner Murphy, remarked in 1909: "There is nothing more perilous to the normal standards of social feeling than the presence of a large and distinctive class of a closely related population too ignorant and too weak to protect itself."[1] After Reconstruction, the Southern state became again, in time, not only a white state but an embattled white state, and every white citizen became an official of that state charged with one primary duty: to keep the Negro in his place. I do not think this overstates the average Southern white's feeling of duty in regard to the Negro. When duty is mixed with passion, as so often it has been here, the total effect is almost disastrous.

That it has not been totally disastrous is due to the fact that the white did not lose entirely his sense of responsibility for the welfare of the Negro. The habits adopted through more than two centuries did not become inoperative when the Negro was set free. But the gap between the races was widened, and race became a more important factor than it had ever been.

It should be pointed out that the motivation for putting the Negro back "in his place" was more than the desire for either economic benefit or the satisfaction of injured pride; it was also the fear, felt certainly by many of the leading whites, of the general breakdown of society; the basic fear of chaos. Some four million Negroes, the main labor force of the South, had been set adrift. From having been the solid base of the South, they had become, almost overnight, a fluid mass, sweeping aimlessly across the land. It was highly important that this mass be stabilized. The leaders of the South had always been sensitive to order and had relied heavily upon law and the Constitution. They had had to. In the democratic, freedom-loving air of America, slavery was a volcano, and any man who built his house upon its slopes had to be sensitive to the least tremor. When the volcano erupted, in war, occupation, and Reconstruction, the first idea in the minds of Southern leaders was to bring out of this chaos some kind of order; and since the Negro out of his place seemed the chief evidence of the disorder, putting him back into his place seemed the prime necessity.

But though to attain this end the South used force, and sometimes used it brutally, it is significant that it was not satisfied with force alone. It elaborated the earlier myth of the loyal, devoted, and happy Negro servant. Look especially at the writings of Joel Chandler Harris and Thomas Nelson

Page. Though these appeared during the years when the Negro was being put back into his place, they do not hint of this. What they say is that the Negro in his place is where he longs to be; that he is happy to be the Atlas of the South.

The modern liberal is apt to dismiss this with the comment, "Lies!" This is an oversimplification. There was lying going on. There was the attempt on the part of whites to hide from their own eyes and from the eyes of unfriendly and powerful Northerners a grave injustice. But there was also the admission that the Negro was basic to the life of the South and the hope at least that he might be satisfied here. They overdrew the picture, of course. But the emancipators had overdrawn it on the other side. It is our task to try to discover the living truth behind these caricatures.

William Alexander Percy (writing recently it is true but trying to recapture the mood of the post-Civil War years) says: "On ex-slave and ex-master it dawned gradually that they were in great need of one another—and not only economically, but, curiously enough, emotionally."[2]

It is worth noting that the South moved only slowly and hesitantly toward segregation. It had sufficient power from 1877 on, though there was indeed the attempt at a force bill in Congress as late as 1891. Without question, the fear of federal intervention affected the South's caution in instituting segregation, but its own inner doubts were also a deterrent. Most of the segregation laws were passed between 1890 and 1910. It is significant that as late as 1898 the Charleston *News and Courier* was arguing strongly against the adoption of segregated railway coaches. It said, in effect, that if this foolishness went on we should soon have segregated eating places, etc., etc. Well, it went on, and grew more foolish; but in spite of all the turmoil preceding it and incident to its beginning, it began very slowly. There was considerable pressure in the South *against* this division of the races.

And even when the division was made, it was not made absolute. I am not speaking of the fact that whites and Negroes continued to associate, especially in economic relationships; to have stopped this would have been impossible; it would have cut the economic taproot of the South. I am speaking of the fact that whites and Negroes attempted to maintain a personal quality in their relationships. These personal relationships may have been warped and incomplete; they are still warped and incomplete. The fact remains, however, that the whites, with the Negroes agreeing, attempted to maintain a kind of personal relationship.

This did not have to be done. Men may associate coldly and impersonally, purely for business purposes. Not only did the South not attempt to achieve this aloofness, it never occurred to the South to attempt to do it.

But since this demand for some personal quality in his relations with the Negro became confused in the mind of the white Southerner with the personal quality of the Christian religion, we will discuss it further elsewhere.

Here we have still to note that the growing division between the two races, the result of the emancipation of the Negro slave, had an effect which, though in the beginning damaging to the unity of the South, would, by the middle of the twentieth century, begin to release powerful, positive forces. These, as we shall see at the close, may bring to the South a unity it has not yet known.

Segregation, in separating the Negroes from the whites, drove the Negroes back upon themselves. But not entirely upon themselves. Though the benefits they received from the majority group, the whites, were skimpy, they did receive benefits; and it must be remembered that the whole society was poverty-stricken almost until World War I. In the early years after the Civil War, when there was practically no public education, the churches, in the South as well as in the

North, were actively concerned to educate the freedmen. Especially during the first years, religious leaders among the whites often expressed the idea that now that the Negroes had been freed they had to be educated, if only for the safety of the state.

In 1896 came the Supreme Court's Plessy *v.* Ferguson decision, which found, in effect, that "equal but separate" facilities in education were constitutional. Actually, the public schools, such as they were, had never been integrated, except very briefly and slightly in Louisiana and South Carolina. Also, segregation had been spreading through public life for some fifteen years. The Supreme Court merely recognized the temper of the country. The decision, however, gave the green light to segregated education and the South began to build schools with almost religious fervor. It also built schools for Negroes, though of course far more sparingly and indeed stingily. Yet the fact of education, however poor, had its implications: sooner or later Negroes would recognize that they were American citizens; and when enough of them recognized it, and when they became important enough to the rest of the country, they would in turn be recognized as American citizens.

But this would take place only because the segregation was incomplete. The Negro, though educated separately and poorly, was educated in the essentials of American life. There was another effect that followed segregation: the Negro was driven in upon himself and his leaders were driven with him. There could have been established a system of partial segregation, by which the most talented Negroes would have been skimmed off to become effective parts of the white group. This would have left the mass of Negroes without real leadership. But segregation as it was applied in the South forced all Negroes, no matter how talented, to remain together, and it is this absolute quality of the system that has resulted finally in such racial leaders as Thurgood Marshall, Martin Luther King, Jr., and, unhappily, Muhammed X. All of these have been created by segregation. But, whereas Muhammed X is fighting to maintain and indeed widen the division that created him, the other two are using the understanding and sometimes wisdom gained within the system to break it down. So the divided and dividing South of the late nineteenth century has created out of its most extreme division the very force that may in time close not only this division but the others also, and make of the South the place it has always dreamed of being.

CHAPTER 22

UNSPOTTED BY THE WORLD

Finally, in our consideration of the flaws in the structure of the South, we come to religion. As we have seen, there has long existed here the gap between culture and religion, between this world and another. No society, of course, ever bridges this gap completely; even individual saints fail to do so, as they are the first to admit. The South, however, did have a continuing sense that the two worlds belonged together, and at least tried to build communities that might image faintly the City of God. It failed because, though it loved the world, it did not love it enough to realize within its temporal forms its eternal spirit. Though it remembered better than other American regions the Heavenly City of Saint Augustine, the outlines of that city had been almost obliterated even in the South by the onrush of the individualistic modern spirit. Hastening into the modern world, the South had established on the base of slavery an economic order lifted out of the past and to be justified, if at all, only in the religious air of the lost medieval world. Even while Southerners insisted that the status quo was sacred, they were undermining it by their individualistic western adventures.

When, under the pressure of the Civil War, the South cracked up, it cracked along the existing flaws, and its religion was the most fundamental of them all. Moncure Conway, after admitting that there was in the 1850's an antislavery religion in the North, said that as a Virginian he knew there was a proslavery religion in the South.[1] The South went into the war, therefore, not only telling itself—as people generally do—that its cause was sacred, but also insisting that slavery, the core of that cause, was sacred too. The extremity of this claim suggests its shallowness. The great majority of white Southerners owned no slaves. So far as slavery was concerned, the Southerner fought, not to defend it, but to protect himself against the vague but frightening dangers that might follow its abolition. Even more than this, he fought to defend a land he had come to love deeply.

But as the outlook darkened, the Southerner began to doubt whatever cause he had. After Lee's thrust into Maryland had been stopped at Antietam in September, 1862, this doubt spread. We must remember that, with rare exception, at no time since the Revolution had thoughtful Southerners in moments of quiet been able to convince themselves of the justice of slavery. It is true, most men repressed these doubts as war approached. But not so the great Charleston Unionist, James L. Petigru. Asked how the conflict, then opening at Sumter, would end, he replied: "Alston, don't you know that the whole world is against slavery? So, if the South is to fight for that, rest assured it is lost, never mind which side wins."[2] In December, 1864, another South Carolinian, Fred A. Porcher, writes: "Are we not fighting against the moral sense of the world? Can we hope to succeed in such a struggle?"[3] Colonel Fremantle, of the Coldstream Guards, recalling in his *Diary* his visit to the South in 1863, indicates that Southerners realized the general condemnation that slavery brought upon them. "But somehow, with the irony of a Greek tragedy, they struggled along, sensing that 'their peculiar institution' might ruin them, yet never knowing [how?] to rid themselves of it."[4]

This sense of tragic doom is replaced at times by a sense of religious guilt. Mrs. Cornelia McDonald wrote from Virginia also in 1863: "If we do come out of these trials and our nation is established . . . we will go back to the old corrupt way . . . money-loving, courting power, striving for the things which in all ages have been the ruin of nations, till God shall again lay his hand upon us and we be again plunged into war and misery?"[5] When, in August, '65, all had been lost, she wrote: "I felt that God had forsaken us, and I wished, oh! I wished that He would at one blow sweep me and mine from the earth."[6]

Perhaps the strongest expression of this doubt was contained in a letter from "A Poor Woman" of North Carolina to Governor Vance of that state: "I believe slavery is doomed to dy out that god is agoing to liberate niggers and fighting any longer is fighting *against* God."[7]

Summing it all up, Bell Wiley, Southerner and Civil War historian, comments as follows: "When the tide of war turned against the South the guilt complex became more oppressive." And again: "As Confederate fortunes declined, a considerable number of Southerners became convinced that in clinging to slavery they were defying the moral sentiment of the world, and the consciousness of disapproval by Christian people everywhere made them extremely uncomfortable."[8] Only a score of years ago, Ben Robertson, writing from the strongly Calvinistic piedmont of South Carolina, recorded the deep wound that defeat had brought to the South: "The surrender at Appomattox broke us economically, but it did us a far deeper injury than that: defeat put us spiritually on the defensive. We have been punished for eighty years for defending black slavery."[9]

The preachers generally were the most stubborn defenders.

They had cause to be: They had stuck their necks out farthest; it was they who had preached that God was on the South's side. The South's failure, then, became God's failure—or his treachery.

Of course, it is not surprising that such a religious people as the Southerners should have had their faith sadly shaken by defeat. Gildersleeve says, "There were those in the South who, when they saw the issue of the war, gave up their faith in God, but not their faith in the Cause."[10] Most men probably managed to keep at least a modicum of faith in both. Summarizing Confederate attitudes after the war, historian Thomas J. Pressly says: "However much in happier days they had cited victory in battle as evidence of Divine favor, Southerners, like most humans in similar circumstances, were unwilling after the war to believe that physical defeat signified any lack of merit in themselves or in the principles for which they had fought. . . . Like vanquished men in all ages who feel that might has unjustly triumphed over right, Confederates looked to the future for justification."[11]

We must remember that by this time the South had convinced itself that it had not fought to defend its property in slaves or the institution of slavery, but principles of liberty and native land. Slavery could therefore be destroyed—and maybe good riddance—without affecting the truth of the cause. Writing in the 1880's, the Southerner George Washington Cable commented that while slavery continued to exist, men defended it as necessary and just; when its necessity had been disproved by military defeat, they ceased to defend its justice. But this did not make them cease to defend the justice of what by then they had come to consider the "Southern cause."

Whether or not defeated Southerners lost their nominal faith in God, like all peoples after great military effort, they lost, at least for a time, all clear standards of action, and entered a period generally to be characterized by the adage "Every man for himself and devil take the hindmost"—the devil in this case being the Yankee. You could keep ahead of him, or you could join him. Some did one, some the other, some both. Meanwhile, we may remember that the Yankee was erecting at the same time that tawdry structure called by Mark Twain "The Gilded Age."

It was this breakdown of society, the result of war, defeat, and Reconstruction, that over the years drove the wedge even deeper between the formal religion of the South and its general life. In the tense years preceding the war and during the war itself, the preachers of the South had forgotten their earlier insistence that the concern of the church was "spiritual" and other-worldly, and had permitted themselves to bless from the pulpit, first, slavery, and then the total Southern cause. As we have seen, the defeat of the South put them in a quandary, from the effects of which we still suffer. Though white Southerners today have generally forgotten why they want the preachers to stay out of politics, this is one of the reasons: a hundred years ago the preachers made a terrible mistake. So deep was the wedge driven then between religion and the total life of society.

However, as we have seen again and again, there are no absolutes in the South. Where they seem to exist, as, for instance, in the 1962 pronouncements of Barnett of Mississippi and Wallace of Alabama, they are really peripheral and are the expression, not of native character but of the too-great complexity of the total situation. From the beginning, the Southerner, desiring to possess the world in its richness, avoided the stripped life of the Puritan and the Yankee. Partly because of this acceptance of the world, partly because of the challenge of these other Americans, the world became too complex and broke up. At his best, he is still concerned to put the pieces together; at his worst, in his demagogues, he appears to solve his problems with a lying simplicity.

It is inaccurate, then, to say that the Civil War defeat drove a solid wedge between religion and the total life of society. Though the "personal" religion of the ante-bellum South was made even more "personal" by defeat, it was still the preachers, and lay religious leaders, who exerted the chief efforts to keep whites and Negroes within one religious community. Even during the war itself, there was a movement, led largely by churchmen, to reform slavery by increasing education, ending absentee ownership, recognizing slave marriages, and forbidding the selling of children away from their parents. This, says Bell Wiley, was an expression of the humanitarian impulse that dated back to Jefferson but which had been driven underground by the abolitionist movement.[12] After the war, when Negro church members wished to withdraw and organize their own churches, there was rather consistent opposition on the part of white churchmen. Granted that the Negroes wished to withdraw because they were second-class members in these churches; granted that the whites were in part motivated by the desire to continue such control as they had; it is only just to recognize that they were also motivated by their conception of the inclusiveness of their faith. They certainly did not see men as equal, but they saw mankind, however brokenly, as one. In this over-all view, they had set themselves strongly against certain Southern scientists, who, in the late ante-bellum period had argued that Negroes were not really human, or were incompletely human. It is the inclusiveness of the Christian view, which somehow brings all men together in God, however unequal they may be in this world, that has both haunted and inspired the mind of the South.

As for illustrations of the white opposition to the founding of Negro churches, take the following. In 1866, the South

Carolina Presbytery, of the Presbyterian Church in the United States, issued a paper, agreeing regretfully to the petition of certain Negroes that they be permitted to organize their own church, but adding: "The ground of color is a schismatical foundation on which a church may not be built. The same principle, of course, would admit the organization of a white man's church into the membership of which no colored person could be received. . . . We greatly desire . . . that our churches in this Southern country should be composed as hitherto of men of both colors."[13]

Ten years later, even after the upsetting days of Reconstruction, the Right Reverend William B. W. Howe, speaking to a convention of the Episcopal Church in South Carolina, said: "I ask you not as Carolinians, but as representatives of the Church in Convention assembled—if the two races in this State, under adverse influences, are drifting asunder, one from the other—shall the Church of God catch the evil infection, and instead of trying to put a stay to it, rather add fuel to the flame?"[14]

Continuing the fight, E. M. Seabrook, an Episcopal layman, said in 1887: "To make a *Christian Church a race Church,* is to attempt to put back the hand on the clock of time over two thousand years . . . *and this is the nineteenth Century!* It cannot be done."[15]

But it was done. Done so well that what church historians may finally rank as one of the most heretical actions of the Christian church is still accepted by many white Southerners as an essential part of Christianity. But it came to be accepted after the fact and because of the fact. The fact produced the justification. In fairness it must be said that the Negro communicants usually produced the fact, their segregation was self-imposed, the schism was created by them. The schism occurred, however, because the whites had never accepted the Negroes into anything like complete Christian fellowship.

Our image of war and defeat as a wedge widening the earlier split in the South between the church and the world, or religion and culture, becomes somewhat confusing here. The establishment of racial churches was an admission, on the part of both whites and Negroes, that their religion was not the inclusive structure its founder had claimed, that not only could it not close the gaps of the world, it extended and deepened those gaps. The church was not cut off from the world, nor unspotted by the world, but was merely one aspect of the world. The basic division was in the hearts of men; war and defeat widened this division.

When we leave the question of racial churches, and consider further what defeat did to religion in the South, we shall see what we began to note earlier, that it became more and more concerned with the individual, less and less concerned with the social order. Except in the formal days of the eighteenth century and the great seaboard plantations, religion had always tended to be personal in the South. This was because life tended to be personal, mainly a matter of strong individuals, or loyal family groups, in a largely unstructured world, constantly changing under the lure and the fact of the frontier. The most striking expression of this religion was the frontier revival and camp meeting. It is true, this type of religion had some direct impact upon the social order: temperance societies, better schools, some concern for slaves. But these attempts consisted only in modifying society, not in really changing it. During this same time in the North, religion was expressing itself in various radical movements ("isms" they were scornfully called in the South) of which abolitionism was only the most widespread and influential. The presence of slavery prevented the Southerner from tampering with the social order.

The last nationwide revival of ante-bellum days occurred after the depression of 1857, and probably as a result of the hardships suffered during that depression. Called the "Great Awakening of 1858," it was continued by the South throughout the war, especially among its armies. It reached its peak as the South approached disaster, that is to say, after the defeats of Gettysburg and Vicksburg, in July, 1863, and especially while the armies were in winter quarters during the following winter.

If these defeats, if shattered regiments, if the continuing threat of death found expression in the Confederate armies in such revivals, one would expect that the loss of the war, the occupation of the land, and the racial revolution of Reconstruction would either drive the white Southerner away from religion or lead him more deeply into it. As we have seen, it drove some away, either in lust for gain at any price or in loss of faith. Most men, however, it brought together in that rich but limited personal religion they had always known. As John Wade says in his study of Longstreet: "At last, they were all one in the South now, all one, all glad enough in this undependable world, in this too troublous time, to fall back upon the sure Refuge, and to surrender up to that Refuge all care and all necessity for planning. . . . Ah, they had learned in catastrophe, these people, that somewhere God must square life in accord with justice, lest otherwise it prove unthinkable."[16]

The temporary loss of political control during Reconstruction and the later regaining and maintenance of control by unscrupulous means drove men more than ever into the citadel of a personal and moralistic religion. Bishop Haygood, of Georgia, said in 1880 that the basic sentiment among all Southerners was religious. And in 1908 Edwin Alderman remarked that "The fancied home of the cavalier is the home of the nearest approach to puritanism and to the most vital protestant evangelicism in the world today."[17] This puritanism, unlike that of early New England, had no strong intellectual structure, though it did have a solid base of dogma. The South has never insisted upon intellectual structure; in the bleak days following the Civil War it would have insisted unavailingly. Nor, as we have seen, was this late Southern puritanism concerned with the social order. It avoided the core problems and dabbled around the edges with a bunch of blue laws. That is, until, under the purifying influence of a war to make the world safe for democracy—and maybe everything else—it spread its eagle wings and put over the Prohibition Amendment of 1919.

One expression of this personal religion was the stoic mood we have already discussed as being important in the antebellum South. This was a personal religion in that it was detached from social forms and available to any man courageous enough simply to bear life as it was. If the cultural leaders of the South gravitated toward Stoicism during the decline of the South, much more might they adopt it after the South's destruction. To cultured men, to polite and restrained men, who for a while yet still wore the mantle of leadership in a world ruined perhaps beyond repair, this might seem the one available pose. Most men were too rough and unrestrained to adopt it; furthermore, most men did not carry the burden of leadership. Such men might find at least temporary escape from daily frustration in the uninhibited forms of popular worship. The leaders, however, at least so long as any aristocratic leadership remained, might find their strength in an almost pagan courage, in their ability to remain in their place though the heavens should fall, and, after Reconstruction, in their satisfaction with the Negro's being now back in his place and the world beginning to turn again somewhat as of old.

To return to the spate of blue laws promulgated by puritanical Southerners, the churches did move, on two general occasions, into a constructive approach to public life. During the 1880's and '90's, they generally supported the new industrialization—cotton mills—with religious fervor. But this was not then so radical an innovation as we now recognize industrialization to be; for the cotton mills were intended for the whites alone, and were but the extension to them, through the factory, of the attitude which had formerly been most evident on the plantation in relation to the Negro. Following this, and beginning about 1900, there was an almost evangelical drive for public schools. This grew out of an economy strengthened by textiles—and also by better farm prices—and out of a political situation that included the fact of segregation, now assured by the Plessy *v.* Ferguson decision of 1896. It was in no sense a criticism of society; it was instead a pushing of society more rapidly along the course it was already following. This was essentially a course of benefiting the whites in part at the expense of the Negroes.

If during the last century the white churches of the South have avoided the core problem, the racial, because it was so close, intricate, and inclusive as to be overwhelming, much more so have the Negro churches, the destiny of whose members lay so largely in the hands of the whites. If the whites had been made one through the disastrous failure of the Confederacy, the Negroes had been made one through the long frustrations of slavery and the all-but-complete putting out of the light of freedom that had blazed up briefly during Reconstruction. They were also made one by the insistence of the whites, who kept them in one place. Unhappy cellmates, then, in this prison-house of the world, they continued to turn, as they had turned under slavery, to a God who had to be just to right somehow the injustices of life. The Negro could do little to change this world, but he could prepare for life in another, in anticipation of which he experienced the joys of heaven, and may have enjoyed, in his starved life, the anticipated terrors of hell. He but followed the white in this;

but, perhaps because of his nature and also because of his lack of any middle-class success to harden his sense of moral order, he followed with more abandon. He had no puritan theology to make him hate the world, nor as yet any success to make him prudent in handling it. He took it when and where he found it, but most of the time he had to get along without it. "Honey chile," said the old nurse to her white charge, "in this world you's got to learn to want and not git." So he continued to want, and to live without getting, and to lay his burdens on the Lord.

As we have seen, the white too was trying to do this; he too had learned "that somewhere God must square life in accord with justice"; but, for certain reasons, he could never quite absorb the lesson. First, because he was an arrogant, stiff-necked Anglo-Saxon—and proud of it! Second, because he had not been defeated greatly enough or long enough: there was always one more chance of getting back at the Yankees. As of now (1964), in the mind of Wallace of Alabama the chance still exists. Finally, because of this chance of continuing and—maybe, who knows? Southerners are romanticists—someday winning the quarrel with the Yankees, we have refrained from quarreling with ourselves, that is, with God. We have assumed that God's ideas of justice were the platitudes we accepted, and that, in time, He would show His hand by supporting our cause.

The Negro's ideas of justice were not platitudes; he had won them by suffering injustice. When he pleaded with God for justice, he pleaded wholeheartedly. When he left with God the problem, he left his heart there. We shall see later how this trust, the result of great unhappiness, has produced in the favorable climate of today an active faith that is moving mountains—including such hard-core states as Alabama and Mississippi.

CHAPTER 23

"SOME OF MY BEST FRIENDS . . . ."

At the moment, however, we need to consider the curious personal and pseudopersonal bond between the white and the Negro, which has continued to exist even until today, though far more tenuously now, within the racial divisiveness caused by segregation. We are considering this relationship presently because it is in part really religious and in part considered by the white South to be more religious than it is. Its existence is one of the best illustrations of my earlier statement that there are no absolutes in the South. Even while recognizing the widening gap between the races caused by Civil War defeat and Reconstruction, we must examine the frail bridges that the South built across it.

The South calls these bridges personal relationships. Their existence underlies the claim of the contemporary white Southerner, often heard since 1954, that he has the kindest personal feeling toward the Negro, indeed that "some of his best friends are Negroes." Here again the liberal mutters "Liar!" It isn't so simple. Your Southern white probably has a fair average of sincerity. The truth is that, because of his nature, which values personal relationships, and because of certain details in these white-Negro relationships, he believes that they are truly personal, that is, free, and therefore of great value.

Perhaps I should say here that I'm speaking of the more fortunate white people of the South, those who state the ideals and more or less consciously support the culture. This is the group that has been called, in a phrase a bit too telling, "the gentle people of prejudice." There may be grounds for preferring the tar-and-feather racist to the gentle racist; at least one knows where he stands; but there are also grounds for preferring the latter. Anyway, I'm not talking now of bitter racists. What has failed in the South has been close to the heart of the South: its religion, its basic outlook on life, its too great emphasis upon the "personal." The bitter racism of roughnecks, blue collar or white, is only a symptom of this basic failure.

It was to be expected that the Negro would not lament the weakening of these personal relationships, the so-called "breakdown of communication" of recent years, as much as the white would. He was not losing nearly so much; in addition, he had an increasingly clear vision of what he was trying to win: a wider justice. In such a struggle, it was good strategy to disregard the costs. But the more thoughtful Negro—not the "Uncle Tom"—has known, and increasingly is realizing that there was some reality in these badly flawed, indeed, if you wish, pseudopersonal relationships; and he may come to realize—and the South with him—that these relationships were essentially distortions or aberrations of the age-old Southern interest in people themselves.

We shall see how this basic interest has been distorted. We have mentioned that the white South, in instituting racial segregation, kept even interracially a degree of personal relationship. If the white Southerner really disliked the Negro enough, he would have made his dealings with him cold and impersonal. The Southerner did not even attempt this, nor did it even occur to him to do so. (He did play with the idea of entire separation from the Negro by sending him back to Africa.) One of the basic myths was that the Negroes were "our people," and, therefore another myth, that they were happy in their estate. They had to be happy, because we who created the myth were happy, and we didn't like unhappy people around us.

However that may be, the South, in pushing the Negro back into "his place," never intended, at least in the minds of the "better" whites, to push him beyond personal relations. Consequently, the strange situation we have today, and out of which we are violently moving with but the vaguest idea of where we are going.

What makes this relationship seem personal is the air of freedom that touches it and sometimes suffuses it. It is, superficially, a homely relationship, a relaxed, friendly relationship; at its best a courteous relationship; the business of the meeting somewhat incidental; the play of small talk, of anecdote, of farm and family always present. It is no surprise that the best of the Southern whites have been deceived by the quality of goodness that inheres in these relationships. When the Southern white says he is personally interested in the Negro, certainly in the Negroes he knows best, he means it. Furthermore, because he feels free in this relationship, he assumes that the Negro feels a like freedom. I am sure the Negro does, though not to the same degree. But is it freedom? The air, the only air, in which persons can develop?

As a matter of fact, no. As a matter of fact, its true name is irresponsibility. It seems free because of the boundary walls of segregation. When two accepted equals meet, they are apt to be cautious in the gambits they make. Each has to consider how far the play may lead, what may develop from it, especially whether one may be taken advantage of! But within the strict walls of segregation, one does not have to bother about this. The gambit may be easy and relaxed; the play will stop at the wall.

For instance, the white landlord or employer—this is the

typical situation—may express immediate interest in the family, in the wife and the children of the Negro employee. This may be economic prudence; it is also a part of the interracial code and an expression of Christian concern. The landlord will back this concern by actual help in evident distress or in crisis, but not in the continued low-level need of the employee's everyday life. The employer is personally interested in his employee and his family; but he does not feel bound to extend that interest into the world in which the employee lives, nor to seek such changes in that world as would give the Negro employee the same general chance that his white employee has. His friendliness is limited to the alleviation of evident distress; it is not extended to any modification of that world which, largely, creates the distress. It has in it, so far as it goes, a quality of reality, but it does not go far. It is, if you please, an over-personal relationship. Its goodness is not built into the total structure of society.

What, therefore, springs up in the easy air of freedom has but limited growth because of its shallow rootage. This shallowness rests upon a shallow understanding of the necessities of personal life.

The Negro participant in this relationship, occupying the inferior position, shows less irresponsibility. He is also less fooled by the pseudofreedom, because he is more evidently bound by the situation. The irresponsibility he shows consists of a set of particular irresponsibilities with which he counters the basic irresponsibility of the white. The white sets up and maintains the total irresponsible situation; the Negro is irresponsible in many particular words and actions. He faithfully promises his employer that he'll be at work on an important job at sunrise the next day when he knows already that at that hour he'll be fishing for catfish miles away down the river. But he does this in the most pleasant manner. Why bother the white man with what he'll learn at sunrise anyhow? Might as well let him sleep tonight. The white man concludes that the Negro is irresponsible, and accepts this as a fact of life. He doesn't see that this irresponsibility is merely a poor answer to his own inclusive irresponsibility. The Negro steals from him a little time, some trifling goods. But the white man has stolen from the Negro a large part of his livelihood and of his life. He does not see himself as irresponsible or thieving. He is a pillar of the community, elder in the church, cashier of the bank. It is doubtful if the Negro thinks him irresponsible, for it is the white who defines irresponsibility. But he does know that the white is arbitrary and sums it up in the proverb "White folks is white folks." Then, playing in his little way the game the white folks taught him, he baits his hook at sunrise far from the field in which he swore he'd be working.

The reason I am emphasizing this flaw in personal relations is that the South is nominally Christian, personal relations are of the essence of Christianity, and the white South is inclined to equate with Christianity, not only the general personal relations extolled by its culture, but even these doubtful personal relations between the two races. And, if we go a little further, we shall see exactly how a wedge splits the fabric of the South here, a split but poorly bridged by these frail "personal" relations.

We may say that these relations are truncated because they do not extend above the level of pleasant words and particular kindly deeds. They do not grow into the public world, to be expressed there in social justice. High above this homely and limited good will, however, there also exists in the South, though far less extensively, a feeling essentially of Stoic respect felt by some whites for some Negroes, perhaps even by some Negroes for some whites. We have already spoken at length about this, especially as it existed under slavery, and there is little need for more than a mention of it here. This is the respect brave men feel for other brave men who hold firmly whatever positions life has assigned them, who bear unflinchingly the burden and heat of the day. For those who take this view; brave enduring men are somehow a part of the eternal order of nature; not children of God, whom we actively love; but sons perhaps of thunder, whom we respect. Why should we force upon them even the things we hold to be good? Their essential nature, and ours, is to stand bareheaded under the stars. Worldly position makes no difference, nor culture, nor even color. "A man's a man for a' that."

As we have seen, this attitude has for a long time suited the most cultured leaders of the South. So long as the Negro had little chance of advancement, it has suited a small Negro group. And this implies a personal relationship, even though on a high, other-worldly plane. When this attitude is verbalized among white "Christians," it becomes an aspect of that spiritual Christianity into which the white South so happily fell in late ante-bellum days. Of course, all men are brothers, runs the argument; spiritual brothers in God. In this world, however, there are divisions. What God may do in another world, only He knows. Here we will wish our colored brethren well and may even hope to see them beyond segregation on the Farther Shore, where, as the Scriptures tell us—we do not say this, of course, but the thought lies like a pearl in the shadowy recesses of our minds—"where there is neither marrying nor giving in marriage." Thus insured, we leave these things to God.

As we leave outside our care, at least so far as the Negro is concerned, the whole range of life which lies between homely good will at the bottom and stoical respect at the top. This is to put it too mildly. We're not only unconcerned about this, we make it a point of seeing that the Negro participates in this world only at second hand. This world contains the whole area of public life, economic, educational, professional, political, recreational, and religious (though it is the Negro himself who originally willed absence from the last). It is the world primarily of institutions, not of simple person-to-person relationships. It is therefore a world whose law is justice, for, as Emil Brunner says, "Justice is the law of institutions, love the law of persons." There are, of course, no completely just institutions; but it is the justice they do exhibit that gives them the power they have; when insufficient justice remains, the institution either collapses or is destroyed.

This is the world within which a man must live if he is really to become an effective person. For the white man in the South, there is such a world. And into it is structured much goodness: a considerable chance at economic advancement and a rising standard of living, a considerable chance at the best education society is providing, a considerable chance at professional skill and even at political power. For the Negro these chances are far slighter. The white has tended to push the Negro clean out of this world and force him to build, along its borders and with what snippets of culture and economic power permitted to him, a segregated Negro world. He has done astonishingly well with what he has had, but he hasn't had much. And it is the white who, even while priding himself upon his personal, indeed, his Christian relations with the Negro, has seen to it that he didn't have much and therefore not much chance of really living in this world.

But, in order really to live, men need much more than bread, much more even than political power. Men need honor, as Simone Weil points out in *The Need for Roots;* and it is in this public arena, this same middle world between homely kindliness and Stoic respect, that honor is gained.

"This need is fully satisfied," says Miss Weil, "when each of the social organisms to which a human being belongs allows him to share in a noble tradition enshrined in its past history and given public acknowledgement."[1]

So far as the Negro is concerned, this need has been generally not only overlooked but denied. And this despite—or perhaps because of—the historic Southern emphasis upon honor. This is in general the Southern emphasis upon public life, upon the public character of a man, his reputation, his honor. It is connected, of course, with the existence of an aristocracy, possessing its own code, the purpose of which was both to hold its members together and to set them off from lesser men. Under the influence of this aristocracy, the lesser men also developed a code, rough and ready but still effective.

This Southern emphasis upon honor, upon public relations, has appeared in certain particular ways. Perhaps most important has been the honor of belonging to a family. Important also was the honor of belonging to a profession, especially the legal profession, and, closely related to this, the honor of political leadership. These honors were goods in themselves. Doubtless, they also paid off, but even without that they were good. It takes no study to conclude that the South has been very careful to keep the Negro out of the field of honor. The cotton field, yes. The field of honor, no. In its limited sense, this was reserved for the most select whites; in its general sense, it was reserved for the selected white race. These gained honor by belonging to families with histories. The Negro was either denied a family, or was discouraged, both economically and morally, from forming one. The whites were honored in their several professions, each of them deeply rooted in the past; the Negroes were told to go to the outskirts of society and build their own, from the ground up.

Finally, the whites had the honor of being part of the culture of the South, however faded or legendary that culture might have become; it never occurred to them that the Negro also was a Southerner. Indeed, this is a shocking idea even now; there is something almost sacrilegious about it. How could the Negro belong to a sacred race that in this sacred land enacted sacred history!

The South has been poor but proud. Indeed, for a while it was proud of being poor, but, now, in better circumstances, it begins to be proud of becoming rich, an attitude equally unhealthy. But, beyond economic failure or success, the South has always put a high value upon the whole concept of honor and pride of place. Its Stoics may have been willing to honor the Negro in his place, but it was a poor and fixed place, and most whites simply did not honor him there. More plainly, they did not respect him. And they very carefully excluded him from that world in which he might have gained respect. They were friendly to him, somewhat as to a child; at the other extreme some of them granted him Stoic respect; but they allowed him but limited entrance into the great middle world between.

It may be asked by those who wish to defend Southern race relations, "Is not kindness Christian? And is not respect for man's immortal soul Christian?" Yes, kindness is a part of Christian compassion, but Christian compassion includes far more than kindness. Yes, a respect for every man's immortal soul is Christian, but, again, Christian compassion sees man's immortal soul as clothed in space and time. In brief, Christian compassion both pushes personal kindliness out into the institutional world of justice and brings Stoic respect down into this same middle world. Christian compassion believes essentially in the Incarnation.

It is doubtful if racially prejudiced Southern "Christians"

do. In the wide middle world, in which men work out their lives (where God, too, is working), the white and the Negro in the South are pretty effectively separated from each other; race relations hardly exist. It is doubtful whether this split in the structure of the South was made worse by the Civil War or not; there had never been much relationship in this area. But what we can see here is another instance of the flaws or gaps in the social order of the South, of which we have spoken so often. The basic gap here is between religion and life. The basic lack, a vision that brings the two together, that sees in the church the distillation of the spirit which permeates society and in the social order the varied expressions of this spirit.

In the beginning of its history the South had hints of such a vision, a faint sense of two worlds existing together, one within the other. But it was never clear, never complete. The South did not produce the theologians and metaphysicians to complete it. Worse than this, the South rested its economy upon chattel slavery and, later, upon segregation. More than anything else, this split the vision in two. On one side, an individualistic and with some a stoical religion, on the other, a highly social public order, in which men cherished the honor of belonging to human associations. But how was the honor of earth related to heaven's honor, how was Southern courtesy related to Christian courtesy? The South simply could not answer the question, indeed it could not even produce the men to raise it. Why? Because of the Negro, present but excluded from earthly honor. For he, too, was a man, as both Stoics and Christians admitted, and therefore a worthy citizen of the Great Universe. But since he, a man, was excluded from the honors of this world, what standing had these honors in the sight of God? However good they might be for living, they weren't much good for dying. They might have formed a structure of grace, a stairway leading to God. Unhappily they did not. Even today, the South is looking for the unity it never had. Out of the division itself, perhaps out of the very people whose presence provoked the division, may come at last the healing.

CHAPTER 24

IMPOSSIBLE PANACEA

But before this can happen, the South must pursue to the limit its old, accepted method of dealing with divisions, the political. It was its engrossment in this method that had been important in bringing on the Civil War. The loss of this war, with the resulting augmented political power of the North and the new political power of the freedmen, instead of warning the South of the danger of relying so heavily upon politics, caused it to rely still more heavily. Commenting upon Allen Tate's novel *The Fathers,* Walter Sullivan says, "The Southern weakness of believing that the highest good of man is the good of politics had not, before 1861, developed to its destructive logical conclusion."[1] The weakness appeared during the war itself, and was one of the chief causes of defeat; the South was torn by bitter political divisions. "The Confederacy was relatively well-off with respect to military command," says Bell Wiley. "Its crying need was for political guidance; for a dynamic leadership that would draw its discordant elements together and make available for effective use the last ounce of available manpower and material strength."[2] And again: "While Lee complained repeatedly of the raggedness and barefootedness of his men in the war's last winter, Vance hoarded in North Carolina warehouses '92,000 uniforms, great stores of leather and blankets, and his troops in the field were all comfortably clad. This was States' Rights carried to its mostly costly extreme.' "[3]

Jefferson Davis, devoted Southerner though he was, could not control the divisive political forces of the South. Probably no one could have. And Davis was too much the soldier to be a masterly politician. A graduate of West Point, he had distinguished himself in the Mexican War and liked to think of himself as a military leader. But even while he concerned himself overmuch with military affairs, the Confederacy was being eaten away by the canker of states' rights.

Another instance of the conflict between military and political leadership appears in a correspondence carried on in 1864 between the Southern general Longstreet and the Northern general Schofield. Longstreet felt that the politicians had got the South into the war and would fight to the bitter end unless the military leaders took a hand in political action. It is significant that Longstreet, even while a soldier, was turning toward political methods to gain Southern ends. Schofield, less politically minded (and also, perhaps, feeling himself on the winning side), replied "that it was not his part to deal with such matters, which were properly to be discussed by the Executive in Washington."[4]

Longstreet, like a Southerner, was turning to political methods when military methods proved unsuccessful. Lee, another type of Southerner, accepted the preeminence of politics, however disastrous he felt them to be; he was simply the loyal Virginian, engaged in defending his state and his cause within the strict confines of the social and political code. Thomas J. ("Stonewall") Jackson, was still another type. With the intensity of the Scotch-Irish, he became a passionate soldier of the Lord, a pure fighter driving toward victory against whatever odds: "Kill them, sir; kill them all!"

But there were too many, even for Jackson. The South,

defeated because its politics had been unable to encompass the nation and, during the war, even itself, now, during the course of Reconstruction and Redemption, became politically one as it had never been before. Out of military defeat came a kind of political victory. All the breaches, all the gaps, were supposed to be healed; politics made all Southerners one. All white Southerners, that is. Now, for the first time, the racial division was not only accepted but accentuated, and a solid white South was built vis-à-vis a Negro South. This was an extension of that ante-bellum attitude in which the white cherished freedom partly because of its contrast with the enslavement of the Negro. But because the divisions in the South were deeper and more dangerous than they had ever been, the attempts to heal politically all these divisions but one were more desperate.

Given the importance of political life in the ante-bellum South, and the weight of political pressure exerted upon the South by the victorious North, this emphasis upon politics was inevitable. But it made many strange bedfellows and caused many strange unions, however brief. The white aristocracy, in form at least the leaders of the ante-bellum South, had been backed against the wall by the loss of their property in slaves. Many of them now gave at least tacit support to the new underground power organization, the Ku Klux Klan. Like most of the white South, they too were reduced to deceits and threats and violence. The Klan had been organized in Tennessee, in 1866, as an innocent fraternal order among former Confederate soldiers. Its possibilities for control of the Negro were soon recognized, however, and it spread across the South, with General Nathan Bedford Forrest as probably its first commander, or Grand Wizard. As early as 1869, however, General Forrest is said to have recognized the danger and ordered the dissolution of the Klan. The formal organization disappeared in 1871. It should be said for upper-class

Southern whites that they realized very soon the danger of the Klan and tried to rid the South of it.

Many of the aristocrats failed economically; some fled from the South, to eke out their years or perhaps even to succeed in foreign lands; some turned their faces to the wall and drank themselves to death. Those who succeeded in the postwar South often did so by accommodating themselves to actions contrary to their code. For instance, in race relations they had often shown little personal prejudice against the Negro, however much they had exploited him. Now, with the end of Reconstruction, the Federal troops gone and the Southern whites back in power, they were inclined to align themselves with the mass of whites and against the Negroes. They "were determined," says Harry Williams, "to retain their estate by maintaining the disciplines and the devotions of Reconstruction. They would do this by the surest means they knew—by recalling the past, the great past with its radiance and the immediate sad past with its dangers just averted. . . . It was an admirable arrangement to head off any economic stirrings on the part of the masses."[5]

Williams summarizes as follows Vann Woodward's comments on this moment of Southern history: "The Redeemers tried by invoking the past to avert the future. The Politics of Redemption belonged therefore to the Romantic school, emphasizing race and tradition and deprecating issues of economics and self-interest."[6]

Yet the South was never entirely successful in uniting all whites against all Negroes. The divisions between the whites were too great. The postwar leaders of the South turned for financial backing to the only source immediately available, the financial interests of the East, and aligned themselves with these, and especially with their gigantic outreach in the South through railroad companies. In the long run, this may have been for the good of the South, but one of its immediate effects was to channel immense sums into the pockets of Southern promoters. While this was going on, the average Southerner, who was a farmer, was finding himself in increasingly dire straits. Out of this disparity between the leaders and the masses grew the Populist Revolt of the 1890's. This revolt, which began in the Midwest as a reaction of the farmers against the similar predatory activities of the railroads and banks there, rose to the height of bitterness in the South. Here the economic issues were confused and intensified by the race issue. The best-known leader of the Southern Populists was Tom Watson, of Georgia, who tried to weld poor white and Negro farmers together on the ground of their common exploitation by the conservative forces—landlords, merchants, banks, and railroads. For a while, Watson succeeded; but the coalition he established was soon overwhelmed by the conservatives who, because of their situation, could control more Negro votes than the Populists. For the conservatives lived mainly in the old plantation area, in which most of the Negroes resided; and when the conservatives found that their economic and political supremacy was being challenged by the Populists, they unhesitatingly threw the massed Negro vote against them by the use of bribes, threats, and deceit. Also, because it had been the Populists who first used the Negro vote, they succeeded in tagging them as "nigger-lovers," and thus drew the white vote away from them.

This suggests that the racial division, at least between the conservatives and the Negroes, was not nearly so great as the conservative leaders had permitted the common whites to believe in the early days of Redemption. When the conservatives found themselves in danger of losing political and economic control, in spite of the lurid memories of Negro control during Reconstruction—memories that they encouraged—they used the Negro vote to save themselves.

Even while they were doing this, however, they were turning, with the help of embittered Populists, then in process of defeat or already defeated, to the total disfranchisement of the Negro. Out of the struggle among the whites, therefore, there came a greater determination on the part of whites in general to deepen the political difference and division between whites and Negroes. At the same time, the economic conflict among the whites was not resolved. To be sure, defeated Populism did find expression during the following decades in certain qualities of Progressivism in the Democratic Party, but these reforms were relatively mild, urban, and out of touch with the poverty-stricken farm group. Negatively, however, it found expression in the rise of the Southern demagogue. These men were spellbinders, inheritors of Southern eloquence, able to make the word stand for the deed, building, sometimes for their own purposes and even cynically, upon the ignorance and frustration of the white masses. Their readiest weapon was fear of the Negro. They played this racial division for all it was worth. The distinction of Huey Long was that he was the first of the demagogues to speak for the masses without playing on racial prejudice. But in 1900 Huey Long was still a third of a century in the future.

The over-all purpose of Southern politics for the last hundred years has been to create, out of a sadly divided South, a solid South. But the politician, being himself a deeply divided Southerner, has sought in politics an impossible panacea. Unable to face his own inner division, he has tried to create a solid South by ignoring certain divisions and by stressing others. Some of this action has been malicious or cynical, some of it the confused reaction to frustration.

Forgetful of the sentimental and economic bonds that tie the South to the nation, the politician has developed within the South a sense of being separate from and opposed to the nation. Granted that national policies, especially in the period following the Civil War but continuing somewhat into the present, gave him reason to encourage this attitude. He has caused the South to pay a high price for the sense of separation he has cultivated. In happier times the South approached a sense of oneness with itself without estrangement from the Union; during the last hundred years the Southern political leader has unfortunately cherished estrangement in the futile attempt to reach oneness.

Attempting to heal the traumatic division of the Civil War, the political leader has helped to increase the trauma. For he never understood what had happened, and was therefore unable to heal the breach even within himself. Guarding himself against Northern political influence, he accepted almost gladly Northern financial aid and at times control; that is, the Southern leader reached for the new non-Southern industrial future with eager, grasping hands. At the same time, however, both to ease his own conscience and to lessen for the underdog the pains of economic change, he praised in glowing terms a lost and golden past. He recalled it nostalgically even while he was "rigging" the future. The more brutally the politician was thrusting the South into that future, the more he praised that past. There was nothing in this to heal the trauma of war and defeat. He didn't know how to do it, and therefore he used defeat to his own advantage, even while insisting that the New South and the Old South were one.

As a consequence of this extreme reliance upon politics, politics became in a sense a religion, and devotion to the Democratic party became the first article of the Southern Creed. This was the culmination of Jefferson's belief that politics encompassed the destiny of man; that public, political life was the whole of life. The white Southerner of course had his private religion, nominally Christianity, but he was to be saved or lost in this world by politics. It is interesting to read Thomas Bailey's discussion in *Race Orthodoxy in the South,* published in 1914, and see what stress he puts upon "blood" and race as a prerequisite for voting. Voting, he says, is not related to democratic processes; it is related to racial kinship. Bailey is unhappy that the Negro cannot vote, but seeing voting rights as he does, he feels it is impossible.

So a means, politics, became an end, and a part of life took on the weight of the whole. This is idolatry. It was the intention of the politicians that politics should unite the South. For some decades indeed there was the semblance of unity. The heart of the South, however, was confused still further, and the divisions within it went unhealed or even grew wider.

It should be noted that along with the growing concern with politics went a growing indifference and even disgust. Frances Leigh, recalling in the 1880's her life on a Georgia rice plantation in the late '60's, remarks with surprise that "neither in my letters nor in my memory can I find a single instance of political discussion, or attempt to rebel against the new state of things, or desire to interfere with the new rights of the Negroes." They talked only rice. "I never heard it suggested to prevent the Negroes voting but only to get rid of them and get reliable labor in their place. The war was over, the Negroes free to vote."[7]

This attitude was in part the result of recent military defeat, moral letdown, and the feeling that each man should save himself. Some of these same men may later have entered political life. A "South Carolinian," however, writing in the *Atlantic Monthly* in 1877, said that Southern businessmen have never had much to do with politics, considering it unfitted for practical men, and leaving it to "fiery and oratorical aristocrats." Criticizing this attitude, George Washington Cable, writing about 1885, said that we could not accede to commercial advisers and let politics alone, leaving merely to time the settlement of so basic a question as racial disagreement; time alone would settle it in blood.

The South, of course, did not leave the question alone, but tried to settle it by political action. We do know, however, how sick of politics many white Southerners were by 1890. This is suggested by the satisfaction with which they greeted the new state constitutions and statutes designed to disfranchise the Negro: now they would not have to steal votes any more. With the exception of a few individuals, they simply disregarded the fact that the constitutions and statutes were the biggest steals of all.

Now, with the Democratic primary rendering the Negro's vote ineffective, together with the moral weariness resulting from long participation in such a "dirty" game, many Southerners withdrew any real concern from the political field. They went to the rallies, of course, and shouted for the speakers, and voted; but for most of the time they left politics to the politicians. These, more than ever before, became a special class, separated from the deep, disturbed heart of the South, mere dealers in words. Now, more than ever before, the danger inherent in a mannered culture became apparent. Words and gestures may reveal to the public eye the essential man; but if the social structure weakens or gives way as it did in the South, they may reveal nothing but themselves. In politics they may become sheer demagoguery, as too often they have in the South.

But why did the decent white people of the South—of whom there were many in spite of social disaster—permit the demagogues? In part they were outvoted; in part they belonged to the total social and racial system that created the demagogues; and in part, as Howard Odum says, they were simply disinclined to interfere. "Many professional and business men and women," says Odum, "as well as many special groups, appeared to feel that too much energy and trouble were required to interfere with the prevailing mode. It was, they felt, easier to go along without 'hurting people's feelings.' "[8]

So the majority of the whites, many of them poverty-stricken, were led to believe that they were fine brave fellows together. The Negro was something else again, and life consisted solely in the whites sticking together against the Negroes. It is remarkable that any concern was left for the Negro or any concern on the part of the Negro for the white. The fact that there was, and is, suggests the comprehensiveness and resiliency of the Southern character. Though the white Southerner cheered his politicians, he did not believe all he heard. It was a good show, and in his frustrated life, he relished it. To some degree, unhappily, he acted upon the racially inflammatory words; harsh lives flowered in violence; but, more than is generally realized, the white and the Negro returned to their daily lives to live with considerable decency like neighbors together.

CHAPTER 25

BITTER FRUIT OF DIVISION

With the South thus divided—past from future, the region from the world, whites from Negroes—and with the whites held together only superficially in a "solid" political South, we naturally hear increasingly a tone of extremism and bitterness that is the very opposite of the moderation of the early South. Let us examine this bitterness and violence and relate it to that early moderation. We shall consider first the situation among the whites.

It must be admitted that the South has always been in a sense immoderate. It maintained slavery, an immoderate stand in an increasingly democratic world; and it was led finally to an immoderate defense of slavery in a disastrous civil war.

The fact remains, however, that the Southerner, with his realistic acceptance of the complexities of time and space and of a community deeply founded in time and space, was basically a moderate. He may still be. For a long time, however, he has given the impression of being an extremist. It is probable that the basic extremism, the basic error, of slavery led him finally into the extreme attitudes of the past century.

This extremism, however, this undue attention to the part, whether of time, or space, or a single race within a biracial society, has resulted in part from the breakdown of that large and proper concern with the whole that marked the earlier society of the South. With the collapse of the whole, men did not generally change their entire attitude and become rank individualists; they merely transferred to whatever parts remained a devotion more befitting the whole. As we have seen, the slave-based Southern way of life had become even before the Civil War a matter of religious faith. Such fragments of this life as were left by the war and Reconstruction commanded an even greater, a fanatical devotion. The white Southerner has loved not wisely but too well. His expression of this love has confused him still further. For, in spite of the selfish interests and prejudices that in part motivate his actions, he can always tell himself with some truth that he is working for a cause greater than himself—his race, his land, his time, especially that golden time that is lost and must therefore be cherished so that it may not be lost forever.

This tendency to extremism has also been strengthened, as we have suggested, by the long-continued poverty of the South and the accompanying bitterness. Admitted that the poverty was in part the result of a stubborn refusal to compromise, to come to terms with the new order, its long duration strengthened the bitter resentment. For even the poorest of Southern whites was never in any sense a peasant. He had no feeling of a human lot and a plot of land handed down from father to son through the centuries. He was drawn by the geographical frontier, he was adrift on "the frontier the Yankees made." Though he was more inclined than his Northern counterpart to accept custom and the changeless life, he was for the most part a struggling man, trying both to keep his head above water and also to find if possible some solid ground on which to stand. If he gave up, it was with bitterness against the land and the world that had defeated him, not in calm acceptance of the impossibility of success.

Yet even among these immoderate, bitter, and violent people, there often remained a quality of acceptance, of relaxation, of languor perhaps, which related them to the more acceptive South of the past. The languor may have been due in part to poor and insufficient diet, a mark of their poverty. But the easy, relaxed acceptance was the mark of a man who, in spite of defeat and hardship, still felt himself in some degree at home in his community. It never has taken much to make a Southerner feel at home in the world. One of his basic assumptions is that he is, and he tends to be faintly surprised and angry when he learns at times that he is not. This is a part of his agreeableness; he expects you to agree with him. If he finds that you do not, he is apt to turn quickly to violence and try to ram agreement down your throat. Having always lived in a closely knit society, or at least retaining the faint memory of such a society, he has little experience of agreeing to disagree.

This suggests that the violence of the South is by no means solely the result of the bitter defeats and frustrations of the last hundred years. The basic causes of violence itself have always been here. We can summarize them briefly. First, the violence of the land itself, the electric atmosphere, the sultry heat of summer exploding into tornadic wind- and thunderstorms. Second, the violence of slavery, a violence largely hidden but there, the mailed fist within the gloved hand. Third, the long continuance in the South of the frontier, by definition relatively lawless, and the renewed frontier of the post-Civil War period.

Fourth—but this is more complex—the feudalistic structure of the South and the attitudes engendered by it. Whatever feudal qualities existed in the South were faint reminiscences of medieval feudalism; that had evolved mainly as a means of physical, even military, defense, and violence was of its essence. But more important than this direct tie with violence was an indirect tie. As we have noted, the Southerner is not as much of an activist as the non-Southerner; he lays relatively more stress on being, less on doing. But his being, his identity, depends upon his place, his status. Who he is depends upon where he stands. In a highly activistic society, a man's being is closely related to what he has done, and therefore any challenge to his being is less close and intimate than in a more contemplative society, where a challenge is apt to be a challenge of the man himself, a challenge, as the South would say, to his honor. To such a challenge an immediate and violent response seemed appropriate. The law could protect a man's goods, only the man himself could defend his honor.

Now, if there was something in the very structure of the South that predisposed men to violence, the collapse of this structure would increase this disposition. For since a man got his identity from his place in the structure, the collapse of the structure would make all men unsure of their identity; and since he had been accustomed at need to defend violently any attack against his inner self, his honor, now, in the new chaotic world, he might have to defend his uncertain self at any moment.

It is his long experience in a social order by which he both defined and limited himself that has caused the Southerner since the general collapse of 1865 to defend fanatically any fragment of this order. For in defending such a fragment—the past, the land itself, the white race—the Southerner has been defending himself, his very identity. The more fragmented the order he defends, the more desperate the defense and the nearer to violence.

One of the chief fragments was the church. The church itself was highly fragmented, the most typical and numerous of these fragments being the Baptist, with its almost complete local autonomy. Though members of individual churches and so-called fringe sects did not defend their churches and sects with actual violence, they often defended them in the spirit of violence, casting into outer darkness all who were not of their particular faith. It is only fair to say that these people were generally aware of the overarching mystery of life and of its inexplicable grief. Yet what they emphasized was a set of moralisms having to do primarily with man's private life. The public world might go to ruin; here on this little island they would find safety. Granted the real neighborliness that was expressed and cherished, granted the periods of joy during which salvation shone briefly among them, it was a hard and narrow religion, cut off from the world, more filled with fear of hell than hope of heaven.

And being in its inner spirit as violent as it was, it could do little to restrain the actual violence that appeared so frequently in the surrounding world; for instance, the violence, the extremism of the racial conflict. This brings us to a consideration of the effect upon the Negro of the widening gap between the races caused by the South's defeat.

The presence of the enslaved Negro was probably the basic factor that divided the South within itself and split it off from the nation. The vague realization of this fact was probably part of the Southern postwar desire to send the Negro back to Africa—or anywhere. The dominant white desire, however, was more realistic: to segregate the Negro, to keep him in a sense by himself and in his place. If he could no longer be distinguished as a slave, he could be distinguished as a peasant or peon. Though peon is theoretically closer to free citizen than slave is, actually the freed Negro was farther from the whites than the slave had been. Basic cause of all the divisions, he was now made to feel more than ever his separation from the rest of society. That this separation probably resulted in less bitterness than that created among the whites is due to several causes.

In the first place, though the poverty and physical hardship of the Negro was greater than that of all except the poorest whites, he was less imbued with the American ideal of success, and therefore less embittered by his long failure to attain it. Again, he had less emotional and no financial interest in the ante-bellum order, and less concern, therefore, to lavish upon a particular fragment of that order. In fact, except for his churches, he had had no desire for or hand in accomplishing this particular fragmentation of the South into two separate races. He certainly did not desire segregation. Furthermore, he was clearly aware, both from emancipation and the political events of Reconstruction, that he was of some importance to the nation itself; this awareness has helped to sustain him during the lean years and has stimulated his efforts during recent decades. There was a great community, immortalized in Mr. Lincoln, to which somehow he belonged. This realization lessened the bitterness he might have felt in his hard, unjust situation. At least his leaders knew that, despite all evidence, he was on the make; the great charters of the Declaration of Independence and the Constitution would finally include him. The Emancipation Proclamation would not be at last in vain.

That violence became a red thread in the narrow segregated pattern of Negro life was to be expected. The whites, who largely controlled matters, were violent among themselves and toward Negroes. The Negroes, finding it mortally dangerous to express violence toward whites, turned against themselves the anger created by hardship and by the insolence of the whites and outdid even the whites in violence. But I suspect that their violence was a simpler thing, a matter often of impulse and but little involved with that sense of identity, the loss of which has so often driven the white Southerner to violence. It is true that the Negro, who was, like the white, a member of a relatively nonactivist society, also tended to find his identity in his place; but his place had been for so long such a poor and unchanging one that he could take little or no pride in it. He was, therefore, forced to turn to God and find a place in heaven. There no one could attack him. Here on earth men might step on his toes or crush him to the wall, but they could not touch him in his identity.

I overstate the case. There has always been more than impulse in the violence of the Negro. It has been in part, like that of the white, a frantic attempt to discover his identity. For the essential insolence of the white consisted just in this: that he denied identity to the Negro. Racial identity, yes; personal identity, no. Every Negro man or woman was seen first as a Negro man or woman. By and large, the person simply was overlooked. Segregation was a curtain—cotton, perhaps—whose essential function was to veil from the white the person of the Negro, leaving only the race visible. That it did not completely succeed was due to the complexity of interracial relationships in the South.

Now, if one's race or group has been historically important, and if, in addition, one is aware of this importance, one may find considerable satisfaction just in racial or group identity. But to expect the Negro in America, at, say, the close of the nineteenth century, disadvantaged and ignorant as he was, to find such satisfaction is to expect the impossible. It is only recently, and among extremist groups like the Black Muslims, that he has made a definite attempt to use his segregated status to strengthen his racial identity. And it should be noted that among the Black Muslims, the intention is to channel individual violence into group violence if violence should be considered necessary.

But this is a contemporary and doubtful remedy. Historically, there was but one essential way for the Negro to prevent the accumulation of bitterness that would naturally result from the ill treatment and the insolence he received from the white. That was religion. For his religion, as I have said, assured him of a place outside the judgment of men; and only this assurance has made it possible for him to be as involved in violence as he has with relatively so little bitterness.

I know this makes religion sound like the opiate of the masses. Maybe. But there is a time to be patient. Suppose the present revolution in race relations had been set off fifty years ago. What good would it have done? Who beyond the Negroes would have supported it? Only destruction would have resulted. What was wiser then than to learn patience? As we shall see later, this long discipline is now paying off, and creative action, remarkably lacking in bitterness, is taking place.

I am not saying that all Negroes have made this use of their religion; nor that they have had no sense of place here and of identification through place. There have always been strong class feelings among Negroes, even during slavery. I am only saying that the Southern Negro has a deeper assurance than the Southern white of a place beyond the reach of men, and that consequently the violence he falls into is less involved than the violence of the white, who is acting out of that complex notion of defending one's inner self, one's identity.

In brief, the old Southern community meant far less to the Negro than it did to the white, and when it fell apart he was but slightly tempted to worship the fragments, especially since he saw beyond the South the larger world of the nation looming on the horizon. Unlike the white Southerner, he could accept this world wholeheartedly: he was no states'-righter who had to be brought back into the Union.

Never having been troubled seriously by the divisory Puritan conscience, never having had to hate the world because he publicly misused it in exploiting an entire race, the Negro possessed a freedom unknown to the white to absorb the more positive values of Southern life, to carry them with a remarkable degree of perseverance through the collapse of the Southern order, and to hold them for the time when he should be able to speak with authority. We stand now on the verge of that time.

PART III

Its Present Possibility

CHAPTER 26

SPATIAL FAULT

The last twenty years. Since the beginning of World War II the South has stepped out of a long period of uneasy somnolence into a world of revolutionary change. Though this change has widened some of the gaps, there is a happy possibility that this is fairly temporary and that the final result will be a healing of the breaches within the South and between the South and the nation. First, then, let us look at the spatial fault, mainly as it appears in the mind of the white Southerner. This is that flaw which for more than a century now has led the Southerner to overvalue the local at the expense of the national.

Together with this movement toward a more deeply and truly united Southern mind there will go, naturally, a lessening of intensity and a return toward the more moderate mind of the early South. As the Southerner discovers a larger whole upon which to lavish his concern, that concern will grow less intense.

For the present, however, the intensity seems greater than at any other time within this century. Since 1954 the general image produced by the South is of a horseman mounting and riding off furiously in all directions at once; a sort of Paul Revere without a message. Never within my lifetime has the

Southerner been more Southern: never more declamatory, never more in the camera's eye, never, apparently, more determined to resist. Where beyond the South can you match Faubus and Barnett and Wallace? Faubus of Arkansas, first of the recent demagogues, Barnett of Mississippi, center of the fiasco at Oxford, and Wallace of Alabama, standing in the schoolhouse door at Tuscaloosa facing the might of the federal government. Southerners all. But what a Southerner is, and what he is supposed to do besides resist, nobody knows. We do know that when he acts it will be in part for the effect—the grandiloquent words, the noble gesture, the limelight. How much he really believes what he says, God knows. Certainly our Southerner doesn't.

This burst of Southernness began during the racial tensions of World War II. It was aggravated by the appointment of the President's Fair Employment Practices Commission, which was supposed to place Negro stenographers in all Southern business offices. It was carried a step further by the Report of President Truman's Civil Rights Commission, in 1947, a report that spoke out clearly against segregation. Then, like tinder, it responded to the match of the Supreme Court school decisions of May 17, 1954, and May 31, 1955. Between these two dates there appeared the white citizens councils, whose chief job has been to build bonfires and dance around them. Nor have things been helped by the Civil War commemorations, in progress since 1961. These are for the most part but remembered bonfires and what they whisper to our hearts while saying nothing to our heads is "Resist, resist."

The apparent effect of all this has been to widen the gap between the South and the rest of the nation, the gap that caused the Civil War, separated the South from the nation during that war, and has kept it in a twilight zone for a hundred years. But, as we have pointed out so often, you must look beneath the surface if you wish to see what is really happening in the South. The South is a great land for words. Indeed, a land of great words. Unfortunately, people who study how to use words in order to facilitate human relations, may under temptation use them to confuse and disrupt the opposition—and, unintentionally, to confuse themselves.

If we disregard, therefore, the shrill cries of the councils and the antic poses of certain governors, we shall see in operation several forces that are closing the gap between the South and the rest of the world, especially the rest of the Union; closing what I have called the spatial flaw. There is first the growing nationalism of Americans resulting from two world wars and the Korean conflict. As the nation needs its citizens more, and as they need a strong nation more, they find within it the lodestar of their interest, and the sense of nationalism is deepened. We have recalled how "Fighting Joe Wheeler," though he still carried in his mind the image of the Yankee as enemy, was actually leading a charge against the Spaniards. And I remember that when I entered the army in 1917 almost directly from Massachusetts (where I had been in school, and where, absent for the first time from the South, I had realized intensely my Southern identity) I did not enter as a South Carolinian or a Southerner; I entered as an American. The Southern difference that I had felt so nostalgically in Worcester was now submerged beneath my American identity.

In the second place, the spatial fault is being healed by the growing industrialization and urbanization of the South. This force has been in operation since the inception of the New South in the 1880's, but only during the last twenty years has it been producing revolutionary changes. Finding itself more industrial, the South begins to ask for tariff protection; the cotton mills of South Carolina want protection from imports —in this case, Japanese—as much as the mills of New England ever did. As the productive life of the South becomes more mechanized and industrialized, and incidentally urban, it becomes more national; and Southerners, increasingly dependent upon this mode of life, become increasingly national themselves.

As a part of this increasing industrialization, there is the growing number of national businesses with branch offices or even with main offices in the South. There are more than three thousand such in the city of Atlanta alone; and in the lobby of, say, the Piedmont Hotel there, at ten o'clock of a weekday morning, it's a safe bet that a fair proportion of the strangers passing by are only two hours out of New York by jet. There is vastly more business in the South than ever before, vastly more national business, and the business code is beginning to shoulder aside the old Southern codes of the leisured manner and the absolute commitment. In Atlanta, now, men transact business at lunch—*"O tempora, O mores!"* Even the Southern Regional Council, champion of the best in the South, sometimes does this! As for the absolute commitment, fewer and fewer Southerners cheer Wallace as he draws a line in the sand in front of the schoolhouse door, spits in it, and says to the approaching federal marshal, "Thus far shalt thou come and no farther." Quietly they turn aside from the show, and ask themselves, How much will the traffic bear? What will it cost?

Well, for one thing, it is apt to cost millions in federal appropriations, especially for military bases in Southern states. And this possible cost, and the desire to avoid it, and to gain the federal dollars, is another reason why within recent years the spatial flaw between the South and the nation is being healed. Mississippi has a law demanding segregated hospital facilities. Several years ago, because of this, a federal appropriation of eleven million dollars for a veterans' hospital there was held up; Mississippians temporarily forgot their commitment to segregation, and the eleven million came in.

I don't mean to make fun of Southern commitment. It's one of the finest qualities we have. Like courage, it is valuable in itself. We hope that a man will commit himself in a good cause and be courageous in a just fight. But first of all, we ask for courage—one of the pagan virtues—and for the ability to lay everything on the line. In the last analysis, we are all gamblers, living by a leap of faith. We have to leap. Only, I wish we would look a little more closely before we do. Wallace does not really know what he is defending by his little line in the dust. Nor what chances there are of success. When a man commits himself regardless of the cost, he usually does so in the belief that, though the present world may be against him, the order of the universe is in his favor, and will someday bring his efforts to a successful conclusion. The segregationist does not believe this; he is fighting a holding battle; fifteen or twenty years is his limit. He is not really going anywhere at all. He is inclined to admit this in private; but when he starts drawing lines in the dust it is something else again.

It was this commitment to the hilt in the Civil War that cost the South disaster; I daresay if it could have foreseen the cost, it would not have made the commitment. But most of the time since, the South has been too poor to bother much about cost. It had nothing, it could lose nothing. Why not get the shot-in-the-arm effect of commitment to any cause whatever? But now, with millions at stake, rash commitment—or maybe any commitment—becomes expensive. In brief, the better the business of the South, the more will the Southerner insist upon better business. If some force is not interposed to stop this trend, we shall become at last run-of-the-mill Americans, with too much know-how for the know-what. We shall see later whether any such force exists.

As for the nationalizing effect of military bases in the

South, it is hard for a Southerner to resist this appeal. Historically, he's a fighter anyhow, and nothing could please him more than the spending of vast sums of national money within his borders on military projects. It has even been suggested by some of the wild segregationists that we could now seize these installations and challenge the national government. Sumter fell. Why not Jackson, Benning, Bragg, etc., etc.? Such people, like true religious devotees, believe because it is impossible. Believe, that is, enough to talk about it. Not to do anything of course. The South has yet to learn certain basic lessons of the Civil War. She did learn, however, that it is not possible now for a state to secede.

The South has also been drawn into national circles and the South-Union fault lessened by the success of the Democratic party, for a hundred years now the Southern party, though always with some national support. Beginning especially with the administration of Woodrow Wilson, and increasing tremendously since Franklin Roosevelt's election in 1932, this party, with its largely Southern control of chairmanships in Congress, but with powerful backing especially in the urban areas of the nation at large, has permitted the South to exert tremendous, perhaps undue influence, in the national government. And now the South has Lyndon Johnson. The possession and exercise of this power have given the South a clear stake in the nation and have helped to close the fault between the South and the nation.

But beyond the nationalizing influence of industry, of business, of political power, there is another influence, more subtle and generally unrecognized. This is the deep and largely unconscious desire of the Southerner to be an American. A hundred and fifty years ago he was inclined to think of himself as *The* American, possessor and defender of the true faith. But as the federal Union grew away from him, he tried to leave it, and was whipped back into it. Worse than this. Whipped back into a nation now, no longer merely a federal Union, but far more un-Southern than the Union from which he had felt constrained to withdraw. He returned, therefore, with sadly mixed emotions: guilty because he had defended slavery, which, after its destruction he felt no real need or desire to defend, guilty also because he among Americans was the only one who had failed; but still hopeful that he would be received back into that national fellowship which long before he had felt so strongly. And not merely that he might get something from the Union, but that he might contribute his share to it. In recent years, some Southerners have said—too shrilly—that they care nothing for the Union, they want only to be left alone. Do not believe it. This is the cry of men who deeply want to be considered. Faulkner said of the Mississippians that they feel lonely and isolated from the world. Increase this feeling enough, and such people, making a virtue of what they consider a necessity, will exclaim that they have no wish to belong to the world. They thus deny their deepest desires.

It must be remembered that, for a long time now, with one general exception the South has had little opportunity to contribute anything of its own to the nation. The exception is the literary renascence of the past generation. Through William Faulkner, Robert Penn Warren, Eudora Welty, John Crowe Ransom, Allen Tate, Cleanth Brooks, and others, the South has created and interpreted a rich and vital world. This would do much to assuage the hurt of the Southerner if only he knew it had happened. But the South has never had a creative literary tradition; it is only now doing what New England did a century ago. Literature generally has been sentimental romance. So that now, when creative writers begin to reveal the heart of the South, the average Southerner, if he hears of it, is apt to feel that such revelations, tawdry or tragic, are a reflection upon the region and therefore should not be approved. Though undoubtedly these writers can help the South to understand its place in the nation and the world, the Southerner himself will have to bring to the writings a more disturbed, acceptive mind than he now has. The disturbance has begun. How much acceptance as yet, we don't know.

To turn from art back to that favorite Southern sport, politics, the South's inability to send a Southerner to the White House for a century is the most glaring illustration of its failure to contribute to the life of the nation. It is not difficult to understand why a Southerner has not been elected president since the Civil War; but this does not assuage the hurt represented by the fact. One of the basic things any self-conscious region wants is to make its contribution to the larger whole. The South has an intense sense of identity; it would like to contribute of itself to the life of the nation. For over a hundred years now it has been unable to offer anything of its own that the nation has been willing to accept.

Except of course its fighting fury, contributed freely in the world wars and in Korea. Interestingly, the South was more enthusiastic about the Second World War than the First. Perhaps the twenty-five intervening years had brought it closer to the nation. Anyhow, such total commitment was what the South had long been trained for. It was most happy when fighting; it didn't have to think about its problems. Southerners were now proving their American character.

Now that Lyndon Johnson, a Southerner—a Texas Southerner—has by a tragic turn of fate become President, the South will have the chance of voting for him for a second term. Undoubtedly his origin will bring him many Southern votes, and if he is elected, the South will have some pride in having one of its own in the White House again. However, it should be recognized that the sense of isolation and national unimportance is felt most keenly in the Deep South, which has been most isolated by history, and Lyndon Johnson, though a Southerner, may arouse in many Southerners the feeling that in his liberalism he has betrayed the South. In their view, his election would put a Southerner in the White House, but not a true Southerner, not one of the old breed.

Within recent years, certain Southerners have upon occasion traveled North and tried to persuade the Northerner to accept that aspect of the Southern way of life crystallized in segregation. Doubtless the motivation of such trips has been the desire to strengthen the position of the South by persuading the non-South to legitimize this Southern practice. Of course, there are segregationists all across the American scene; no one would deny this. But it's bootleg stuff; under the counter. There's no more chance of selling it over the counter in 1964 than there was of selling slavery in 1864.

The fact that Southerners should try suggests how lost they are, how cut off, how deeply concerned to close somehow the gap that separates them from the nation. This concern is but one of the forces that, against diminishing obstacles, are making the South again at home in the nation.

CHAPTER 27

TEMPORAL FAULT

As for the present condition of that temporal fault that cuts across the life of the South, we have a more complex matter. For time is more complex than space. Space runs outward physically from where the observer stands; there are physical roads that lead through it, physical landmarks along these roads. The world of time, on the contrary, is a world of the mind; physically, we exist only on the razor's edge of the present. Our hopes assure us of a future; our memories of a past. But only imagination or memory can take us into that future or that past.

In the early days of the South, as we have said before, past and future were woven together into a rich present: the Southerner moved out of the past into the future, seeking not a radically new world but simply a better, larger world. We have seen the crack caused in this world by slavery as it intensified both the future and the past, and, in place of a creative tension within time, set up a deadly conflict. The modern democratic spirit warred against the medieval. This conflict eventuated in the Civil War; and, as a result of that war and its aftermath, a gulf opened in the mind of the white Southerner between past and future. Is this gulf being closed?

In general, yes. But very slowly, incompletely, and in a

sense mechanically. The mere passage of time, the succession of the generations, and the greatly improved standard of living have together drawn off from the mind of the white Southerner much of the bitterness that, eighty-odd years ago, made him imagine, as a balance to that bitterness, the golden world of the ante-bellum plantation. But now, the greater the number of split-level suburban homes, the less need to recall—or imagine—the columned mansions. As better homes and jobs become available, we are too much concerned with obtaining them to recall a lost past.

The trouble with this attitude is that the past is never as lost as situations like this suggest. The great plantation houses are mostly gone, the plantations with them, but underneath the surface of our lives there exist attitudes, interests, and motivations that began and took form in that lost world. Some of these may be good, some bad, but their presence alters what we do today, both our actions and our responses; and our ignorance of them lets us slip into situations in which, regardless of our material success, we cannot be happy.

What I am saying is that we forget the past consciously a long time before we really forget it. Also, it seems to me regrettable that people should simply let slip from their memories as great and creative a past as the South has had. I must admit that this easy forgetfulness belongs to the American Way. Having had such diverse histories, Americans incline to overlook them all and find their unity in the future, in the American Dream. Though this may be a source of our strength, it is also, as I have suggested earlier, a source of our weakness. It makes us overidealistic, shallow, uncertain of ourselves. Like adolescents, we swing quickly from confidence to despair. In our ever-upward-and-onward American course, we have forgotten the failures and tragedies that have always dogged the footsteps of men, even our own in our European setting. We therefore lack that stability which the recognition of such tragedy would bring.

Now, the South—at least, the white South—being more homogeneous and conservative than the rest of the nation, has never been inclined to forget its past. Herein has lain its strength. If it begins to forget now, however, it not only denies a basic characteristic, but also exhibits a failure greater than that of the typical ahistorical American. For the Southerner has experienced here, on this soil, tragic reversals of fortune and the continuing hardship of life. Therefore, he doesn't have the excuse for forgetting the past that other Americans have—the three thousand miles of ocean lying between them and the Old Country, between them and the numerous Old Countries from which they came. Southerners have been defeated here, and, if they cannot remember creatively their history, it is solely because they are not men enough to understand it; which is to say, to see it all hanging together, its successes and its failures, its exploiters and its exploited, its two so different races so closely intertwined. It has been suggested that W. J. Cash, author of the excellent *The Mind of the South,* took his own life because he could not bear to contemplate the paradoxes and contradictions he had uncovered. I hope that the time will come, and that before long, when Southerners in general will be able to contemplate their past, and know it, and be able to realize within the conflict, partly because of the conflict, a creative spirit—a spirit of the whole, the spirit of Southern culture itself—moving to resolve the conflict and make of the South what it dreamed, though brokenly, of becoming.

As of now, however, we tend either to forget the past or cling unwittingly to it. We tend to forget the ante-bellum past; most of us cling unwittingly to the immediate post-bellum past. The myth of the plantation house is fading; the succeeding myth, "the Negro in his place," still has widespread appeal, especially in the Deep South. How the Negro can remain "in his place" in a highly competitive, mobile industrial society, has not really been asked. He was the key man in our agricultural past; we are reluctant to face the fact that he is an important man in our industrial future. Governor Terry Sanford, of North Carolina, was the first Southern governor to face clearly, in 1963, this fact. He brought the Negro up to date in the thinking of North Carolinians by recognizing that the industrial future of the state depended in part upon the industrial future of North Carolina Negroes. This idea lies just below the surface in much of the South, but nowhere else has it received clear statement by a political leader.

The white Southerner generally is still separated from the Negro by what in a sense is a temporal gap. The Negro he sees is not the Negro of today but that mythical figure that arose out of the turmoil of Reconstruction and Redemption. The Negro still appears before the white as in a frozen moment of the South's history. He is the most evident present embodiment of that history. This is doubtless one of the reasons why the white South is so disturbed by the Negro's getting out of his place. (Only one, of course. A most important reason is the economic.) A region that has attributed so much importance to the past necessarily fears, in a rapidly changing time like the present, the loss of that past. So long as the Negro is unchanged, something of the past is unchanged.

It is in part simply this fear of a rapidly changing South that has brought forth in recent years the flurry of Confederate flags, and, the centennial of the Civil War coming just at this time, the fireworks of memorial actions. The golden legend of the South took compelling form during the years when the South was first striving to bring in a "foreign" force—an industrial order, which, inevitably, would supplant the old plantation order. The refurbishing of this golden legend is occurring now during the years in which the South is driving toward a total acceptance of this industrial order. The more we change, the more we try not to change. The stranger the world of today, the more appealing the world of yesterday.

But it's a nostalgic appeal. A kind of homesickness. The sentiment of an immature people, who, absent from home for whatever reason—fate? their own desire?—have not yet discovered in their present the world they remember from, or imagine in, their past. The South is still a long way from home. It cannot go back to the old place. But neither can it create a new place for itself until it sees in a truer and more creative light its own past, until it understands the home it has lost.

It tends to see its past, especially its ante-bellum past, in a heroic, not a tragic, light. The feudal aspect of the ante-bellum South, together with the feudal myth, encourages this view. This is the South of romance, of ladies and gentlemen, of the "chivalry," as some of them called themselves. This is the heroic South that fell before overwhelming forces. Its fall is symbolized by the fading blast from Roland's horn in the woods at Roncevaux.

But what has this to do with us today? Especially, how can this interpretation of the past bring the Negro into the life of the South today? He is here, but, in a view like this, here by force, not by the fact that he belongs here.

The tragic view, on the contrary, shows Southern whites and Negroes as opposed, intermingled, and cooperating from the beginning: bound together in good and evil, each the cause of the other's woes and joys. Largely because of the Negro's presence, the white Southerner has come to differ from other Americans, has engaged with them in violent conflict, and has been defeated and overrun. By this defeat the Negroes were nominally freed, but actually remained for another century the most exploited group in a region itself nationally exploited. Only the tragic view does justice to the greatness of endeavor, of defeat, of failure, and to the awful complexity of human life revealed by the history of the South.

So far, however, the white South has been unable to accept this tragic view. To accept, and forgive, what history has done to it. For this is to accept its own flawed nature and the flawed nature of its heroes. This is to deny that our history was merely romantic or heroic.

And yet the South has in its experience the making of the tragic view. Vann Woodward is touching upon this when he points out that Southern history has created the Southerner: he alone, of all his fellow countrymen, has suffered military defeat, regional poverty, and a conscience never really free from guilt because of his treatment of the Negro. Largely because of these defeats and burdens, the Southerner—and, excluding the matter of general guilt, the Negro Southerner, too—has a deep sense of the flaws and contradictions of life. He has always feared abstractions. He probably felt uneasy about them from the beginning; under the economic and moral pressure of the North he came actively to fear them. The abstract plans for the future, the blueprint, may be perfect on paper. He can see this, but he has learned the hard way that the best-laid plans "gang aft a-gley." He still has much of the drive of the American pioneer. Indeed, in his rapidly expanding economy, this drive may at times be stronger than in the rest of the country, in which great economic achievement has been more common. Yet there is usually the afterthought of the uncertainty of any future, and, indeed, a question of the simple goodness of pure economic achievement. Maybe it is true that "life is more to be enjoyed than to be used." His hesitancy is also moral because of his long experience with the Negro: with his attempts to justify the system; to live with the wrong; to find, or create, some goodness within the structure. Granted that this led him into duplicity; it also led him into an understanding, deeper than he is aware of, of the terrible complexity of life, of the impossibility of final judgment, of the necessity of accepting the imperfections within ourselves and the world, and yet of holding on to some light in the darkness.

But this, you say, doesn't sound like the Southerner. True. This is almost the exact opposite of the mythical Southerner: stubborn, brash, extreme, devil-may-care. And indeed, perhaps a majority of white Southerners accept this national opinion of themselves. Even their own newspapers play it up. This mythical Southerner is the newsman's best friend; he is always doing something worthy of front-page headlines. The persuasive, hesitant, complex Southerner makes no headlines, makes no news.

I have already spoken of the extreme Southerner and pointed out that he is the product of a basic Southern interest in public life combined with long-continued disaster that drove him toward extremism. He is not, in my opinion, central in the South; on the contrary, he stands near the outskirts. To some degree, of course, he is a pole, which balances the opposing pole of the moderate. Harsh circumstances helped to create both; the one became belligerent and exclusive, the other conciliatory and inclusive.

But, as I have said, the South is easy to attack and hard to defend. In the democratic atmosphere of much of the modern world, it has maintained such impossible racial structures and backed such impossible public figures that no one needs to know anything else about it to justify a full-scale attack upon it. Yet this is not all of the South; indeed, this is not, I think, the heart of the South. But how understand, and present, and defend that quiet, more inclusive heart?

It seems to me ironic that the South, which always stressed

the importance of public life, should have created and maintained a public life so easily subject to harsh criticism. We should have done better where we tried so hard. Perhaps we tried too hard. Perhaps our temper and the nineteenth-century world tempted us to try too hard. We tried to resolve all our problems in public. Did not politics comprise the total destiny of man? We disregarded the moral and private underpinning of public life. We quarreled too much in the forum, too little with ourselves and with God in our closets. But it must be admitted that we faced in the abolitionist an opponent who had in the past done some quarreling with God and who had come out of it deeply assured that he and God were together and that together they would sweep us from the field. This desperate situation put us in the field, but, though we also dragged God with us—as men always do—we weren't quite so sure of His presence as were his long-time associates, the Puritan abolitionists.

If this leaves American history mixed up, that's where it is. Which side was God on? Which side was right on? Both, of course. Did the right side win? The side won that in the democratic and industrial atmosphere of the nineteenth century had to win. But the extremes of corruption that entered American life when, following the defeat of the South, the new industrialism came to unrestrained power, certainly gives point to a common Southern comment of that time: This is what we were fighting against.

So much for the irony of our public life. We return to our point that the character of the Southerner is to an unusual degree moderate and malleable, but emphasize the point that he does not really see himself in this light, and certainly does not understand how historically he developed like this. He may think of himself as a conservative; but about as far as he gets with this self-image is that he is opposed—he thinks—to the radicalisms of great cities and especially of the national government in Washington. Inclined to move more slowly, more hesitantly, more doubtfully, and, finally, more understandingly, he does not see this ability as his most important characteristic or realize that this sense of life's tragic complexity marks his essential quality as a Southerner.

In brief, he does not realize that his Southern nature is his human nature. He senses at times the feeling that he is different from other Americans; but this mainly makes him self-defensive and angry. If he could see himself as a human being, involved in life's painful complexity, and could realize that it is his life as a Southerner that has so involved him and so shaped him, he could accept his Southernness, not only without chauvinism but with gratitude.

We are the complex products of our tragic past, but we fail quite to make the connection. The past is something else, back there; the Negro, too, is something else, back in Reconstruction; and we are here, enormously attracted on the surface by the economic possibilities opening before us, but frightened in the depths because our past does not sweep us forward or because, in the person of the Negro, it sweeps us where we are afraid to go.

CHAPTER 28

CHURCH AND WORLD

Slavery and the loss of the Civil War split the church in the South widely from the world. Only recently has this gap begun to close. This is partly due to the fact that the church is one of the most conservative of institutions. All institutions tend to be conservative. Established to perform some function, with the passage of time they necessarily take on as part of their function the conservation and extension of themselves. This may become in time their sole function. The church is especially subject to this law because it represents the eternal in time. Since the eternal does not change, it is easy for the church to assume its own changelessness. It forgets that it is itself in time, and must change with time.

Within recent years the church in the South has been called "the last stronghold of segregation." Who is going to oppose segregation in the church? Those who are actively fighting segregation are for the most part Negroes. It is the Negro who suffers most from it in limited educational, economic, professional, and political opportunities. But the church was segregated by the Negro's own will, and he has made of his own church a powerful institution, in which all the positions of power are held by Negroes. Among the whites, only a handful of liberals is going to fight for the desegregation of the church. Most of the members are satisfied with the present situation. Since the Negro is exerting little pressure for church desegregation, the white feels only slight twinges of conscience in maintaining a segregated church. After all, what harm is being done? Religion being so much a matter of another world, what difference does such a custom make? We are all spiritual brothers, however separately we may worship.

The truth is, however, that, though the church may try to imply that religion is of another world, it is never able to make it so. According to Paul Tillich, religion exists wherever man is ultimately concerned, and such concern expresses itself in some way in all of man's activities. The church in the South has not been, as it has usually assumed, separate from the world. In larger social issues, it has been hand in glove with the world. Its members today are a large proportion of the citizenry, and wherever it has refused to criticize the world, it has lived by worldly standards. One of these standards has always been the playing down of racial conflict, and, because of this basic attitude, the playing down of all conflict, the insistence upon agreeableness, regardless of basic agreement. Or, rather, the assumption of basic agreement. Gentlemen are still crying, "Peace, peace," long after another Southerner, Patrick Henry, warned that there was no peace. Peace is the product of justice, the great prophets said, but who in the South could afford to read the great prophets? An interesting illustration of the acceptance by the church of the social standard of agreeableness appears in the sentiments expressed during the day of public prayer observed by many of the churches of Little Rock on October 12, 1957, shortly after the school-integration disturbances of that year. The general tenor of these prayers was, "O Lord, we whites and Negroes have been disagreeable to one another. Make us agreeable again." The church was seeking here the form of reconciliation. It was trying to save its manners without mending its morals. There was practically no admission of the prior need of reconciliation with God. It hadn't quarreled with God.

In conserving itself, therefore, the Southern church has been a prime force in conserving the manners and mores of society. With such an attitude, strongest within the white church but existing also within the Negro church, the Southern church is moving but slowly toward its proper goal, the healing of all division, and its attitude during the last twenty critical years has changed less from its earlier attitude than have the attitudes of other segments and groups. This attitude has been changing, however, both because of changing economic and political conditions and of a changing theological climate.

The growing industrialization and urbanization of the South bring social problems which, in the agricultural order, either did not arise or could be handled by the individual or the family. The church finds it increasingly necessary to engage in forms of social work. Some years ago a presbytery of the so-called Southern Presbyterian Church debated the question of recommending to the denomination that it withdraw from the National Council of Churches. It so recommended. Yet almost while this action was being discussed, one of the largest churches in that presbytery was using a staff member from the National Council to make a local survey to determine what that church should do about the social situation in the mill district of the city. The presbytery as a whole was defending the older theory; the individual church was coping with the new situation. This is rather like the South: do what you have to do, but be certain you put the right words on it. It's how you name a thing that really counts. The influence of the Negro may be at work here: words are magic.

As for the influence of changing political conditions, the influence of the Supreme Court decision of May 17, 1954, in the school cases is the most striking. Strictly speaking, the action of the Court was not political; yet, in the largest sense, it was. It came as the end of a series of legal decisions; and both they and it came when they did, not because the Constitution had been amended, but because the total national and international situation had changed. There was an increased sense of the worth of the average man instilled by the Depression, there was the growing economic and political power of the Negro, and there was the rising world conflict between democracy and communism, with the consequent need to defend democracy both abroad and at home. In the largest sense, therefore, the 1954 decision was a political decision. Actually, it makes no difference for our argument whether you call it political or legal; it was a situation outside the church that affected opinions within the church.

Partly as a result of this decision, the leading churches of the South have issued through their highest courts or assemblies statements supporting the decision, urging compliance, and expressing some stand—stronger here, weaker there—against segregation. It should be noted that the statement issued by the Presbyterian Church in the United States—the "Southern" church—though adopted after the decision, was actually written by its committee on social action before the decision. One should not make too much of this timing, however. The decision was impending and it seemed likely that it would be the kind of decision it was.

But the fact that the leading church bodies of the South have officially condemned segregation, and have tried therefore officially to close the gap between the races caused by segregation, and also to bring a generally other-worldly religion to grips with the social structures of this world does not mean that particular local churches have generally followed suit. Here and there a single church has, and the number continues to grow. But Protestantism, which is predominantly the religion of the South, is nonauthoritarian. Assemblies and conventions may advise but not require. Within the last ten years, the opposition by local churches to the standards set by the highest leadership of the church has been more evident than the compliance. For the most part the leadership has been ignored; here and there dramatic opposition has flared up. This has sometimes resulted in a local pastor's losing his job.

Though there are clergymen, especially in the groups that have poorly educated leaders, who accept generally the mores of the South, including segregation, apparently a majority of the preachers agree with the stands taken by their supervisory bodies. As a consequence, the gap between pulpit and pew has become marked in recent years. It must also be said that the pulpit has lost much of the influence that it had in the nineteenth century. For one thing, the preacher was once the educated man; now he is one among many, often less educated than some of his congregation. Therefore, when division occurs between pulpit and pew, the pulpit has less chance of riding down the opposition.

One of the favorite charges hurled against the pulpit during the years of the segregation controversy has been couched in questions like these: Who are you getting your instructions from, God or the Supreme Court? How is it that segregation is a sin now when it wasn't twenty years ago?

Such questions occur only to people whose nominal religion has been pretty effectively separated from their total life. This has been the situation in the South. There is the Bible, separate from the world. There is God, who spoke to men in times past, and whose words are preserved within the Bible. If the preacher is frank in countering this opposition, he has to say: "I hope I get my instructions from God, but they come to me by way not only of the Bible, but also of the Supreme Court, the local newspaper, presidential elections, and international conflicts. Segregation may have been as great a sin twenty years ago as it is now. I did not denounce it then, however, because I had not heard God's voice sufficiently clearly through these various earthly channels. Now I can hear that voice clearly enough to be bold in announcing it. Segregation is the sin of this generation, and woe be to him who refuses to grapple with the sin of his generation."

Such a frank statement probably wouldn't help that particular preacher, but it would be one step toward closing the gap between the church and the world, and toward making clear to men that the teachings of religion apply not merely to another world and to the preparation of individual souls for transport thither, but also and more importantly to this world, a world of living men and women, and to all the social structures they build in the hopes of living more happily together.

Finally, theological developments, it seems to me, are bringing the church closer to the total life of the world. The social-gospel movement that was influential outside the South around the turn of the century made little impact within the South. Today, with the increase of social problems in an urbanizing and industrializing region, the question of the pertinence of Chistian teachings to society at large is being increasingly raised. Yet this question is being raised in a theological climate that, in its neo-Calvinistic aspects, has put renewed emphasis upon sin and grace. Therefore, the church in the South, necessarily giving more concern to social problems, is yet restrained by its entire Southern history and by the emphasis of contemporary theology, from going overboard in the adoption of a shallow social gospel. The problem in the mind of the church in the South is still man, though it is now increasingly man involved in all his institutions. This, to use Paul Tillich's terms, is man involved in the structures of grace and the structures of sin.

The time is ripe, then, for Southern churchmen to consider the South and its problems in the light of Christian doctrine. It would certainly be one function of the church in the South to reveal to Southerners, white and Negro, how their historically gained sense of life's tragic complexity is a human sense, and how it fits those who have it for life in the world. Especially would it be one function of the church to interpret the tragedies of a region in the light of Christian doctrine. This is a part of the church's prophetic mission.

The church in the South has always pointed out the relation of individual tragedies of Christian faith. The key words? "In the darkness comes the light." There is a cross at the heart of life. Love suffers, and dies, and is born again. Love continually creates life.

The church in the South needs to apply this vision to the region itself, and teach men how the disappointments, the frustrations, the failures of a group are among the general means by which men are either destroyed or saved; how these common events, this structure of history, are means of grace or judgment.

The Negro has learned this lesson far better than the white man has. He realizes in his condition the essential human condition. The white man still feels that the American condition of success is the human condition, and that somehow he, in his lack of success, is incompletely human. Yet this very lack of success has taught him, at the best, moderation, the ability to live with incompleteness, amid imperfections, to love life however flawed it may be. The church, however, has not told him that this quality is a mark of his increased humanity, and that its presence is a mark of the grace of God.

The question arises here about the racial sins the white South has committed and, consequently, of the justice of its being defeated and thwarted. And now I suggest that out of this—judgment of God, you may call it—comes the grace of God? Exactly. Within God's judgment lies always the possibility of grace. It does not matter finally how and why a man is defeated. The important question is, what becomes of him then? Christianity speaks to defeated men; perhaps only to defeated men. "Come unto me all ye that labor and are heavy laden." The Negro in America was defeated and thwarted, unjustly. The white Southerner was defeated and thwarted, in the broad sense, justly. It does not matter now. Though defeat caused in some whites extremism and bitterness, it caused in others a deeper, more understanding attitude. Herein is God's grace revealed.

We should thank God for this, thank Him even for the defeats and the hardships, of which this is the best fruit. Thank Him for a past that makes possible this present and a greater future. We should not thank Him for the evil our fathers did, or that we still do, hoping that out of sin more grace will abound. We can thank Him, however, for the wonder of life, where judgment may turn to grace and where also, unhappily, grace may turn to judgment. We have this sense of life in the South; we have received it from history; but nobody tells us what it means.

The church, representing eternity, might reveal to us how in the present the regional past still exists, and how indeed the future lies all about us. It might reveal to us eternity within time, and help to restore that coherent sense of past and future which the South in its dawning possessed. It might interpret the culture of the South in terms of Christian doctrine, and not merely support, largely by inaction, the current regional absurdity.

CHAPTER 29

STONE THE BUILDERS REJECTED

It is now time to ask: What is the Negro doing to close these painful rifts? The reader may ask, incredulously, how the Negro, the cause of the divisions, could possibly be instrumental in closing them. There's a saying that the hair of the dog is good for the bite, meaning we may live by what we die by. In my opinion, this is the curious and complex paradox that is now taking form in the South. If this should occur, it would be the supreme paradox of a region noted for its paradoxes, and would be, at least in this sense, a most Southern event.

Let us notice first that the Negro, though the basic cause of division, was always far less conscious than the white of the divisions he caused. The reason for this is that, for the most part, he did not will these divisions either directly or indirectly. Except in the matter of his church, he did not directly will separation from the whites. As for the spatial and temporal conflicts that haunt the mind of the white South, and which have come into being because of the Negro's enforced presence as an exploited man, these either do not exist for the Negro or exist in a much less critical degree.

Unlike the white Southerner, he has had little cause, until recently, to feel separated from the nation. Recently he has become aware of nationwide discrimination. Since states' rights were maintained mainly to keep him in subjection, he could not be a states'-righter. Since the whites who held him in immediate control were proud and self-conscious Southerners, he could not be, at least consciously, a Southerner. Since his emancipation, and what security he has had, have come mainly from the national government, he is naturally first of all an American. For these several reasons, he is less aware than the white of any conflict between his feeling for the South and his feeling for the nation.

There is, however, some conflict and ambiguity. To continue the comparisons, the white, especially if from the Deep South, knows how he feels about the South but may be uncertain how this can be harmonized with his feeling about the nation, or, to state it differently, how in the light of his feeling about the South he does feel about the nation. The Negro is fairly clear as to his feeling about the nation; he doesn't know how he feels about his immediate community, the South. He hates it so much that he leaves it; he loves it so much that he stays; or he loves it and hates it, and leaves and returns. He loves it as men love the fields and woods of their childhood—unless those years have been too bitter; he hates it for the sufferings and indignities it has inflicted upon him. Like most men, he is probably more clearly aware of what he hates than of what he loves, hatred demanding a focus foreign to the expansive nature of love. He finds himself at home in the genial physical climate of the South, and there is something—he doesn't know what—in the human climate that attracts him; but he is rebuffed by the harsh political, economic, and social winds that blow against him.

The essential problem of the Southern white in this matter is, how am I an American? The essential problem of the Southern Negro, how am I a Southerner? Neither one is clearly aware that the problem exists. But it does, and is a part of the problem of identity: Who am I?

At this point, the Southern white is in a slightly more assured position than the Southern Negro. For the white identifies himself more clearly and closely with and by the things which lie immediately around him, and is vague about the things which lie farther away. About these, however, men are always somewhat vague. The Negro, unable to identify himself so clearly with and by the things which lie around him, is forced to depend more heavily upon things far away. But distant things are more abstract and less convincing than things close at hand.

There are, however, several facts in history and perhaps also in his character that help the Negro to compensate for the weakness of his identification with the South. And these raise the question of the Negro's use of the past, and, more particularly, the question, whether there lies athwart the mind of the Negro that kind of fault that makes it so hard for the white to use his past effectively.

Such a fault exists, but it is far less serious in the case of the Negro than in that of the white Southerner. The white Southerner, remembering lost honor and greatness, is not yet able to fuse that part of his history with the failure and frustration of the past hundred years and the widening future opening presently before him. He is ambivalent: he looks with nostalgia toward the past and with hope toward the future. Behind the Negro lies a past, in the eyes of the modern democratic world, lacking in honor, indeed disgraceful: chattel slavery and second-class citizenship. He feels very little, if any, nostalgia for this past; his eye is on the future; he is not ambivalent. Yet, like the white, he is not yet able to make effective use of this past. He would rather forget it, and live solely on hope. But hope without memory is a shadowy thing.

Attempting to strengthen this hope, many Negroes leave

the South. To some degree, the hope is strengthened, for the North is supposed to be the Land of Freedom, and certainly the legalized disabilities are fewer there. But they are there. And now the Negro finds himself among a people who have always lived largely upon hope and with few memories. John Erskine used to say that the typical American, having no common history, tended to find his history in the future. This atmosphere of hope untamed by memory intensifies the Negro's hope; and, when he finds himself still disadvantaged, he turns quickly toward revolution. This desperate urgency is one of the things that make the racial problem more difficult in the North than in the South. Ideally, the white Northerner, priding himself upon freedom, should be proud that this newcomer demands freedom now; but even a white Northerner does not want to change faster than he wants to change, especially if he is one whom the change may hurt financially.

We have spoken of the fact that the attitude of the Roman Catholic Church toward slavery made it easier in South America for the slave to move out of slavery than in Protestant North America: there, slavery was a misfortune, not an index of a man's worth; here, in an atmosphere of individualistic freedom, it was a disgrace, and its memory also tends to be disgraceful. Therefore, the Negro is strongly tempted to forget it.

As he is tempted sometimes to be a little ashamed of the spirituals, the richest fruit of his unhappy life. I think, however, that with his growing strength and self-respect, this attitude is passing; as is also his need for apologizing for his experience under slavery. His coming strength will lie in his acceptance, indeed in his conscious affirmation of his past. For the fruits of that past still live in him, and it would be as self-defeating to disregard the good fruits as it would the evil. Whites at least are clearly aware of the evil fruits among Negroes, though they are generally too proud to recognize these as fruits of the condition imposed upon the Negro by the white. But it is the good fruits I am chiefly concerned with because we have so far thought too little about them.

Though the Negro has contributed richly to American culture in jazz and the blues, his spirituals express most clearly the wisdom he has learned in hardship and dishonor. To what degree he is conscious of this wisdom, no one knows. As we shall see, he tends to express it in his actions. At this point again, he resembles the Southern white, who has gained a rich sense of life's tragic complexity without understanding that this is what makes him a Southerner. But the Negro is nearer to basic wisdom here than the white because, though he has not yet come to the place of being deeply proud that he has endured the indignities of life on the American scene, he has at least come to the point of realizing that life is this kind of thing, where, as Samuel Johnson said, "much is to be endured and little to be enjoyed." He learned this mainly here in America; he will be strengthened as he realizes that this is the kind of American he is.

Let us go back now to the question as to how the Negro has been able to identify himself with the South in spite of the fact that the culture has been at least nominally white and he has not been welcomed into it. He has gained a measure of success here because of his ability to make much out of the little that was given him. He had within himself a quality of wholeheartedness that permitted him to establish his home in a not too friendly land.

In the first place, the Negro has never been too much disturbed by the split that extreme puritanism causes in the world, dividing the spirit from matter, driving some men toward God without the world, others to the world without God. He never was this kind of extremist. In spite of all frustration, he found pleasure, sometimes joy, in the moment.

He loved the world about him so much that out of both its lights and its shadows, and with certain rather backhanded gifts from the whites, he built his Christian faith. Out of his own vibrant love of life, he found things to love even in a strange land and a hard existence. He bent to the blows of life but kept on the whole a steadfast heart. The religion that the whites rather belatedly and halfheartedly offered him spoke of a God of love. The apparent miracle is that he could accept this version of deity from the hands of a people who showed so little love toward him. The fact that he did accept it suggests his ability to make the most of whatever life offered. It also suggests that, in spite of the exploitative system of slavery, there was in its operation sufficient humanity and kindliness to make possible the acceptance by the Negro of the idea of a God of compassionate love.

But the Negro's exploited situation prevented him from accepting too easily the present physical world. He did not succumb as did the white; social, economic, and political forces prevented this. He had to live largely by hope; he had to refer his life to the future, perhaps even to an other-worldy future. He did not make this reference, however, because of a puritanical distrust and hatred of the world; he did it because of the poverty of the world that even in its poverty he loved. The whites, of course, encouraged him to do it: it kept him quiet in hardship, and quieted also their own consciences.

Yet, giving the Negro a taste of Christianity was like the later Southern "error" of giving him a taste of education. It was never intended in the post-bellum period that the Negro should read Patrick Henry and develop a passion for freedom; but in our generally democratic atmosphere this follows the ability to read. So it had never been intended in the ante-bellum period that the Negro should learn of prophetic justice and add to his proper learning of obedience to those in authority—"Servants, obey your masters"—the "improper" demand for fair play and social justice. The white man so carefully silenced the voice of social justice within himself—being unable to listen to it—that it hardly occurred to him that the slaves might be moved by the great story of the Israelites' flight from Egypt. But they were. They saw themselves as God's people; and, though they still worshiped a God of love who, if they trusted him, would save them in heaven, they also began to worship a God of justice who would save them here on earth.

The essential point is that the Negro, through his character and his experience, made a closer connection than did the white between his Southern experience and the eternal kingdom of heaven. He was both induced and forced to see another land in this. This land admittedly was not his either economically or politically, and he lacked therefore a certain rootage in it that the white developed. But it was his really; suffering made it so; the only way he could live in it was to see in it something of the love and the justice of God.

For the most part, then, the Negro did not will directly or indirectly the temporal, spatial, religious, and racial divisions that debilitate the mind of the white South. Insofar as these exist, they were largely imposed upon him. Being less affected by the divisions, he has attained more completely the unity the South aimed at. Forced to live at the bottom of Southern life, largely untempted by the drive for power that corroded the white Southerner and dissolved the Southern community, he was able to realize in himself, better than the white, the unity the white dreamed of but was unable to attain. He was but slightly infected by the proud individualism of the white Southerner: it was not in his tradition nor was it suggested by his situation; it had little chance to grow there. He was not afflicted by the puritan sense of God *versus* the world: he accepted as from God whatever homely goodness life brought, and saw even the injustices of society as finally under God's control.

The Negro has revealed his aptitude for the virtues of the South in his manners and in his religion. As for the manners, he helped to create them. It is probable that he brought from the highly traditional life of Africa a strong feeling for the importance of form: there were proper ways to do and say things. In the slow-moving physical and social climate of the South, the whites too, though they were affected by the modern drive toward the future, were favorable to a leisurely, mannered life. It is true, they developed a racial etiquette to keep the Negro in his place. The Negro, with his traditional feeling for manners, accepted this and used it in part to keep the white man in his place; that is, to restrain the exploiter, to bring him under a degree of control. The white tended to accept this control, even though he often realized it was being imposed upon him. As I have said, he, too, had a feeling for manners. He was also aware of the terrible need for order, restraint, accepted modes of action in a society based upon violence. Out of these good and evil motives, out of need and desire, the mannered life of the South developed, and the Negro was at least an equal contributor with the white to the final result.

We have spoken of the Negro's pervasive religious sense, his sense of the mystery (sometimes of the magic) of life, a sense that the white Southerner also has maintained longer than other Americans. Together with this emphasis upon manners and an inclusive religion, and influenced by the personal, in a vague sense feudal, society of which he was a part, the Negro developed to an unusual degree the virtue of loyalty and the ability to commit himself completely to a person or perhaps even to a cause.

With this equipment the Negro in the South came to the period of World War II. In the segregated society in which he had lived for sixty-odd years, manners had deteriorated and personal loyalty had dimmed. Yet the core of the old virtues existed. Now, after long and patient waiting, he was drawn by national and international forces toward the mainstream of economics and politics.

But the Negro has done more than wait. Considering his general poverty, and the poverty of the South, he had done remarkably well in preparing himself for American citizenship. He had produced several great leaders who had outlined for him his aims and methods. Outstanding among these were Frederick Douglass, Booker T. Washington, and W. E. B. DuBois. The last two disagreed sharply with each other; Washington was during his lifetime the more influential; but it is probable that each drove home the lesson that both the condition of the Negro and the state of the times demanded. Washington was for compromise with the whites and for job training for the Negroes. In 1895 this was the only way to get any support, and Negroes certainly needed job training. Unfortunately, the craft jobs disappeared or were seized by the whites. Nor was the successful Negro accepted as Washington had predicted. DuBois had no patience with compromise. Even while Washington was at the peak of his influence, he was preaching the demand for complete citizenship, especially for equal political rights. Washington did not accomplish what he had promised, but certainly he aided his race tremendously and sustained some hope within them. The drive for complete equality, which DuBois led, and which found one of its most effective organs in the National Association for the Advancement of Colored People, operated mainly in the legal realm because it was there that, because of the Constitution, advance would be easiest. Slowly but fairly surely the legal battles, beginning with that against the Grandfather Clause, were won. This decision, handed down by the Supreme Court in 1915, outlawed the so-called Grandfather Clauses, which, in most Southern states, had effectively barred the Negro from voting by requiring that all voters be descended from persons who had voted prior to 1867—and practically no Negro was. But now with the coming of World War I, the Negro, being included in the needs of a nation fighting for democracy, inevitably began to demand that he be included in all the benefits of democracy.

It was probably incidental, but in his emphasis upon the legal approach, the Negro was exemplifying the Southern stress upon law, a stress upon both the importance of the word and the need for a traditional legal structure to contain an explosive social situation. Later, in 1960, because of the slowness of legal processes, and especially because of the evident will of the white South to oppose the implementation of the 1954 Supreme Court decision, the Negro began direct action—lunch-counter sit-ins, freedom rides, selective buying, picketing. This kind of action was indeed shocking to the white South, which had carefully cultivated the myth that the Negro was happy, a myth that could still be "believed" so long as contrary evidence consisted only of a relatively few scattered legal cases, promoted by a "foreign" organization, the N.A.A.C.P. Belief became more difficult when student demonstrations spread like wildfire across the South.

But more amazing than the fact of the demonstrations was the character revealed in the demonstrators. Let me say it in so many words that there may be no mistake; it was a Southern character. So far, this has not been generally recognized, or more accurately, admitted by white Southerners; indeed, it has not been recognized by many Negro Southerners. This is to say that Negroes as yet hardly recognize themselves as Southerners.

Why should anyone expect them to? Nobody stops to define terms here; Southerners are white. Since Negroes are evidently not white, they cannot be Southerners. Since they are striving so hard to wrest from white Southerners certain rights that the whites have reserved for themselves as privileges, they have no cause to think of themselves as Southerners. They are Americans who are striving to gain the rights of Americans in the South.

But more than this, why should they think of themselves as Southerners? There is one basic reason: because they are. "Speak of me as I am," said Othello. Only as we recognize what we are can we gain what we want. Southern Negroes undoubtedly think they want American rights; I doubt if they realize that they want them in the Southern context, with a Southern flavor. That is, I doubt if they realize that they want these things as Southern Americans. To speak perhaps in shockingly concrete terms, they want more fried chicken with the grits and gravy. And why not? Why should a man deny his tastes?

But I know. Because it has been too often assumed by whites that this was all the Negro wanted: fried chicken and watermelon. All I'm saying is, there's no sense in denying what truth there is in the image men hold of you as you expand and dignify that image. Doubtless Calhoun liked fried chicken and Webster baked beans. I can support Webster without taking up baked beans. One doesn't have to change his tastes with his politics.

It is my belief that what the Negro wants in the South, and his method of trying to get it, are both strongly Southern. First, as to what he wants. So far as he wants justice, this is a desire created in him by the unjust life he has suffered here and, more importantly, by his interpretation of the prophetic quality of the religion the South taught him. He took the religion of the South as it was presented to him, in all its emphasis upon individual salvation, personal devotion, and commitment, and he has added to this the unrecognized prophetic element in Christianity, the inspiration for which he found, not in the life of the South—except by contrast—but in the Bible the South claimed to believe. He has brought the personal commitment, which the South knew, to the cause of social justice, which the South did not know. During the past century, the white South, too, has suffered political and economic injustice and discrimination at the hands of the nation. Yet, for evident reasons, it has not been able to relate this to its religious base. The Negro, suffering a far greater injustice, has been able to interpret it in the light of his religion.

But the Southern Negro wants more than justice, more than "cold justice." He wants to belong completely to the community. In seeking this, he is seeking what he has, in however limited a degree, already found. Always occupying an unjust and unhonored position in the community, he has yet been a part of it. He wishes now to be more completely a part. He does not generally desire to abbreviate the rights of others as he extends his own. The community is his home; he wants only a fair place in it, a fair chance to improve it and improve himself in it. This mood can be seen in all the attempts of Negro demonstrators to come to peaceful terms with the whites, to leave them a chance to save face as they necessarily retreat, to improve the common community, not to destroy it.

I remember an instance when a group of whites and Negroes, students mainly, were considering plans to desegregate a local theater. Some action had been suggested; it was opposed on the grounds that it might ruin the theater manager. With that, one of those present, not a Southerner, exclaimed passionately, "We don't care if it does ruin him! This is a moral cause!" He was voted down. The majority were not in favor of simple moral causes; they wanted to maintain the community, even while they improved it.

The ends sought, therefore, are Southern ends; or, if you

prefer, national ends with a Southern flavor. What of the means used to gain these ends? Even more than the ends, these, too, are Southern. The nonviolence is Southern only by contrast. Forced to endure patiently and for a long time the possibility and the fact of violence, the Southern Negro, ready at last to move, takes his cue from the temper of the South and adopts in nonviolence a method he is basically prepared to use and the white basically unable to oppose. Should the Negro use violence, the white would remember the old Southern need for order and the old fear of slave insurrection, and in violent reaction forget any whisper of conscience. But when the Negro uses nonviolence, the white is nonplused. The Negro is saying dramatically that he is dissatisfied. But according to the myth he should be satisfied, indeed happy. At this point the conscience of the white begins to trouble him.

Undoubtedly, some whites are driven to desperation by their inability to cope with nonviolent demonstrations, and so become violent themselves. But the technique is generally suited both to those who use it and to those against whom it is used.

Nonviolence is a way of acting. A manner. This brings us to the importance of manners in the recent attempts of Negroes to effect social change. Their good manners were noted from the beginning of the demonstrations in 1960, noted indeed in contrast to the manners of certain whites who opposed them. One of the leading Southern segregationists, Editor James Kilpatrick, of the Richmond *News-Leader,* was reduced to Latin by his dismay at the contrast between the quiet manners of Negro sit-inners and the crudities of the white bystanders. "Eheu," he said, "that the South should witness Negroes teaching whites manners." But the South has always witnessed this without really understanding it. Who taught whom the manners of the South? I can still hear the voice of my Negro nurse, "Child, aint you 'shamed?"

Again and again through the last several years, we have seen Negroes, mainly young but now including many adults, bearing taunts, obscenities, even violence, in a quiet, reserved manner. Occasionally they have resorted to violence, but this has been rare. Yet whites should not be complacent about this. The Negroes have been patient, far more patient than whites would have been, but we cannot ask them to be patient forever. Even God is not patient forever. It is probably true, also, that many Negroes have adopted nonviolence as a technique, not as a faith, and if the resistant whites make the way too hard, they may throw away the technique with disastrous results, not only for themselves and their local communities, but also for the nation at large, trying to maintain its position of democratic leadership in the modern world. So far, however, they have generally maintained dignity and reserve, and in doing so have illustrated Southern manners at their best. Attempting to overthrow Southern racial etiquette, they are using Southern manners to do it. It is this use of the South to change the South that confuses and renders relatively helpless the white Southerner. It is clear that Negroes should not sit at lunch counters with whites, as these Negroes are trying to do; but it is also clear that men should act with dignity and reserve, as these Negroes are doing.

Yet, though this is Southern manners, it is also, perhaps even more than the participants realize, the expression of religion. Here we have the faith that if men are patient God will reward them; if men will suffer for a cause God will use their sufferings. Here we have a fusion that has not been accomplished in the South before, indeed a double fusion. On the side of religion, the fusion of personal faith and social justice, which the South had never been able to make; and, added to this, a new religious attitude expressed in the best manners of the South. All this appears in the young Negro who leads the present Negro advance.

It is significant that white students appear increasingly with the Negroes, either in actual cooperation or in other actions indicative of their sympathy. Outside of Mississippi and Alabama perhaps, the passage of the generations has softened the conflict; a more liberal knowledge of history and of modern needs has increased the concern of many white students for the racial problem. It must be admitted that great numbers of white students are still indifferent, and some bitterly opposed. The fact remains that a strong desire exists among them for increased understanding of the Negro and increased cooperation with him.

We have in my own state, South Carolina, as a subsidiary of the interracial Council on Human Relations, a Student Council on Human Relations. To this belong students from most of the colleges, white and Negro. The present president is a Negro. This is an expression of the spirit of decency and good form which South Carolina has always upheld ideally; it is also an illustration of how memories are woven into hopes.

Finally, the Negro is bringing into the political life of the South a moral urgency that has usually been absent. We have said that the error of the Puritan in this matter was to thrust ethics into politics without modification. Witness Garrison. The opposite error of the South was to keep ethics out of politics. Witness Calhoun. Even today the South tries to avoid discussing civil rights by bringing up states' rights. The Negro, coming now into public life, brings a long and bitter experience of bondage and inequality, and therefore speaks inevitably in the great words of the Declaration of Independence on freedom and equality. Yet he is no simple idealist, like Garrison. He is a man of the world, a realist, who knows that he must obtain his rights under the political rules. Yet he knows the rules are for the preservation and extension of the rights. This he insists upon; and if we make it too hard for him to speak through the law and the ballot, he speaks to our eyes, our ears, and our hearts through demonstrations. And he is winning because we know deep down that he is right; that the greatest words of our state documents have to do with freedom and equality; that politics is finally a moral matter. Thus the Negro, entering public life today, is healing the age-old breach in the South between the inner and the outer life, between religion and politics.

What we see today, then, in the advance of the Negro is not simply the Negro advancing; it is the South advancing; advancing toward the unification of its culture. The Old South failed because it could not bring together its manners and its morals, its culture and its religion, this world and another. It had the vision faintly, but the adoption of Negro slavery made impossible the vision's attainment. Cracks appeared in the structure. Under the storm of war it collapsed.

But all was not lost. The seeds remained in the soil, strangely but properly in the basic black soil of the South. Partly because they could do nothing else, Negroes learned what the South was trying to do; learned and remembered; and are now ready to tell us what they learned. It's a strange and perhaps Christian destiny. The Negro by his enforced presence here created division. Separated from the rest of society, he became more clearly aware than others both of the cost of separation and of the possibility and the fact of union. He is now in the process of healing the gaps caused by his presence. And he is healing them because he has never denied the richness of life in the pain of life, because he has been able to value both this world and another, to accept all things but always with a grain of salt. He caught the drift of what the South was trying to say, and now, for the first time, he, a Southerner, is saying it.

CHAPTER 30

LAST HURDLE

But will he be heard? "Ay, there's the rub." It's been commonly remarked in the South during the last ten years (among the whites usually lamented) that communication between whites and Negroes has broken down. This means specifically that the Negro is no longer hearing the white. The white never heard the Negro; he didn't even listen; he was too busy telling him.

This is an overstatement. It implies that the Negro has not influenced the white. The whole thrust of this book has been to develop the theme that the Negro Southerner has influenced the white Southerner—both through the racial institutions that by their massive presence have modified the South, and by his own character, which in fundamental ways has changed the whites about him. The white has always heard the Negro, though often he didn't want to; he has certainly tried to keep from hearing the tragic overtones of the Negro's voice. But they did talk together.

The difference during the last ten years is that the Negro hasn't been easily available for conversation. This is a more severe blow to the Southerner than a non-Southerner might think. For in a land where manner counts for so much, it is almost as important that action be accompanied by the proper words as that it take place. It's a deprivation to a Southerner not to talk about what he plans to do, what he is doing, and what he has done. Since the Negro Southerner was going to do most of the doing and reap least of the benefit, he was naturally willing to spend as much time in conversation as possible. Recently, however, he has become aware that there is too much talk and too little profitable action, the times suggest strongly that profitable action is possible, and therefore he is withdrawing from the more or less pleasant conversation. But the white is still getting the message. It isn't that he doesn't hear; he doesn't like what he hears. Or what he doesn't hear. The transit company in Montgomery didn't hear the silver falling in the change boxes on the buses, and the silence was displeasing.

Certainly, however, interracial communication in the South is at present strained and sometimes violent. The old apparent ease is gone. In its place there is more bitterness than many had expected. Not all, however. The Southern Regional Council, the most solidly based interracial organization in the South, with board of directors, officers, and staff biracial, recently issued a statement in which the following sentences occur: "We are little impressed by public opinion polls which reveal Negro bitterness or white prejudice. No informed and intelligent observer has ever doubted the existence of either. Bitterness and prejudice are . . the conditions against which the responsible institutions of American society . . . must contend and which they must rectify."

Expected or not, the bitterness is here, among both Negroes and whites. The question that faces us here is, how can we have any hope of expecting the Negro to act creatively in the contemporary South when apparently so much bitterness exists on both sides of the racial line? And, first, among the Negroes.

I repeat what I said earlier: in my opinion, there is much

less Negro bitterness than one would expect. Theoretically, there should be an enormous backlog of it, built up from the smoldering resentment of centuries. But here again we have an illustration of the fact that the South is not at bottom what it appears to be. Its racial structure is proud and insolent; there is pride and insolence in personal relations; but there is also in these relations a degree of humanity unsuggested by the structure.

Merrill Proudfoot, a white Presbyterian minister, in his *Diary of a Sit-In* expresses his belief in the existence of interracial good will. "I do believe," he says, "that our movement has been not so much to secure good race relations as to realize the potential of those that have long existed. . . . I still think that there is a great deal of good will, that attitudes are not fundamentally hostile."[1]

This good will rests upon Christianity, however distorted. The patience of the Negro rests upon Christianity, as does his present passion. Having learned to wait upon the Lord, now in the Lord's time he moves assuredly into the world. Much of the division, the fragmentation of life that embittered the white became for the Negro a source of strength. I know a Negro Lutheran pastor of Alabama who has taken part in racial demonstrations. He describes and interprets the meetings held in churches prior to many of these. The prayers, the singing of hymns, the rhythmic clapping of hands are mainly for the purpose of giving expression to pent-up emotion so that participants may go into the streets against opposition, and even violence, with calm spirits, "all passion spent." This, I think, is what has always happened with the Negro: through his religion he has sublimated much of the frustration and bitterness of his daily life.

But having said this, we must remember that when reasonable goals have been set, as at present, suffering endured in the struggle for these goals, and widespread and sometimes cruel opposition met, the temptation to bitterness increases powerfully. Negroes are simply demanding that they be accepted as Americans; any delay in acceding to this demand is dangerous. Any delay also makes it more improbable that the Negro will be able to make a creative contribution to the life of the South.

As for racial bitterness among the whites, it, too, is far less than it seems to be. A part of the opposition is not to the Negro, but to what is called "outside interference." This was true during Reconstruction, it is true now. The Negro is in part the occasion of bitterness; he is by no means simply the cause. Rightly or wrongly, the life of the South has been more often and more forcibly interfered with than the life of any other part of the country. Also, trying to estimate racial bitterness among the whites, we are fooled by the violent opposition of several Deep South states, which naturally makes the headlines. Indifference or acceptance do not. South Carolina is also Deep South, and many people on the outside expected violence. It has not occurred; and it has not occurred partly because that state discovered another Southern heritage: decency, orderliness, respect for law. This image from the past was brought out and refurbished because the leaders read correctly the meaning of the extremism of Arkansas, Mississippi, especially Alabama. They saw both its futility as regards integration and its danger as regards the economic future of the state. It is true, there has been, and there is, mean legal and economic infighting in South Carolina; but violence itself, even the suggestion of violence, is quickly condemned.

We should recognize, also, that the bitterness of opposition to integration increases with the spread of integration. This is inevitable. As the segregationists lose, they become increasingly desperate. The intensity of their opposition is a mark of their desperation. Whatever they say, they know better every day that integration is coming: the public opinion polls in the South show a steadily growing sense of its inevitability. Of course, desperate men applaud George Wallace. What else can they do? And, after all, George Wallace has adopted the proper pose: undying defiance. This is how the South likes to think of itself. Overwhelmed perhaps, but never giving up. This is, after one hundred years, the tawdry heritage of Gettysburg: the brilliant charge in the afternoon, the frozen moment among the guns on Cemetery Ridge, and then the night. There may have been time for such a charge in 1863, if for nothing else, a splendid page in the history of war; George Wallace charging now begins to look ludicrous. Ludicrous and too expensive. If this is humor, it is costing the South and the nation too much.

Perhaps this is the time, if ever, to comment upon the most publicized, the most expensive, and the most tragic instance of violence that has occurred in the South: the assassination of President Kennedy, in Dallas, on November 22, 1963. Actually, Dallas is on the border of the South, between the Deep South and the Southwest. Furthermore, the supposed assassin was not strictly a Southerner or a Westerner, and the fatal shot could have been fired at any place in the nation. There was bitter opposition to the President all over the country. Yet the shot was fired in Dallas, and it is not unreasonable to inquire if the location had anything to do with it.

The violence of the South, or the Southwest, is basically American violence: the violence of a young people who have just emerged from a frontier society. But having said this, we have to add that the frontier lasted longer in the South than anywhere else, and that it was sharpened there by what W. J. Cash called "the frontier the Yankee made," and by the new racial frontier that resulted from the freeing of the slaves. For with emancipation the races stood in a new relation to each other, with much uncharted ground between them. Also we should add that Dallas, lying on the border of the West, lies on the border of that frontier where widespread violence has been most recently expressed. It may be that there the frank racial prejudice of the South met the propensity to violence of the frontier West, the smoldering of an old frontier met the clear violence of a new.

One thing is sure. The most flagrant opposition to the federal government has appeared during the last ten years in the South. This is due primarily to the racial issue, secondarily to the failure of Southern leaders to realize that state sovereignty went down the drain with the Civil War. When a Jewish synagogue was bombed in Atlanta several years ago, the *Atlanta Constitution* pointed out that those who were really guilty were the political leaders of the South who had urged violent opposition to the enforcement of the segregation decision of 1954; and when four children were killed in the bombing of a Negro church in Birmingham in 1963, other Southerners pointed out that this was an inevitable sequence to the violent opposition Birmingham and the state of Alabama had offered to desegregation.

What can be said then is this: since 1954 the South has offered more opposition, some of it violent, to the federal government than any other section of the country; President Kennedy was the leader in the proposed civil rights legislation that seemed to be aimed chiefly at the South; his assassination, therefore, was a logical, though terrible, conclusion of such violent opposition. The assassin may have been moved to act when he did and where he did because of the widespread and sometimes bitter opposition in that area and in the South in general.

On the contrary, there may have been no such connection. But men who sow the wind should remember the whirlwind.

CHAPTER 31

BY GOD'S GRACE, THE SOUTH

Meanwhile, here is the Negro trying to tell us what the South really is. Will he be heard? In a certain sense, he is already being heard. The South is yielding, however grudgingly and erratically, to his demands. Also, as I have suggested, the yielding is due in part to the appeal of the Southern manner in which the demand is made. But the South is hardly conscious of this. To what degree can it become conscious? To what degree can it permit itself to become conscious?

The question may be raised, If it is yielding, what difference does it make whether it recognizes the Southern element in its reason for yielding? Because this is the beginning of the recognition of the Negro as a Southerner, the beginning of his complete acceptance by the white South. He does not want to be accepted by the white South? He merely wants his abstract rights as an American citizen? As reasonable as this sounds, I do not believe it. The Negro, like all of us, is a part of all that he has met, and he has lived, for three centuries now, in a region fearful of abstractions, whether of right or of wrong, concerned with individuals and with groups of individuals in communities. The value of the concrete community is one of the most fundamental things he knows, and he is concerned, therefore, to be accepted more completely into that community. Not just as it is, of course. His entrance would change it radically. But it would still be community he sought, for that is what, however poorly, he has found.

As to his acceptance by the whites, they have long accepted him as a pseudo- or imitation-Southerner, and have smiled condescendingly or scornfully as they said, "He copies us." They have not been ready to recognize that he also created the South, that they have "copied him," or rather, that that entity called the South was hammered out by black man and white man working together.

Booker T. Washington was aware, more than half a century ago, of the nature of the Negro's contribution: "The Negro has contributed, not merely his labour, but something also of his inner life and temperament to the character and quality of the South."[1] And Howard Odum says: "The story of the Negro in the South becomes, from the moment of his coming to complicate the picture, the most decisive fact in the architecture of Southern culture."[2]

If the South should yield merely to the economic and political pressure of the advancing Negro, certain material values would be enhanced: the standard of living would be raised, our politics would be more democratic and, we hope, just. But concerned as I am with the inner health of the South, I would ask, what improvement would this make in that health? For the South is suffering, as the Negro Southerner especially is suffering, not simply because of long-continued and widespread material poverty but also, and more importantly, because of spiritual poverty, especially the inability to create anything both characteristic of itself and acceptable to the nation. We have noticed already, as an exception to this, the South's recent literary contribution, together with its unfortunate inability generally to appreciate it. We have noticed also the contribution the Negro has made to music, out of his poverty, perhaps even because of it. The poverty of the South as a whole is especially damaging because of the great contributions made by the South at the founding of the Republic, and during its first fifty years. "Sorrow's crown of sorrow is remembering happier things."

To be sure, the improvement of the standard of living in the South will, almost of itself, make the Southerner more American, and might even persuade him to accept without reservation the straight American religion and simply forget that he had ever been a Southerner. But if he does this, he takes on also the weaknesses of the American religion, its shallowness, its rootlessness in time, its fluctuation from sentimental optimism to sentimental despair. As he does this, he makes impossible the acquisition of that wisdom that lies in his understanding and development of the Southern style. It seems to me sheer waste to throw away so much only to gain—more shares in General Motors!

I recognize that simply raising the standard of living in the South would be a contribution to the material life of the nation. But this is the same contribution Americans are already making. It carries no gift from the heart of the South; it's no Southern contribution. It is therefore important, to the South first, then to the nation, and perhaps to the world, that the South understand itself, and understand thereby the gift it has to offer.

It is important, then, that the South understand the Southern reasons for its increasing acceptance of Negroes. As I have pointed out, the white South finds it hard to resist the demands of the Negroes partly because these demands bear the stamp of Southern manners and express the spirit of Southern religion: racial etiquette goes by the board, but the concerned, the conciliatory heart is there; the religion extends the old Southern image of love and a kind of justice between individuals into the entire social structure, but it is still

Christianity, the religion of the South, with prophetic justice emphasized.

The South, adept with words, has been saying more than it understood. It needs now to see these words in modern dress, incarnate in the contemporary air. Feeling once a sense of paternalistic community, and expressing the racial understanding that underlay the racial injustice, it spoke of "our people," "our white folks," "our colored folks." Now that "our colored folks" are advancing inevitably into a more democratic world—an advance which we, caught up in a worldwide struggle with communism, have to desire—it is not expecting too much of ourselves that we should recognize in the fact and especially in the manner of that advance a contemporary expression of the old Southern style. "Our fathers would be shocked," we say. But we are not our fathers, but our fathers' sons; and all that they can reasonably require of us is that we face the demands of today with the best wisdom we have, including what they taught us.

That wisdom, as I have suggested, is very complex. It includes the knowledge of failure, of human imperfection, of sin if you wish. Generally, it includes the experience of life as tragic. But there is a world of difference between failure interpreted as the experience solely of oneself or one's group and therefore implying injustice, and failure interpreted as the human lot. According to Robert Penn Warren, the South is, unhappily, too keenly aware of failure in the first sense. In this sense, the Civil War and the whole complex of defeat becomes for us the Great Alibi, the great excuse for whatever is wrong today. Whatever is wrong, whatever is too difficult, we attribute to those events. This permits us to face the difficult present like automatons, without need for thought, our reactions already determined. But this unhappy, this negative interpretation of failure, lies only a hair's breadth away from its second, its positive interpretation as symbolic of all human failure. The closeness of these two contrasting interpretations reminds us of Browning's lines:

Oh, the little more, and how much it is!
And the little less, and what worlds away!

But this is like the South, where good and evil lie down together.

The wisdom of the South also includes the fact of an old sympathy, of which I have often spoken, between whites and Negroes. This sympathy makes possible a reasonable cooperation of all Southerners in our contemporary world. America needs this wisdom. It is not too much to say the world needs it.

To use a modern phrase, it is possible that during the last three hundred years the South has been a pilot project learning—at terrible expense it is true, but learning doesn't come easy—how to do within a limited area what now has to be done in the world if civilization is to survive. But who set up the project? No one. The South did not. The nation did not. Nobody intended this. The South intended an increased production of tobacco, rice, sugar cane, and cotton. The nation intended increased profits. But it so happened that white Southerners were nominally Christians, of a certain general temperament, affected in certain ways by the climate, and that a certain way of life naturally developed here, a way of life which, though based upon selfish interests, began to show, either because of the evil or despite it, certain virtues. These virtues now begin to appear publicly, most clearly in the lives of the Negroes, who have suffered the most and have therefore lived the most. The Southerner who is true to his religious heritage will be inclined to say that this has happened because of the grace of God. The South has been God's project.

Of course, in this view of divine providence, the world itself is God's project. Only, God's hand is more evident in the South than in most other regions. Beautifully evident. In late ante-bellum days, the South, badly on the defensive, called God to its aid, and insisted that even slavery was His project, a means used by Him to reveal to heathen Africans his encompassing grace. When slavery was destroyed, this interpretation failed. The failure may have been due to shortsightedness, to forgetfulness of the fact that a thousand years in God's sight are as a day that has passed. Perhaps it is time for the church in the South to take another look at the old doctrine.

If the Negro in slavery became a Christian by the grace of God, then perhaps the white, through defeat and frustration, might become a better Christian by the same grace. Out of God's effective judgment upon slavery might come the realization of God's grace. Few Southerners have ever doubted it was best for slavery to go; being religious, they were ready to admit the going was God's will. But they have failed to carry through their earlier belief that God permitted slavery in order that the Negroes might be Christianized, and to recognize that Negroes under this discipline might become better Christians than their teachers the whites; it never occurred to them that God's grace might be so extravagant as this. The South, though religious, is still largely ignorant of the working of grace and judgment in society itself.

It will take the church, the best of the church, to interpret the lesson. "But if the church read history so badly in 1860, how can anyone expect it to read it better in 1960?" Well, a century has passed. If the Southerner has learned something through defeat—and he has, though he hasn't quite got to the point of seeing that what he has learned is the result of his defeat—if he has learned something, then maybe he has learned something in his church; maybe his church has learned something. Maybe his church could become aware of the religious significance of the Southerner's experience. Since Southerners are typically churchmen, this would mean that Southerners would become aware of the religious significance of their experience.

Since the lesson to be learned is so fundamental, I doubt if it can be learned on a level more shallow than the religious. I doubt if the Southerner—the white Southerner now—can accept the Negro completely into the community merely on the ground that the Negro is exemplifying at present certain positive aspects of Southern culture. The Negro sees far better than the white the religious significance of what he is doing; indeed, he is more aware of its religious significance than he is of its cultural significance as an exhibition of Southern manners. The song "We shall overcome some day" has a deeply religious ring. Even the method of nonviolence, though perhaps also a reaction against Southern violence and therefore good strategy, is in the Negro's mind based upon Christian teaching and example.

The Southern white is as religious as the Southern Negro. Until he, too, realizes the religious significance of what is taking place, he will hardly be able to see it in its deepest and most creative significance. But his church, in attempting to discover and reveal this deeper meaning, has at least this much to begin with: it is, for better and worse, a cultural church, and the more strictly religious interpretation of the cooperation between the two races in the South can rest and build upon the more strictly cultural unity that appears in manners: the prevailing dignity and reserve of the Negro, the pervading sense of the importance of means, of manner, of manners.

The church in the South, then, has the chance to make use of the cultural similarity between the races in its attempt to unveil the vision of the religious significance of race relations: to interpret the biracial South as God's Project. But the deeper meaning lies not in the culture but in the historical events. What happens is prior to how we take what happens, to our manner of response, though indeed the manner is both a partial cause and a part of what happens. The question I wish to raise here is this, Can the church use the similarity in manners between whites and Negroes, an evident aspect of our culture, as a means of revealing the religious unity of the South and the operation of God's grace and judgment within it? Or, contrariwise, must the grace and judgment be made to rest directly upon the historical events, and, when thus established, made more rich and significant by reference to manners? In my opinion, the second alternative is the more workable.

I am saying that it is both easier and also more important to make clear the bond of humanity among Southerners, white and black, than it is to make clear the bond of culture. To know ourselves as men is more important than to know ourselves as Southerners.

Put like this, there is no arguing the matter. Man is more basic and more inclusive than Southern man. What complicates the matter is the high valuation put upon the term *Southerner* by the white Southerner, and the urgency, therefore, that he think of the Negro as a Southerner. Men need to extend whatever sense of brotherhood they have. This is especially true of Southerners, who react weakly or adversely to abstractions but strongly to concrete situations.

I'm afraid, however, that so far as we let the term *Southerner* stand between us and the term *man,* feeling it more important to be a Southerner than a man, we shall resist pretty effectively any attempt to bring others, specifically Southern Negroes, within the sacred confines. I almost added "of the white race," and probably this should be added, for, as I have said, *white* and *Southern* are so intertwined in our history that it is a little surprising to realize that the Negro, too, is a Southerner.

We are willing to grant his similarity of manners, but we can do this and still feel that he presents only a copy—excellent or poor—of what we, by precept and example, have taught him. But when it begins to appear that he was, with us, the co-creator of these manners, and sometimes even our teacher, we begin to develop a strong resistance, for this would be to make him our equal in the warm interchanges of Southern life. I'm afraid, therefore, that we shall come to accept him as a Southerner only as we accept him as a man.

To accept him as a man is, in a sense, to accept him as an equal. That is, if we accept ourselves as men. Unfortunately, most people do not. Most people think they are special instances, radically different from the run of mankind. Only through actual defeat, or through the imagined ultimate defeat that death brings, is it possible for most people to realize their humanity. Defeat, especially in its ultimate form death, is the great equalizer, the great humanizer.

I have already pointed out that when it comes to defeat, Southerners, Negro and white, have resources not available to other Americans. In the experience of defeat, Negroes are our equals, perhaps our superiors; certainly, they have been able to make better use of defeat than we have. If the whites of the South could realize and accept their defeat as a mark of their humanity, an indication of their participation in the common human doom, they would see all about them the faces of Negroes who had also participated, even more deeply, in that doom, and they would turn to them, as men in distress always turn to their fellows, seeking the outstretched hand, the encouraging word.

This has happened many times in the history of the South. In times of trial and defeat, individual whites have sought aid, and most of all comfort, from individual Negroes. I recall the case of a white woman, race-conscious to the bone, who fell outside her home and injured herself so badly that she could not move. There was no one near but the Negro maid, who tried her best to help her mistress up the steps, but could do nothing. Then, waiting for chance help to appear, they lay crying in each other's arms, racial difference forgotten in suffering and sympathy.

In such moments of distress, whites have let down their guards before individual Negroes, assured that they would be understood. For they were bringing their suffering to men and women who were old in suffering. On a shallower level, I have learned it is much easier to talk to Negroes publicly about the tragedy of life than to whites. They know what I'm talking about; they have admitted it. The whites, being also Americans, whose duty it is to succeed, hate to admit life's tragic quality. But when tragedy comes, they may well unburden themselves more freely to a Negro acquaintance than to a white.

This sense of brotherhood in failure marks already the white fraternity of the South. But the stoic quality we have spoken of makes the white far more tight-lipped in personal crises than the Negro. The Negro is wiser, as the white admits when he turns to him for comfort.

> *Give sorrow words, the grief that doth not speak*
> *Whispers the o'er-fraught heart and bids it break.*

And that passionate Spaniard Unamuno says that if only we would go into the streets and cry our grief aloud, something might be done. But your Southerner is not a passionate Spaniard. He is a combination of the coldness of the north and the warmth of the south. The coldness is more apparent in the white, the warmth in the Negro, but each influences the other. Southern whites and Negroes, separately and together, have suffered the tragedy of life. The Negro has accepted it better; admits it, talks about it. The white is still inclined to think he has been defeated because he is a Southerner, and the cards are stacked against Southerners—the "Great Alibi." Though the Negro too has not resolved the modern tragedy of being himself in a world for so long white, he has accepted the general tragedy of life, and it is in part this relaxed acceptance that draws the white to him. For the white senses within himself the need to accept, but finds himself unable to do so.

Which suggests that there may be some truth in the contention of the Southern white that he likes the Negro. On the surface, this seems absurd. You like or dislike individuals, not entire groups. But suppose the Negro is temperamentally more warm and relaxed than the white. This very quality might attract the white Southerner, who is generally of the colder north European stock. The often unspoken afterthought of the words "I like the Negro"—*in his place*—may be put there, then, not from simple pride, but from a mixture of pride, longing, and the fear of yielding. There may be, as James Baldwin suggests, a love affair between the races.

Whatever the truth here, it is the place of the church in the South to recognize the tragedy of Southerners, and to explain the mercy and the judgment of God in the total life of the region, revealing especially how, through failure and defeat, there has been established a common bond between Southern whites and Negroes. But this bond cannot be effective until the whites admit defeat, as the Negroes long ago have done. And this is not simply to admit that our fathers failed, that slavery was a mistake, that the Confederacy was properly defeated. It is to admit that we ourselves have failed; that we should not have permitted the racial injustice to go on; that we have been selfish, overprudent, cowardly. No matter how the blame should be distributed, we have failed.

This is what the church has always told us about our personal lives and we have been inclined to accept it. Even from the beginning, we were inclined to accept both the world and ourselves as imperfect. We need only apply these teachings to our history and to our society.

But this is hard, for, in effect, this is for the whites to ask forgiveness of the Negroes and the Negroes of the whites. No matter who is to blame, we have injured each other. It is harder for the whites to ask forgiveness, for we have inflicted greater injuries upon the Negroes than they have upon us. The greatest, the essential injury was simply our assumption that we were different from and better than Negroes; the economic discrimination was incidental to this. And now we may heal this injury—so far as men can ever heal the injuries of life—simply by admitting, in thought and action, that we are not better; that we, too, have failed; that we are equals in failure, as all men are. This is simply to admit that both we and they are human.

Once we admit this, once we stand together on this old religious ground, we can take the further step of admitting that not only the defeats inflicted by life but also the very nature of our culture has brought us together; that not only are we men together, we are also Southerners together. It is important first of all to be a man, a human being. But a man is more than a stoic figure bareheaded under the stars. A man is also—to speak in terms of the region we are concerned with—the lazy speech of the Southerner, the winy tang of the turpentine forests of Georgia, the heavy red clay of Georgia hills on one's shoes, the strength of Atlanta's Stone Mountain in one's heart, and—to be a little absurd—the mists that float forever around the Atlanta airport in one's eyes. There is no naked universal man. There are only men wearing the garments of Asia or Europe or the United States or the American South. There is no reason why we should not love the garments we wear, and the way we wear them, provided we remember that at bottom we are all men. Southern whites and Negroes are alike men, but also, wearing as they do the garments of the South with a Southern air, they are alike Southerners.

If we could learn this—and, though it's a hard lesson, under the pressures of the world and of our own South we might learn it—if we could learn this, then, indeed, we might begin to see the South as God's project; or, rather, as that one of God's projects that we understand the best. In this view, we should begin to see the basic wisdom behind the defense of the slaveowners, who, for selfish and self-defensive reasons, but also with a sense of over-arching Providence, brought God into the picture. He was in the picture, in the patience and trusting faith of the Negro, and in the acceptance of life as imperfect and sinful on the part of the white. He remained in the picture through the South's defeat, willing that defeat and the great lessons it spread before us. He was with the Negro when he was shoved aside through segregation, into a sort of Babylonian Captivity, where, partly because he was out of the mainstream, he could both retain the best of the past and prepare through long, hard years for the future. During this period the world was growing increasingly tense, both expressing and increasing these tensions in World Wars. The Negro consequently grew increasingly aware of himself, and the nation increasingly recognized him and invited him to participate in its affairs. The 1954 Supreme Court decision was the great charter of his real emancipation. The forces that wrote it were the will of the Negro, the will of the nation, and the will of the world—though the world did not intend this particular event.

The Negro now makes his public appearance in the South; as we have noted, even this gives him status as a Southerner. There is no doubt that he is now the most important active force in the South: he calls the plays, the whites respond as they can. Happily, he is calling creative plays, drawn from the deep reservoir of Southern history. He is not concerned primarily to overcome the whites, though as the whites resist his participation in the common life, he naturally begins to see their overthrow as his prime motive. He is concerned primarily, as the Southerner has always been, but so often ineffectively, to close the gaps within his life, to hold together in one community citizens who were also responding to the individualistic lure of the modern world.

If the South finds its most creative expression today among Negroes, then, as David Potter has suggested recently, "There is . . . a question whether the Negroes may not have embodied the distinctive qualities of the Southern character even more than the whites."[3] For among Negroes we find most often the best of the past acting creatively in the present. Here is neither the dead past nor the rootless future. Neither the rabid Southerner, the commonly accepted type, lost in the past; nor the driving Southern American, interested only in the future. Here is that happy balance between past and future revealed in the early South. Here the South has returned to its roots, below the fires of war and "the slow smokeless burning of decay," and from these roots puts forth fresh foliage.

Here is a man who wished to be at home on earth, but who found it impossible until, by God's grace, he had become at home in heaven. Here is a man supported by the sentiments of the South but not enslaved by them; responsive to the ties of people and place and community but always aware of the wider ties of earth and heaven—of a universal justice and love.

Here is the man the South was trying unconsciously to produce. The paradox is that his forefathers were brought here simply as means for the creation of Southern ends, and he has become, through a strange inversion of roles, the best exponent of the ends the South was seeking. If he should become generally accepted in this role, the possibilities of achievement for the South are almost unlimited. This acceptance can take place only at the religious level.

Here, then, if anywhere, is the working of God's grace. "Against our will and in our own despite," said Aeschylus, "wisdom comes to us by the awful grace of God." A despised minority, excluded from the common life, returns at last more in love than in hatred to reveal to the majority, not only that possibility of community that has always haunted the mind of the South, but also and far more importantly a vision of the universal meaning of failure and defeat, revealing how men become human through the positive acceptance and affirmation of defeat. The man who was once servant reveals through his suffering to the man who was once master the meaning of suffering, and in this common realization paternalism breaks down and a democracy richer than we have yet known may arise.

In the light of this supreme paradox, all the other paradoxes of the South—and they are legion—appear small. If we can accept this, we shall be on the way to becoming Christians. For we shall understand that Southern history was God's way of leading two originally opposed peoples into a richer life than either could have found alone.

NOTES

Chapter 2 "Early Settler"

1. John A. Doyle, *The English in America* (London: Longmans, Green, 1883), p. 134.
2. Perry Miller, *Errand Into the Wilderness* (Cambridge, Mass.: Harvard University Press, 1956), pp. 11–12.
3. Charles H. Foster, *The Rungless Ladder* (Durham, N.C.: Duke University Press, 1954), opening statement.
4. William Bradford's *History "of Plimouth Plantation,"* printed under the direction of the secretary of the commonwealth (Boston: Wright & Potter, 1898), pp. 95–97.
5. Perry Miller and Thomas H. Johnson, *The Puritans* (New York: American Book Company, 1938), p. 17.
6. Henry Nash Smith, *Virgin Land: The American West as Symbol and Myth* (New York: Vintage Books, 1957), p. 251.
7. Perry Miller, *Errand Into the Wilderness* (Cambridge, Mass.: Harvard University Press, 1956), p. 123.
8. Max Weber, *The Protestant Ethic and the Spirit of Capitalism* (New York: Charles Scribner's Sons, 1958), pp. 157, 158.

Chapter 3 "Inviting Land"

1. John A. Doyle, *The English in America* (London: Longmans, Green, 1883), p. 214.
2. Thomas J. Wertenbaker, *The Old South* (New York: Charles Scribner's Sons, 1942), p. 346.

3. Blanche Henry Clark, *The Tennessee Yeomen, 1840–1860* (Nashville, Tenn.: Vanderbilt University Press, 1942).

Chapter 4 "Dominant Pattern"

1. Harriet Martineau, *Society in America* (London: Saunders and Otley, second edition, 1837, 3 vols.), Vol. II, p. 115.
2. Erik H. Erikson, *Childhood and Society* (New York: W. W. Norton & Company, 1950), p. 244.

Chapter 5 "Basic Error"

1. Howard R. Floan, *The South in Northern Eyes: 1831 to 1861* (Austin, Texas: University of Texas Press, 1958), pp. 97–98.

Chapter 6 "Go to the Ant"

1. Howard R. Floan, *The South in Northern Eyes: 1831 to 1861* (Austin, Texas: University of Texas Press, 1958), p. 153.
2. Rollin G. Osterweis, *Romanticism and Nationalism in the Old South* (New Haven, Conn.: Yale University Press, 1949), p. 52.
3. A. DePuy Van Buren, *Jottings of a Year's Sojourn in the South* (Battle Creek, Mich.: no publisher, 1859), *passim.*

Chapter 7 "Tightening Bow"

1. Sidney Mead, *The Lively Experiment: The Shaping of Christianity in America* (New York, Evanston, and London: Harper & Row, 1963), pp. 4–7.

Chapter 8 "Puritans of the South"

1. Thomas P. Abernethy, *The South in the New Nation: A History of the South* (Baton Rouge, La.: Louisiana State University Press, 1961), Vol. IV, p. 19.
2. James C. Leyburn, *The Scotch-Irish: A Social History* (Chapel Hill, N.C.: University of North Carolina Press, 1962), p. 151.
3. Clement Eaton, *The Growth of Southern Civilization: 1790–1860* (New York: Harper & Row, 1961), p. 314.
4. Mary Boykin Chesnut, *A Diary from Dixie* (New York: D. Appleton & Co., 1906), p. 176.
5. *The Encyclopedia Americana* (New York: Americana Corporation, 1959), Vol. 15, p. 577.
6. Allen Tate, *Stonewall Jackson, the Good Soldier* (New York: Minton, Balch and Co., 1928), p. 215.

7. *Ibid.*, p. 314.
8. C. Hugh Holman, "The Southerner as American Writer," in *The Southerner as American*, edited by Charles Grier Sellers (Chapel Hill, N.C.: University of North Carolina Press, 1960), p. 193.
9. *Ibid.*, pp. 192–193.

Chapter 9 "Earth's Corruption"

1. Allen Tate, *Reactionary Essays on Poetry and Ideas* (New York: Charles Scribner's Sons, 1936), p. 255.
2. Moncure Daniel Conway, *Autobiography, Memories and Experiences* (Boston: Houghton Mifflin Company, 1904, 2 vols.), Vol. I, p. 250.

Chapter 10 "This World and Heaven, Too"

1. Noni Jabavu, *Drawn in Color: African Contrasts* (New York: St. Martin's Press, 1960), p. 54.
2. Allen Tate, *The Fathers* (New York: G. P. Putnam's Sons, 1938), p. 185.
3. Christopher Hollis, *The American Heresy* (New York: Minton, Balch and Co., 1930), p. 177.
4. William Butler Yeats, *Essays and Introductions* (London: Macmillan & Co., Ltd., 1961), p. 340.

Chapter 11 "Stoic Remedy"

1. Walker Percy, "Stoicism Is Not Enough," *Commonweal*, Vol. 64 (July 6, 1956), pp. 342–4.
2. William Alexander Percy, *Lanterns on the Levee* (New York: Alfred A. Knopf, 1941), pp. 74–5.
3. *Ibid.*, pp. 74–5.
4. Gamaliel Bradford, *Lee the American* (Boston and New York: Houghton Mifflin Company, 1912, 1927), p. 233.
5. Douglas Southall Freeman, *R. E. Lee: A Biography* (New York and London: Charles Scribner's Sons, 1934–1935, 4 vols.), Vol. IV, p. 464.
6. *Ibid.*, p. 484.
7. Quoted by John Stuart Bryan, in *Joseph Bryan: His Times: His Family: His Friends* (Richmond, Va.: privately printed, 1936), pp. 166–7.
8. Douglas Southall Freeman, *R. E. Lee: A Biography* (New York and London: Charles Scribner's Sons, 1934–1935, 4 vols.), Vol. I, p. 344.
9. *Ibid.*, Vol. IV, pp. 502–3.
10. *Ibid.*, Vol. IV, pp. 502–3.
11. *Ibid.*, Vol. I, p. 404.

12. *Ibid.*, Vol. III, p. 268.
13. *Ibid.*, Vol. I, p. 346.
14. Harriet Martineau, *Retrospect of Western Travels* (London and New York: Harper, 1838, 2 vols.), Vol. I, pp. 238–9.

Chapter 12 "Sir Walter Scott and the Civil War"

1. Alexander Welsh, *The Hero of the Waverly Novels* (New Haven and London: Yale University Press, 1963).
2. *Ibid.*, p. 55.
3. *Ibid.*, p. 201.
4. *Ibid.*, p. 110.
5. *Ibid.*, p. 94.
6. *Ibid.*, p. 193.
7. *Ibid.*, p. 263.
8. *Ibid.*, pp. 263–4.

Chapter 13 "Poetic South: Its Sentiments"

1. John Crowe Ransom, *The World's Body* (New York: Charles Scribner's Sons, 1938), p. 36.

Chapter 14 "Poetic South: Its Images"

1. C. Vann Woodward, "Southern Identity," *Virginia Quarterly Review*, Vol. 34 (1958), p. 336.
2. *Ibid.*, p. 337.
3. *Ibid.*, p. 337.
4. Hannah Arendt, *The Human Condition* (Chicago: University of Chicago Press, 1958), *passim*.
5. *Ibid.*, p. 50.
6. Quoted by Alfred Kazin, in "The Negro in American Culture," in Mathew H. Ahmann, *The New Negro* (Notre Dame, Ind.: Fides Publishers, 1961), p. 133.
7. Richard M. Weaver, "Aspects of the Southern Philosophy," in *Southern Renascence*; edited by Louis D. Rubin and Robert D. Jacobs (Baltimore, Md.: The Johns Hopkins Press, 1953), p. 28.

Chapter 15 "All That Glisters . . . ."

1. T. Harry Williams, *Romance and Realism in Southern Politics* (Athens, Ga.: University of Georgia Press, 1961), p. 3.
2. Alfred Tennyson, "Morte D'Arthur," in *Poetical Works* (London: Oxford University Press, 1926), p. 130.

3. John Temple Graves, *The Fighting South* (New York: G. P. Putnam's Sons, 1943), p. 200.
4. Hannah Arendt, *The Human Condition* (Chicago: University of Chicago Press, 1958), *passim.*

Chapter 16 "Politics as Religion"

1. David Duncan Wallace, *History of South Carolina* (New York: American Historical Society, 1934, 4 vols.), Vol. III, p. 77.
2. Roger Burlingame, *The American Conscience* (New York: Alfred A. Knopf, 1957), p. 251.
3. William B. Hesseltine and David L. Smiley, *The South in American History* (Englewood Cliffs, N.J.: Prentice-Hall, 1960, second edition), p. 163.
4. Clement Eaton, *The Growth of Southern Civilization: 1790–1860* (New York: Harper & Row, 1961), p. 293.
5. *The Private Journal of Henry William Ravenel, 1859–1887,* edited by Arney R. Childs (Columbia, S.C.: University of South Carolina Press, 1947), p. 17.
6. David Duncan Wallace, *History of South Carolina* (New York: American Historical Society, 1934, 4 vols.), Vol. III, p. 40.
7. Edgar Gardner Murphy, "The Task of the Leader," *Sewanee Review,* Vol. XV (January, 1907), pp. 8–9.
8. Ulrich B. Phillips, "The Central Theme of Southern History," *American Historical Review,* Vol. XXXIV, No. 1 (October, 1928), pp. 30–43.
9. John Donald Wade, *Augustus Baldwin Longstreet: A Study of the Development of Culture in the South* (New York: The Macmillan Company, 1924), p. 190, quoting Miller's *Bench and Bar,* Vol. II, p. 260.
10. Clement Eaton, *The Growth of Southern Civilization: 1790–1860* (New York: Harper & Row, 1961), p. 316.
11. John Donald Wade, *Augustus Baldwin Longstreet: A Study of the Development of Culture in the South* (New York: The Macmillan Company, 1924), p. 191.
12. William Sumner Jenkins, *Pro-Slavery Thought in the Old South* (Chapel Hill, N.C.: University of North Carolina Press, 1935), p. 63.
13. James Ward Smith and A. Leland Jamison, *Religion in American Life* (Princeton, N.J.: Princeton University Press, 1961, 2 vols.), Vol. I, p. 333.
14. *Ibid.,* Vol. I, p. 350.

Chapter 17 "The Tragic Sense of Life"

1. Joseph Haroutunian, *Piety Versus Moralism: The Passing of the New England Theology* (New York: Henry Holt & Company, 1932), *passim.*
2. Perry Miller, *Errand Into the Wilderness* (Cambridge, Mass.: Harvard University Press, 1956), *passim.*
3. Henry Nash Smith, *Virgin Land: The American West as Symbol and Myth* (New York: Vintage Books, 1957), *passim.*
4. William R. Taylor, *Cavalier and Yankee: The Old South and American National Character* (New York: George Braziller, 1961), p. 292.
5. *Ibid.*, p. 55.
6. *Ibid.*, p. 52.
7. Allen Tate, ed., *A Southern Vanguard* (New York: Prentice-Hall, 1947), p. 114.
8. Louis Rubin, *The Faraway Country* (Seattle, Wash.: University of Washington Press, 1963), p. 136.
9. Robert Frost, Introduction to Edwin Arlington Robinson's *King Jasper* (New York: The Macmillan Company, 1935), p. xiii.

Chapter 18 "Pause for Reflection"

1. John Alden, *The First South* (Baton Rouge, La.: Louisiana State University Press, 1961), p. 7.

Chapter 19 "Ghostly Past"

1. Walter Hines Page, *The Southerner: A Novel* (New York: Doubleday, 1909), p. 46.
2. Ralph McGill, *The South and the Southerner* (Boston: Little, Brown and Company, 1963), p. 16.
3. William Faulkner, *Absalom, Absalom!* (New York: Modern Library, 1951), p. 12.
4. W. Somerset Maugham, ed., *Fifty Modern English Writers* (New York: Doubleday, Doran, 1933), p. 1300.

Chapter 20 "Sacred Soil"

1. Basil L. Gildersleeve, *The Creed of the Old South* (Baltimore, Md.: The Johns Hopkins Press, 1915), p. 17.

Chapter 21 "In His Place"

1. Edgar Gardner Murphy, *The Basis of Ascendancy* (New York: Longmans, Green, 1909), p. 123.

2. William Alexander Percy, *Lanterns on the Levee* (New York: Alfred A. Knopf, 1941), p. 275.

Chapter 22 "Unspotted by the World"

1. Moncure Daniel Conway, *Autobiography, Memories and Experiences* (Boston: Houghton Mifflin Company, 1904, 2 vols.), Vol. I, p. 231.
2. *Rice Planter and Sportsman: The Recollections of Jacob Motte Alston,* edited by Arney R. Childs (Columbia, S.C.: University of South Carolina Press, 1953), p. 129.
3. Bell Irvin Wiley, *The Road to Appomattox* (Memphis, Tenn.: Memphis State College Press, 1956), p. 105.
4. Sir Arthur James Lyon Fremantle, *The Fremantle Diary,* edited by Walter Lord (Boston: Little, Brown and Company, 1954), p. 259, notes.
5. Mrs. Cornelia McDonald, *A Diary with Reminiscences of the War and Refugee Life in the Shenandoah Valley, 1860–1865,* edited by Hunter McDonald (Nashville, Tenn.: H. McDonald, 1934), p. 139.
6. *Ibid.,* p. 277.
7. Bell Irvin Wiley, *The Plain People of the Confederacy* (Baton Rouge, La.: Louisiana State University Press, 1943), p. 67.
8. Bell Irvin Wiley, *The Road to Appomattox* (Memphis, Tenn.: Memphis State College Press, 1956), pp. 104–5.
9. Ben Robertson, *Red Hills and Cotton* (New York: Alfred A. Knopf, 1942), p. 108.
10. Basil L. Gildersleeve, *The Creed of the Old South* (Baltimore, Md.: The Johns Hopkins Press, 1915), p. 38.
11. Thomas J. Pressly, *Americans Interpret Their Civil War* (Princeton, N.J.: Princeton University Press, 1954), p. 74.
12. Bell Irvin Wiley, *The Plain People of the Confederacy* (Baton Rouge, La.: Louisiana State University Press, 1943), pp. 95–6.
13. Louis C. La Motte, *Colored Light* (Richmond, Va.: Presbyterian Committee of Publication, 1937), pp. 169–70.
14. George B. Tindall, *South Carolina Negroes, 1877–1900* (Columbia, S.C.: University of South Carolina Press, 1952), p. 196.
15. *Ibid.,* p. 198.
16. John Donald Wade, *Augustus Baldwin Longstreet: A Study of the Development of Culture in the South* (New York: The Macmillan Company, 1924), p. 353.
17. C. Vann Woodward, *Origins of the New South, 1877–1913* (Baton Rouge, La.: Louisiana State University Press, 1954), pp. 170–1.

Chapter 23 "Some of My Best Friends . . . ."

1. Simone Weil, *The Need for Roots* (London: Routledge & Kegan Paul, 1952), p. 19.

Chapter 24 "Impossible Panacea"

1. Louis D. Rubin and Robert D. Jacobs, eds., *Southern Renascence* (Baltimore, Md.: The Johns Hopkins Press, 1953), p. 116.
2. Bell Irvin Wiley, *The Road to Appomattox* (Memphis, Tenn.: Memphis State College Press, 1956), p. 38.
3. Bell Irvin Wiley, *The Life of Johnny Reb: The Common Soldier of the Confederacy* (New York: Bobbs-Merrill, 1934), p. 113.
4. General G. Moxley Sorrel, *Recollections of a Confederate Staff Officer* (New York: Neale, 1905), p. 228.
5. T. Harry Williams, *Romance and Realism in Southern Politics* (Athens, Ga.: University of Georgia, 1961), p. 47.
6. *Ibid.*, p. 47.
7. Frances Leigh, *Ten Years on a Georgia Plantation Since the War* (London: R. Bentley, 1883), pp. 152–3.
8. Howard Odum, *The Way of the South* (New York: The Macmillan Company, 1947), p. 204.

Chapter 30 "Last Hurdle"

1. Merrill Proudfoot, *Diary of a Sit-In* (Chapel Hill, N.C.: University of North Carolina Press, 1962), pp. 176–7.

Chapter 31 "By God's Grace, the South"

1. Booker T. Washington, *The Story of the Negro* (New York: Peter Smith, 1940, first published 1909), Vol. I, p. 7.
2. Howard Odum, *The Way of the South* (New York: The Macmillan Company, 1947), p. 41.
3. David Potter, "The Enigma of the South," *Yale Review* (Autumn, 1961), p. 150.

INDEX